KNIGHT-CAPRON LIBRARY
LYNCHBURG COLLEGE
LYNCHBURG, VIRGINIA 24501

WITHDRAWN

JOHN BUNYAN

Kennikat Press
National University Publications
Literary Criticism Series

General Editor
John E. Becker
Fairleigh Dickinson University

CHARLES W. BAIRD

JOHN BUNYAN
A STUDY IN NARRATIVE TECHNIQUE

National University Publications
KENNIKAT PRESS // 1977
Port Washington, N. Y. // London

KNIGHT-CAPRON LIBRARY
LYNCHBURG COLLEGE
LYNCHBURG, VIRGINIA 24501

Copyright © 1977 by Kennikat Press Corp. All rights reserved. No part of this publication may be reproduced, stored in a retrieval system, or transmitted, in any form or by any means, electronic, mechanical, photocopying, recording, or otherwise, without the prior written permission of the publisher.

Manufactured in the United States of America

Published by
Kennikat Press Corp.
Port Washington, N. Y./London

Library of Congress Cataloging in Publication Data

Baird, Charles William.
   John Bunyan: a study in narrative technique.

   (Literary criticism series) (National university publications)
   Bibliography: p.
   Includes index.
   1. Bunyan, John, 1628-1688–Style.
PR3332.B3   828'.4'07   76-53813
ISBN 0-8046-9162-2

TO CHARLES, IN LOVING MEMORY
" For God giveth to a man that is good in his sight wisdom, and knowledge, and joy."
Ecclesiastes 2:26

CONTENTS

CHAPTER		PAGE
one	INTRODUCTION	3
two	REPRESENTATION: DIDACTIC ELEMENTS	24
three	MIMETIC DEVELOPMENT	57
four	ALLEGORICAL DEVELOPMENT	94
five	CONCLUSIONS	129
	NOTES 138	
	REFERENCES 152	

JOHN BUNYAN

CHAPTER ONE

INTRODUCTION

Professor Henri Talon observed, "Chez Bunyan l'écrivain est né d'orateur,"[1] and it is in the broader sense of this latter term as a spokesman or representative of certain religious ideals that Bunyan consistently described himself. He said in *The Holy City*[2] that he was one of the "foolish things of this world" whom "God hath chosen ... to confound the wise" (I, 282). He consistently emphasized his freedom from nonreligious influences. He pointed out in *Light for them that Sit in Darkness* that he had not "borrowed [his] doctrine from libraries" (III, 114). In *Solomon's Temple Spiritualized* he also averred that he had not "fished in other men's waters" and that the "Bible and Concordance [were his] only library in [his] writings" (III, 224). He emphasized, too, the religious nature of his inspiration. He wrote in *The Holy City*, for example:

> Had I all their [*i.e.* "the learned Fathers"] aid and assistance at command, I durst not make use of ought thereof, and that for fear lest that grace, and those gifts that the Lord hath given me, should be attributed to their wits, rather than the light of the word and Spirit of God.(I, 283)

And of course, he emphasized the religious nature and function of the distinctive "gift" that enabled him to become an Open-Communion Particular Baptist preacher. He reported in *Grace Abounding* that "the brethern" asked him to preach when they "did perceive that God had counted me worthy to understand something of his Will in his holy and blessed word, and had given me utterance in some measure to express what I saw" (p. 83).

He explained and carefully circumscribed these two basic qualifications —the abilities to understand God's will through the Bible and to express that knowledge—as a religious spokesman. First, the gift for understanding God's will. Although he sometimes spoke of himself as an Anabaptist (IV, 182), he rejected the part of the Anabaptist legacy[3] the Quakers espoused: he rejected George Fox's position that "there is a mystical, but Divine, light in the hearts of men; a light which would, if followed honestly and steadily, infallibly lead to God: and that without the aid of either the Bible or any ordinances."[4] This rejection is evident in many passages like that in *Light for them that Sit in Darkness* in which he urged his readers, "Take me to the Bible, and let me find in thy heart no favour if thou find me to swerve from the standard" (III, 114). He said in *The Groans of a Damned Soul* that he depended upon the Bible as "the word of God, all truth" (I, 175) rather than as a human record of divine revelation. His acceptance of the verbal dictation theory, which had been borrowed ultimately from Plato,[5] and which had been widely accepted by Alexandrian and Latin fathers,[6] is evident both from his searching scrutiny of every phrase of the texts he explicated (I, 287-88) and from the explicit avowal in *A Confession of My Faith* that "all the Holy Scriptures are the words of God" (I, 422). More specifically, he asserted in *Of the Trinity and a Christian*, "Suffer thyself... to be persuaded that the Scripture is the word of God... the words of the Holy One; and that they, therefore, must be every one true, pure, and for ever settled in heaven" (II, 534). He asserted in *Some Gospel Truths Opened* the need, too, of divine aid in interpreting the Bible. "Truly the Scriptures... most really and plainly hold out these things," he wrote, "to all those that have received the Spirit of the Lord Jesus Christ. For it is it, and it alone, that can reveal these things" (I, 84). And, finally, he claimed divine aid in understanding the Bible. He consistently appealed directly to the deity in interpreting questionable passages. In *Of the Trinity and a Christian*, for example, he made such an appeal (II, 534), and in *Grace Abounding* he said, "There was not any thing that I then cried unto God to make known and reveal unto me but he was pleased to do it for me, I mean not one part of the Gospel of the Lord Jesus, but I was orderly led unto it" (p. 37). Briefly, then, the gift of understanding was a gift for interpreting an infallible Bible with infallible authority.

Bunyan also described fully his gift for expression or for "utterance." He treated two basic aspects. In some descriptions he clearly implied that neither the matter nor the manner of his utterance was his own. In *Grace Abounding* he compared himself to a "sounding *Cymbal*" in the "hand of Christ," for example, and added:

> A tinkling Cymbal is an instrument of Musick with which a skilful player can make... melodious and heart-inflaming Musick,... yet behold the

Cymbal hath not life, neither comes the Musick from it, but because of the art of him that plays therewith.(p. 91)

Again, he said:

I have also at some times . . . [been] so estranged from the things I have been speaking . . . that I have been as if I had not known or remembered what I have been about, or as if my head had been in a bag all the time of the *exercise*.(p. 90)

It seems clear that he sometimes accepted, as James Anthony Froude pointed out, the conventional theory that the "minister when he preached was . . . an instrument uttering the words not of himself but of the Holy Spirit."[7]

More often, however, he implied that the gift of utterance was under his own control. Possibly he had a moment of recognition like that of George Whitefield, who once admitted, "I have frequently wrote and spoke too much in my own spirit, when I thought I was writing and speaking entirely by the assistance of God."[8] At any rate, he did not usually describe even his preaching in this essentially Platonic way.[9] He usually attributed "inspiration" to the deity in a less exalted sense, implying "encouragement" or "motivation." He said in *Grace Abounding*, for example, "I have been in my preaching . . . as if an Angel of God had stood by at my back to encourage me" (p. 87). And he claimed no such divine aid in the narratives. Even when he described the composition of *The Pilgrim's Progress*, he said he had his "Method by the end" before he said, "still as I pull'd, it came" (p. 2). And in "an Advertisement to the Reader" in *The Holy War* he insisted that, in *The Pilgrim's Progress*, "manner and matter too was all mine own" (p. 253). He illustrated through Mr. Talkative (p. 77) and implied in *Grace Abounding* that some very profane men could "deliver themselves like Angels" (p. 92). He treated the gifts of utterance simply as means to religious ends, saying in *Grace Abounding*, for example, that gifts were "good to the thing for which they are designed, to wit, the Edification of others" (p. 92).

As a religious spokesman, so qualified and so inspired, Bunyan consistently applied essentially religious criteria to literature. He unequivocally repudiated secular literature that produced no salutary effects. Basically, he agreed with many contemporaneous Puritan ministers in condemning the "imaginative literature that appealed to the more vulgar of the public" on the basis that such works were "a waste of time which had better be given to sermons, edifying works, and religious exercises."[10] This agreement is evident in *Sighs from Hell*. He had a repentant sinner there lament that he had thought, "Give me a ballad, a news-book, *George* on *Horseback,* or *Bevis of Southampton:* give me some book that ... tells of old fables; but for the Holy Scriptures I cared not" (I, 166). He did not voice the "highly developed ... theory of recreations" which proscribed "all recreations that in themselves were immoral or impious, or that had no relevance to the calling,"[11] yet he implied that nonreligious literature was relatively insignificant. He raised the question in *Grace Abounding,* for example, whether it was "time to take pleasure, and recreate thyself in anything, before thou has mourned and been sorry for thy sins?" (p. 113). His condemnation of immoral works is clear in *Mr. Badman.* He pointed out that a master could ruin a poor apprentice if he:

> suffers his house to be scattered with profane and wicked books, such as stir up to lust ... such as teach idle ... lascivious discourse, and such as provoke to profane drollery and Jesting; and lastly, such as ... corrupt and pervert the Doctrine of Faith and Holiness.(p. 42)

He clearly drew no sharp functional distinction between literary and other works insofar as their moral and religious effects were concerned.

His attitude toward secular literature as well as his description of his inspiration, knowledge, and gifts as a religious spokesman are undoubtedly compatible with the picture he gives of himself as an author of a fictional narrative in *The Pilgrim's Progress.* He tells the reader explicitly in the "Author's Apology" that his end is "thy good," and he compares himself at length to a "Fowler" and a "Fisher-man" who "ingageth all his Wits" to devise many methods—"His Gun, his Nets, his Lime-twigs, light and bell"—to attain his ends (pp. 2-3). He clearly implies that he is an alert craftsman engaging all his wits to make the fictional narrative serve his religious ends.

His critics, in contrast, have spoken of him and his work in quite different terms. They have "explained" various artistic incongruities and inconsistencies by postulating the existence of an unlettered and largely "unconscious" artist. Bunyan has been described variously as "an Artist in Spite of Himself,"[12] or an "unconscious master" of an art,[13] or "a true artist ... [who] knew nothing of the rules, and was not aware that he was an artist at all."[14] Since Professor William York Tindall published *John Bunyan: Mechanick Preacher,*[15] however, it no longer seems appropriate to refer to Bunyan's "profoundly unconscious art"[16] or his "instinctive habit of dramatizing his intellectual experiences,"[17] or, indeed, to consider that a mere "natural instinct"[18] might have controlled any important aspect of his art whatsoever. Professor Tindall demolished, at least, the legend of Bunyan as a "simple and gifted laborer" in expounding his thesis, that Bunyan "was a typical mechanick preacher and that his writings owe their nature both to the social, economic, and sectarian condition of their author and to the literary conventions of a numerous company of mechanicks."[19] The "simple and gifted laborer" does not appear in the recent studies superseding G. B. Harrison, *John Bunyan: A Study of Personality*,[20] as accounts of Bunyan's artistic development. Professor Talon's brilliant interpretative work, *John Bunyan: The Man and his Works*, emphasizes that *Grace Abounding* is a "work of art" and refers to such qualities as the "formal beauty" of many passages.[21] In *John Bunyan*, Professor Roger Sharrock asserts that Bunyan had "become the self-conscious writer" after the success of *The Pilgrim's Progress*, and he frequently praises such passages as the "consciously ordered set piece"[22] at the end of the *Second Part*. Nevertheless, the "unconscious" or "instinctive" artist lurks in the background of both studies. Professor Talon concludes that Bunyan "felt instinctively that eloquence would be a lapse of taste" in a given context, and that a certain kind of image "springs out naturally."[23] Professor Sharrock affirms that "Bunyan's storyteller's instinct prompts him to drop Sagacity with a disarming naiveté," and that "Bunyan worked without any critical understanding of the potentialities of the various narrative forms he employed."[24]

It is not possible to demonstrate conclusively the accuracy of either of these sharply contrasting positions in biographical terms. The traditional assumption that Bunyan was the "unconscious" artist which still lurks behind these recent major studies involves insurmountable difficulties. Since the degrees of conscious or unconscious activity that may have been involved in the process of composition must necessarily remain a matter of speculation, in fact, the "unconscious" artist cannot be either established or extirpated as a biographical entity. Bunyan's picture of himself as a religious spokesman conscientiously shaping his narratives to religious ends involves similar difficulties. Its accuracy as a biographical statement cannot be verified, of course, because the actual process of composition is not recoverable. Moreover, there are logical difficulties. Logically, the fact that a given work fulfills an author's stated intentions does not establish a cause and effect relationship between the intention and the realization, though it may surely suggest a probability.

If the formal implications of the two positions are considered in relation to the development of Bunyan's narrative art, however, they raise a significant question that is open to investigation. The traditional theory clearly implies that there is no meaningful, coherent pattern in the development of Bunyan's narrative art. Bunyan's picture of himself as a conscientious religious spokesman, in contrast, clearly implies that such a pattern *ought* to be evident if the narratives are considered in relation to his religious ends. These conflicting implications raise a question that can be investigated and answered objectively: is there a meaningful, coherent pattern in that development?

Bunyan's description further suggests that a fuller exploration of his professed goals could isolate or throw light upon the kind of coherent pattern that is possible or probable. Such an exploration has shown that there are unresolved conflicts among his professed goals. It has also shown that there are unresolved conflicts in his comments about allegorical methods. An examination of the narratives in light of these conflicts has shown that similar conflicts are manifest in all the narratives. If the development of the narratives is examined in relation to these unresolved conflicts, it becomes clear that there is a meaningful coherent pattern to the development that has not previously been isolated: both the nonallegorical and the allegorical methods evolve in such a way that the conflict is gradually reduced.

Unresolved conflict is implicit in his description of his professed goals. As a religious spokesman, Bunyan professed four basic goals in both his religious treatises and his major narratives. First, the three basic Ciceronian goals. He professed to inform his readers. He emphasized in *Grace Abounding* that the gifts of expression, though they were "empty and without power to save the Soul of him that hath them," were "good to the thing for which they are designed, to wit, the Edification of others" (p. 92). In the same work, referring to his preaching, he spoke of "labouring to unfold it [the "Doctrine of Life by Christ"], to demonstrate it, and to fasten it upon the Conscience of others" (p. 87). In his writing, he avowed his didactic intentions whether he was teaching children the elements of his faith in *Instruction for the Ignorant* (I, 475) or creating *"Divine Emblems"* (IV, 457), explicating the Bible in *Sighs from Hell* (I, 133) or writing his spiritual autobiography (p. 2), arguing points of doctrine in *Justification by Faith* (IV, 220) or drawing his first allegory from his own "Crown" (p. 1), writing a sermon in the *Jerusalem Sinner Saved* (II, 456) or producing prose fiction in *Mr. Badman* (p. 16).

He acknowledged, too, the need to please his readers. He revealed his recognition of this need most often by implication in defending his use of artifice. He defended his use of certain devices on the basis that they made his message more memorable and effective. In *Profitable Meditations*, for example, he averred, "Men's heart is apt in Meeter to delight / Also in that to bear away the more." He alleged further in defense of verse that it made truth "very quick" so that men "in their hearts do sing."[25] He spoke of *Instruction for the Ignorant* as "wholesome medicine" for the unconverted (I, 475), and he extended the medical metaphor in defending his use of verse: "When Doctors give their Physic to the Sick / They make it pleasing with some other thing."[26] Again, he remarked that he used the dialogue form in *Mr. Badman* in order that he "might with more ease to myself, and pleasure to the Reader, perform the work" (p. 3). He boasted of the novelty of *The Pilgrim's Progress* and emphasized that the book was "writ in such Dialect / As may the minds of listless men affect" (p. 7). Without using the version of the Horatian dictum popular among contemporaneous Puritan ministers, "to profit by pleasing,"[27] Bunyan clearly professed a desire to please as well as to instruct his readers.

Bunyan also professed the desire to *move* his readers. In *Grace Abounding* he acknowledged a duty "even to carry an awakening Word" (p. 87), and in *Ebal and Gerizim*, he voiced the desire to "some impression make / On carnal hearts" (IV, 441); his it was, he said in *Some Gospel Truths Opened*, to urge his readers to "get a very great sense of ... [their] sins" (I, 50), and, as he said in *The Pilgrim's Progress*, to "chuse to be Pilgrims" (p. 172). He professed a desire, in effect, to imitate the good preacher of the *Divine Emblems* who "doth the heart so reach / That it doth joy or sigh before the Lord" (IV, 457). In *Grace Abounding*, he said he was gratified by his flock's "hungerings and thirstings ... after further acquaintance with the Father," their "tenderness of Heart" and "trembling at sin," and he urged them to remember their "terrours of conscience, and fear of death and hell," their "tears and prayers," and their sighs "under every hedge for mercy" (pp. 1-3). In defending *The Pilgrim's Progress*, he pointed out that some things made "Ones fancies Checkle while his Heart doth ake" (p. 170). He said in *Some Gospel Truths Opened* "It [is] meet also to stir up thy heart ..." (I, 46), and he, thus, expressed a desire to move his readers in a variety of ways in both treatises and narratives.

Closely related to the third of these basic oratorical goals, perhaps,[28] yet separate and distinct is a fourth goal. Bunyan undertook to hold a "mirror up to nature," in Hamlet's words, "to show virtue her own feature, scorn her own image." He professed to do this on the basis, essentially, that such a mirror would aid Puritan introspection. Professor Louis L. Martz has demonstrated that self-examination was considered an inseparable part of the art of meditation among both Roman Catholic and Protestant practitioners,[29] but Bunyan did not at all emphasize the devotional aspects of such introspection. Perhaps because he accepted the Calvinistic doctrine of predestination (III, 271), he frequently implied that he would aid those attempting to determine whether they were of the Elect, and he consistently emphasized the critical or rational, rather than the devotional, aspects of such introspection.

He implied that descriptions of various states of the soul, or of the outward manifestations of such states, should aid introspection both in treatises written before, and in those written after, the major narratives.

In his first publication, *Some Gospel Truths Opened,* Bunyan wrote, "I do admonish thee to ... examine thine own heart by the rule of the word of God, whether or no thou hast as yet any beginnings of desiring after religion" (I, 50). In the same treatise, he raised the question, "But how shall I know that I am born again?" He answered it by describing several conditions of belief and states of the soul. For example:

> Art thou born again? Then thou seest, all true peace and joy comes through the blood of the Son of Mary ... But if thy guilt of sin goes off, and convictions go off any other way than by the blood and righteousness of the man Christ Jesus, thy guilt goes off not right, but wrong, and thy latter end will be very bitter.(I, 78-79)

In the same treatise, he wrote, "But ye will say, who are those ignorant persons that shall find no favour at that day? or, how doth the ignorance discover itself? I shall only mention three or four sorts of men...." He then describes a "profane scoffer," a "formal professor," and others (I, 77). Again, in another early treatise, *Christian Behavior,* he said, "There are three things which discover a man or woman too much inclining to uncleanness ... a wanton eye ... wanton and immodest talk ... [and] adorning themselves in light and wanton apparel" (II, 181). The principle that such descriptions should aid introspection seems implicit in these texts.

In *The Pharisee and the Publican,* which was published the year after the *Second Part,* Bunyan wrote:

> Courteous Reader,—I have made bold once again to present thee with some of my meditations; and they are now about the Pharisee and the Publican; two men in whose condition the whole is comprehended, both as to their state now and condition at the judgement.
> Wherefore, in reading this little book thou must needs read thyself. I do not say thou must understand thy condition; for it is the gift of God must make thee do that. Howbeit, if God will bless it to thee, it may be a means to bring thee to see whose steps thou art treading, and so at whose end thou art like to arrive.(II, 318)

Clearly, a reader was invited to understand his own spiritual condition better after reading the description of the "condition" of these two contrasting figures and the explanation of the religious significance of these conditions.

Although he did not use the mirror image in the first fictional narrative, it seems clear that Bunyan applied the same principle therein. He asked prospective readers of *The Pilgrim's Progress:*

Would'st read thy self, and read thou know'st not what
And yet know whether thou art blest or not
By reading the same lines? (p. 7)

Later, when he undertook to write a literal companion piece to this allegory, he explained that he had written so "that thou mayest, as in a Glass, behold with thine own eyes the steps that take hold of Hell," and so that a reader could "discern . . . whether thou thy self art treading in his [Mr. Badman's] path" to hell (pp. 3-4). He also urged, "Gravely inquire concerning thy self by the Word, whether thou art one of his [Mr. Badman's] Linage or no" (p. 4). In both cases it seems clear that his imitations, or representations, of realities outside the work of art were to aid introspection just as the descriptions in the treatises were. Bunyan emphasizes the merely illustrative aspects of these representations so that they seem subordinate to the Ciceronian goals.

Although only the illustrative functions of these representatives were necessary to his argument, this fourth goal introduces immense potentialities. It does so because Bunyan clearly accepts, as the mirror image implies, the mimetic principle of art as an imitation of inward and outward actualities. This acceptance is evident, not merely in the narratives, but in a number of statements about them. The purpose of re-creating the quality and intensity of the process of conversion is clearly implicit in his suggestion that he wrote *Grace Abounding,* "that, if God will, others may be put in remembrance of what he hath done for their Souls, by reading his work upon me" (p. 2). The purpose of presenting an accurate, if somewhat generalized, reflection of contemporaneous actuality is implicit in Bunyan's insistence upon the truth of substance in *Mr. Badman:* "I think I may truly say," he assures the reader, "that . . . all the things that here I discourse of, I mean as to matter of fact, have been acted upon the stage of this World, even many times before mine eyes" (p. 3). And he invited readers of *The Pilgrim's Progress* to enjoy the illusion such mimetic art creates:

Would'st thou be in a Dream, and yet not sleep?
Or would'st thou in a moment Laugh and Weep?
Wouldest thou loose thy self, and catch no harm?
And find thy self again without a charm? (p. 7)

This acceptance is not inconsistent with the assertion that mimetic material may serve illustrative functions, yet it clearly poses an unresolved question of priority and introduces a consistent source of conflict.

To attain the goals so described and understood, Bunyan needed (1) to create an imitation or illusion of actualities outside the work of art, and he needed (2) to make unmistakably clear the religious or moral significance of the mimetic material. He would not have attained his professed goal had he merely created an imitation of a given state of consciousness, or of the outward manifestations of such a state, without either stripping the imitation of moral ambiguity in the process of artistic transformation or stipulating the religious significance of the mimetic material. Nor would he have attained his professed goals if the ethical or religious theme dominated image as it did in the treatises, for such domination would have destroyed the power of the imitation to please or to move, or even to remain an illusion. Both the integrity of the imitation and the clarity of the moral or religious significance were necessary to the attainment of the basic goals Bunyan professed. His professed goals, in effect, demanded that the narratives should both imitate actualities outside the work of art and stipulate the ethical or religious significance of such imitations within the literary context. Or, in other terms, these goals demanded that the writer observe both the mimetic principle, which asks for an imaginative acceptance of illusory experience, and the didactic one, which demands recognition of the stipulated significance of narrative facts.

Conflict is evident in the two basic kinds of narrative technique Bunyan developed to these ends. He developed both literal and allegorical narrative techniques. These techniques differ essentially in that the literal techniques establish *direct* relationships between characters, images, and actions in the narrative and actualities or probabilities outside the narrative; the allegorical techniques, in contrast, establish *indirect* relationships between separate narrative facts and the "real" world outside the work of art.

Literal techniques are essentially mimetic, interpretative, and hortatory. They establish direct relationships by *mimesis*. Details contributing to the vividness or life likeness of the characters, the impression of the life and manners of a society, the concrete realization of the settings, the narrative plausibility of the human motivation, or the re-creation of the sensation of life as perceived by the senses may be said to allude directly to external actualities. Such techniques also establish direct relationships through interpretative commentary, however introduced, which is directly applicable to comparable actualities outside the work of art, and through other oblique suggestions that principles illustrated by the narrative *ought* to be considered in relation to external actualities.

Allegorical techniques in Bunyan's narratives, on the other hand, are analogical in essence. The central metaphors assert identities between external actualities and narrative facts, and they establish relationships between separate images, characters, and actions within the work of art.

Separate narrative facts themselves must be understood in relation to the extending metaphor before they become comprehensible in relation to external actualities. The Hill Difficulty, for example, conveys nothing about spiritual struggle in the "real" world until it is understood in relation to the central metaphor in *The Pilgrim's Progress*. Subordinate analogies, expressed or implied, also stand between narrative facts and external actualities. Christian's armor, for example, says nothing about the value of religious instruction unless it is first understood in relation to St. Paul's figurative statement about the "whole armour of God" in Ephesians, 6:13-17. Neither the external actuality referred to nor the oblique assertion being made about it is clear except by reference to the pertinent analogy. The relationship between separate images, characters, and actions in the narrative and external actualities is, to this extent, indirect.

In this narrow sense, of course, Bunyan, like other allegorists, uses both literal and allegorical methods in his allegories: he establishes both direct and indirect relationships between the two worlds. Christian is depicted in some detail as a representative traveller, often engaged in animated religious discussions with his companions, yet he is the central agent in extending a metaphoric assertion about the process of religious conversion and growth. In a similar way, Moby Dick is depicted in elaborate detail as the object of fictional whalers' pursuit, yet he is a crucial element in a pervasive metaphoric assertion about the self-destructive effects of a search for the absolute. Red Cross is vivid and lifelike as an outraged young idealist when he discovers Una's supposed duplicity, yet his abandonment of Una is crucial to a metaphoric assertion about the deceptiveness of truth during the pursuit of holiness. These separate techniques necessarily involve some of the same sensory material, yet they function in different ways in Bunyan's allegories. The allegorical ones involve analogies and develop further indirect correspondences; the allegorical stipulations are *in* the metaphors, or they are educed from them. The literal techniques imply "reality is like this," or "it should, or should *not*, be like this," and the literal stipulations are assertions about the relationship between the mimetic material and external actuality.

As was mentioned, a central conflict is evident in both kinds of technique. The central conflict involved in the literal or nonallegorical techniques concerns the balance of mimetic and didactic elements. Professor Northrup Frye spoke of a "central dilemma of literature," saying, "If literature is didactic it tends to injure its own integrity; if it ceases wholly to be didactic, it tends to injure its own seriousness."[30]

The illusion evaporates with the integrity in narrative art. That is to say, the pleasures of self-deception, of imaginative participation, of simply watching a fellow human being in action, depend upon the creation of an illusion sufficient to procure "that willing suspension of disbelief for the moment" which, Coleridge said, "constitutes poetic faith." Professor E. H. Gombrich suggests that "illusion is due to the interaction of clues and the absence of contradictory evidence"[31] in representational visual art; in narrative art, in contrast, it is not the absence, but the sudden coalescence of a multiplicity of seemingly contradictory clues that contributes most forcefully to elemental human interest and, hence, to the sense of probability necessary to sustain an illusion. Clues contributing to such a sudden coalescence do not necessarily heighten the illustrative effectiveness of an episode or a character and, of course, may well destroy it by introducing an undesirable complexity. An illustrative effectiveness itself may easily shatter an illusion. An illusion is easily shattered, too, by didactic intrusions that reduce mimetic material to the status of illustrations, impede narrative movement, destroy visual clarity or dramatic immediacy, or, in other ways, either dampen interest in characters and events or inhibit imaginative expansions of meaning. The balance of mimetic and didactic elements directly affects the basic illusion necessary to effectual narrative art.

The conflict that threatens the illusion insofar as the nonallegorical methods are concerned, both in the allegories and elsewhere, is evident in quite different ways in the allegorical techniques. Since the allegorical methods are ways of imitating and stipulating simultaneously, the conflict is essentially one between two separate ways of making a narrative meaningful, or in other terms, of developing allegorical vehicles. Such was the nature of allegory as Bunyan described it that this conflict was transformed into a conflict between the demands of two allegorical principles, the "mimetic" and the "dialectical." These separate, but related, principles need to be seen in relation to Bunyan's own description of allegory.

Essentially, Bunyan described allegory as a didactic or rhetorical instrument, a persuasive way of expressing things known. His description of the allegorical mode cannot be presented in detail because of his terminology. He used the generic term "similitude" to refer to both figurative and literal devices. He uses "similitude" at various times to refer to types (III, 257), figures (III, 257), similes (IV, 86), metaphors (I, 293), analogies (III, 277), exempla (II, 246), parables (I, 72), and, on the title pages, to his allegories. He also ignores many common distinctions between separate kinds of "similitudes." Benjamin Keach, contemporaneous Baptist minister and rhetorician, for example, defines a parable as a "Similitude or Comparison by which some certain Affair or Thing is feigned, and told, as if it were really transacted and is compared with some spiritual thing, or is accommodated to signify it."[32] However, Bunyan ignores the basis here suggested for distinguishing a parable from a metaphor, for he speaks in *Sighs from Hell* of the following lines as a parable (I, 132): "Except a corn of wheat fall to the ground and die, it abideth alone; but if it die, it bringeth forth much fruit" (John 13: 24). Being figurative throughout, this "parable" is "accommodated to signify" some "spiritual thing" in much the same manner that a metaphor is. Again, a more recent writer, Hubert Eveleth Greene, distinguishes a parable from an allegory on the basis that, aside from being shorter, a parable has an explicit moral rather than an implicit one.[33] Bunyan, in contrast, apparently agrees with Keach that a parable may refer to "some other thing in order to instruct, either implicitly or explicitly,"[34] for he refers to four passages as parables in the course of an argument in *Sighs from Hell:* only three of the examples he cites have explicit morals (I, 132).[35]

Despite these difficulties in terminology, it seems clear that Bunyan used the word "allegory" to refer to a work setting forth one thing by another through an extending central metaphor and through a number of subordinate devices. Keach defined allegory as the *"Continuation* of a *Trope,* especially of a *metaphor"* in which *"one thing is said, another thing is understood."*[36] John Prideaux, a prominent Presbyterian Bishop of Worcester, offered a similar definition.[37] Bunyan called *The Pilgrim's Progress,* a continued comparison of a spiritual process and a journey, an allegory, and he justified his practice by saying:

I find that holy Writ in many places,
Hath semblance with this method, where the cases
Doth call for one thing to set forth another.(p. 6)

He also used the verb "to allegorize" to refer to the interpretative process through which he either found the multiple meanings of a biblical text—as he did, for example, in *Sighs from Hell* (I, 135)—or elaborated biblical imagery so that it continued to set forth one thing by another—as he did, for example, in *The Water of Life* (III, 217). It seems clear that he used the word as it was used among contemporaneous biblical rhetoricians to refer to a method of setting forth one thing by another through an extending metaphor.

Elsewhere, Keach pointed out that "Divines" consider allegory "properly or strictly taken" as a "continued Discourse of many Figures together."[38] Or, again, John Smith said, "As a Metaphor may be compared to a star in respect of beauty, brightness, and direction, so an Allegory may be likened to a constellation, or a company of many stars."[39]

A similar idea is implicit in Bunyan's comments about his extended figurative works. In the "Apology" to *The Pilgrim's Progress* he says the "allegory" is "delivered" under the "Similitude of a Dream." He says that he speaks "in *Metaphors*" and implies that the book is a *"dark Similitude"* "borrowed" from *"similies."* He praises the work for presenting *"riddles"* and for presenting *"Truth within a Fable."* He defends his method on the basis that *"parables"* are not to be despised; the *"Prophets"* often set forth truth *"by Metaphors"*; *"holy Writ"* itself is full of *"Dark Figures, Allegories"*; Paul does not forbid Timothy the use of *"Parables"*; and that the *"words obscure"* of his work *"alure"* the mind. He challenges *"nimble Fancies"* to learn to understand the *"mysterious lines"* (pp. 1-6). In the "Conclusion" to *The Pilgrim's Progress* Bunyan urges his readers not to allow his "figure, or similitude" to put them into "a laughter or a feud." He urges them to "Turn up my Metaphor" (p. 164). On the title pages of *The Pilgrim's Progress* and *The Holy War* Bunyan quoted, or slightly misquoted, Hos. 12:10, "I have used Similitudes." It seems clear that a number of subordinate similitudes were to be used in the extension of the central metaphor, or, in Smith's terms, that an allegory could be "likened to a constellation, or a company of many stars."

Bunyan isolated two separate functions of separate "stars" or similitudes: they reveal known truth and they conceal it. First, the ways he said they concealed truth. Much as Martin Luther had spoken of allegories that "beautifie and set out the matter,"[40] Bunyan said, "Similitudes, if fitly spoken and applied, do much set off and out any point that ... is handled in the churches" (I, 293). He referred to the function of "setting off" in *The Pilgrim's Progress* in saying that similitudes could *"Make truth to spangle and its rayes to shine"* (p. 4). The decorative function also seems implicit in his reference to the "inward Rarities" which would "feed the eyes" in *The Holy City* (p. 6). In *Ebal and Gerizim* he alluded to the functions in "setting out" truth in speaking of similitudes that, like "a painting on the wall," would help one understand what Hell was like (IV, 441). Again, he said in *The Saint's Knowledge of Christ's Love* that Christ "condescends to our capacities" in "making use of ... similitudes" (IV, 86-87), and he said in *Soloman's Temple Spiritualized*, "O! what speaking things are types, shadows and parables" (III, 249). Again in the same work, he referred to certain words as being "metaphorical, or words by which a thing most excellent is presented to, and amplified before our faces" (III, 203). In effect, he maintained similitudes "set off and out" truth by expressing it in decorative, graphic, and emphatic ways.

The second basic function of similitudes to which he referred, was, in St. Augustine's phrase, to introduce a "useful and wholesome obscurity."[41] Seen in relation to his comments about biblical imagery, Bunyan's assertion that he used a method like the biblical one in *The Pilgrim's Progress* (p. 6) is itself a reference to such purposeful obscurity. Bunyan consistently implied that the figurative language of the richly metaphoric biblical text constituted a rhetorical facade through which an explicator could discern literal truth. In an early work, *The Holy City*, for example, he observed that certain passages were "but metaphorical sayings under which is held forth some better and more excellent thing." He added, "And indeed it is frequent with God in Scripture to speak of his grace and mercy under the notion of waters, of a fountain, a sea, and the like" (I, 329). A similar implication appears in a late work, *Solomon's Temple Spiritualized*, when he said:

> For since it is the wisdom of God to speak to us oftimes by trees, gold, silver, stones, beasts, fowls, fishes, spiders, ants, frogs, flies, lice, dust, etc. and here by wood; how should we by them understand his voice, if we count there is no meaning in them? (III, 258)

He found in purposeful obscurity much the same values that St. Augustine had earlier found in the obscurity of the Bible itself. St. Augustine surmised that the function of obscurity in the Bible was to stimulate the "appetite"[42] and "zeal"[43] of the reader; Bunyan said in *The Pilgrim's Progress*, *"Things that seem to be hid in words obscure / Do but the Godly mind the more alure"* (p. 171). St. Augustine stated the principle that "what is attended with difficulty in the seeking gives greater pleasure in the finding"[44]; Bunyan clearly implied that, to appropriate Professor E. M. W. Tillyard's phrase, "temporary obfuscation"[45] produced pleasure when the difficulty was overcome. For example, he asked potential readers of *The Pilgrim's Progress*, *"Would'st thou read Riddles, and their Explanation?"* (p. 7). And he cited one of the attractions of the *Second Part* in urging it to *"Freely propound, expound"* those *"Riddles that lie couch't within thy breast"* (p. 173). Both St. Augustine and Bunyan proclaimed the value of obscurity in the learning process, but the value each saw in it differed somewhat. St. Augustine surmised that biblical meanings were shrouded in the "thickest darkness" to subdue "pride by toil," to prevent "a feeling of satiety in the intellect," to enhance a reader's appreciation of the meanings which were discovered with difficulty, and "to exercise and train the minds of their readers."[46] Bunyan suggested in *The Pilgrim's Progress* that meanings conveyed by a *"dark Similitude"* would *"stick faster in the Heart and Head"* (p. 171). Elsewhere, he had Great-heart remark, "I make bold to talk thus Metaphorically, for the ripening of the

Wits of young Readers" (p. 253). Bunyan, in brief, attributed four basic functions to purposeful obscurity: to entice the reader to further exploration, to produce pleasure when the meaning was discovered, to aid the memory, and to train the mind.

Bunyan described two qualities of the vehicle of an extended metaphor. In *The Resurrection of the Dead* he was discussing a passage in which, he said, "The apostle ... descends to the discovery of the manner" of the resurrection through a "similitude of seed." He said this similitude was "very natural, and fitly suiteth each particular" (I, 346). When he was discussing biblical passages which he assumed were setting forth one thing by another, he consistently applied two principles in both early and late works. He applied the "mimetic" principle, the principle that a vehicle should be "very natural," and he applied the dialectical principle, the principle that it should exhibit a precise series of point by point correlations, or "fitly" suit "each particular."

Unlike St. Augustine, Bunyan did not describe an aesthetic moment in which a reader both recognized the significance of a similitude and appreciated its appropriateness, yet, like St. Augustine, he consistently praised the mechanical exactitude he found in passages setting forth one thing by another.[47] In the early work, *The Resurrection of the Dead*, for example, he is treating the "similitude of seed." He makes it clear that the similitude "fitly suiteth each particular" in the sense that there is a precise series of point by point correlations. He says, for example, "the corn of wheat is first dead, and after sown and buried in the earth; and so is the body of man." And a bit later he adds "As to the manner of its change in its rising this similitude also doth fitly suit" and examines additional correlations at length (I, 346). In the late work, *An Exposition on the First Ten Chapters of Genesis*, he proceeds in a similar way. He remarks upon the "fit-ness" of a phrase and adds:

> The wisdom of God, is there to make use of figures and shadows, even where most fit things, the things under consideration, may be most fitly demonstrated. The dividing of the waters from the waters, most fitly doth show the work of God in choosing and refusing....

He then points out a series of point by point correlations between the concrete description and the abstract doctrine (III, 375). He consistently praises passages exhibiting dialectical precision, economy, and consistency.

He also consistently commends passages which set forth one thing by another yet are "very natural," or level with the norm of common experience. Whether he is explaining the typological significance of Old Testament texts, elucidating the significance of separate metaphors, or extending such metaphors, he refers to the qualities implicit in the phrase "very natural." He consistently evinces a noteworthy ability, in effect, to "reason from the properties of things" in a manner more honored in the pulpit than in the theological study.[48] By such reasoning he explains the typological significance of Old Testament detail in both early works, such as *The Holy City* (I, 295), and late ones, such as *Solomon's Temple Spiritualized* (III, 261), both in passages which are primarily narrative, such as those in *An Exposition on the First Ten Chapters of Genesis* (III, 415), and in those which are primarily descriptive, such as those in *Solomon's Temple Spiritualized* (III, 230). When he finds in the latter treatise that Christ is presented "under the similitude of a nail," for example, he reasons from the "natural" function of a nail: "a golden nail, it is to show, that as a nail, by driving, is fixed in his place, so Christ by God's oath is made everlasting priest" (III, 257). In *The Water of Life*, he examines "water of life" as a "metaphor" for the "Spirit of grace, the Spirit and grace of God." He observes, "The words 'water of life' are words most apt to present it to us by; for what is more free than water, and what more beneficial and more desirable than life?" A bit later he proceeds:

> Water of life is . . . most apt to set forth the Spirit and grace of the gospel by. For . . . Water is . . . of a spreading nature . . . Grace . . . may be also compared to water, for that it is of a cleansing nature; therefore grace, and the Spirit of grace is compared to water. . . . Water naturally descends to, and abides in low places [and God gives his grace to the humble] . . . . The grace of God is compared to water, for that it is it which causeth fruitfulness,(III, 203-04)

Still later he elaborates the comparison, and, in doing so, acts on the principle that such elaborations themselves should also be "very natural." That is to say, he assures the reader that his extension of the comparison is "natural" even though such assurance is not relevant to his homiletic point. He says:

> It is as if God should say, Look sinners, look to the bottom of these my crystal streams. I have heard of some seas, that are so pure and clear that men may see to the bottom though they may be forty feet deep.(III, 217)

So described, the allegorical method has great flexibility. It can produce the aesthetic effects both of *mimesis* and controlled recognition, and the instructional effects of both didactic fiction and precise allegorical stipulation. It may establish either extremely short or relatively remote aesthetic distances from the object. The potential effects of narratives in which each of these latter principles is dominant differ greatly. If the "very natural" or "mimetic" potentialities of images and actions are developed within a loosely applied metaphoric framework—as they are in Langland's field full of folk or in Spenser's depiction of Sir Calidore among the shepherds—a pleasing alternation in these varying effects and aesthetic distances is possible. Professor Edwin Honig's generalization is valid in such a case. He says, "In the practical completion of its design, the allegorical work dispenses with the concept of allegory, as something preconceived, in order to achieve the fullest fictional manifestation of life."[49] On the other hand, if the "dialectical" principle, the principle that an image or action should "fitly" suit "each particular," dominates a narrative, the method itself becomes essentially a didactic, rhetorical, or analytical instrument. Such dominance produces three important effects upon a narrative.

When the dialectical principle is dominant in a given passage, or, in other terms, when the method Bunyan described is used more rigorously and systematically, it inevitably turns the passage inward. To apply Professor Honig's phrase, a narrative becomes more like a "self-contained mystery"[50] as the central metaphor becomes more dominant, as subordinate episodes or ideas are developed more consistently through analogies, and as the expressive and aesthetic functions of separate similitudes are unified more completely. It becomes more necessary that a narrative be understood as a unit before it becomes meaningful in relation to external actualities as more images and actions are developed primarily as effective vehicles, rather than as effective imitations.

Bunyan illustrated the process by which a literal narrative turned inward as it, in effect, *became* an allegory in *The Barren Fig-Tree: or, The Downfall of the Fruitless Professor,* a treatise published shortly after *The Holy War* in 1682. Bunyan quotes the "short similitude," or parable of the barren fig tree (Luke 13:6-9) as follows:

> A certain man had a fig-tree planted in his vineyard; and he came and sought fruit thereon, and found none. Then said he unto the dresser of his vineyard, Behold, these three years I come seeking fruit on this fig-tree, and find none; cut it down; why cumbereth it the ground? And he answering said unto him, Lord, let it alone this year also, till I shall dig about it, and dung it: and if it bear fruit, well: and if not, then after that thou shalt cut it down.(II, 245)

As Bunyan interprets this narrative, it contains no detail without a dual meaning; and it exhibits an almost diagrammatic or dialectical consistency among the parts.

The spirit of Bunyan's approach is suggested by Benjamin Keach's statement that "in a similitude there is a manifest *comparison* of one thing with another, and so 'tis a *logical* Argument."[51] Bunyan says, "In parables there are two things to be taken notice of.... First. The metaphors made use of. Second. The doctrine or mysteries couched under such metaphors." He then says the "metaphors in this parable are, 1. A certain man; 2. A vineyard; 3. A fig-tree, barren or fruitless; 4. A dresser; 5. Three years," and so forth. Later he lists the "metaphors" and explains their meanings: "1. By the man in the parable ... is meant God the Father. 2. By the vineyard ... his church. 3. By the fig-tree, a professor. 4. By the dresser, the Lord Jesus...." Assuming that the "doctrine, or mystery, couched under these words, is to show us what is like to become of a fruitless or formal professor," Bunyan, consistently taking the man in the parable to stand for God, the vineyard to stand for his church, and so forth, explains each element in the narrative. He writes, for example, "By the three years, [is meant] the patience of God, that for a time he extendeth to barren professors." He draws many additional conclusions from the changing relationships between the "metaphors" as the dialectic process continues (II, 246-248). Each person or thing that functions as a trope because of the initial analogy is read in a "translated" sense so that one-to-one equations are maintained throughout the closed logical system Bunyan created in interpreting the parable as an allegory. The process is radically reductive; he saw no adventitious detail in the narrative; he interpreted it so that it was completely functional as an allegorical vehicle. Given the identification of each "metaphor," the parable became a separate dynamic system in which separate tropes modified each other in some way.

Rigorous exploitation of the method so described, or in other terms, dominance of the dialectical principle, necessarily restricts the capacity of "very natural" images or actions to become effective imitations. Narrative patterns conveying fundamental insights into the human situation have a logic of their own, and it differs from the dialectical pattern evolving within such a system. Effective representation of external actualities depends upon details suggestive of the world perceived by the senses; such details give substance and authenticity to narratives. They allude to external actualities rather than to other images and actions unfolding simultaneously in the same self-contained dialectical pattern, and they are to be understood by reference to these actualities rather than by reference to other parts of the literary context. This difference in points of reference places a different demand upon each image and action. A "very natural" vehicle may suggest external actualities, may function both as imitation and vehicle, but the necessary dual points of reference—to the actuality outside the work of art and to the dialectical context—severely restrict the number of details contributing only to the vividness of fullness of the imitation. The kind of descriptive and narrative detail that fills the pages of Balzac, or Defoe, or Nashe, in effect, is necessarily excluded because it does not fall into transparent dialectical patterns.

Finally, when the dialectical principle dominates an episode or narrative, the stipulated significance of mimetic, or quasi-mimetic, material becomes unmistakably clear and precise when it is obliquely revealed. The paucity of adventitious narrative detail, detail without analogical function, contributes to the precision and ultimate clarity of stipulated relationships within the dynamic logical system.

The conflicting principles, that a vehicle should be "very natural" and that it should "fitly" suit "each particular," are both manifest in Bunyan's allegories. In both *The Pilgrim's Progress* and *The Holy War*, he imitates external actualities and simultaneously stipulates the significance of such imitations by extending a central metaphor and by using additional analogies. In both he exploits the potentialities of central metaphors and of subordinate ones to reveal truth effectively and to introduce purposeful obscurity. And in both he creates similarly contrasting effects when one or the other of these conflicting principles is dominant.

These unresolved conflicts or questions of priority in Bunyan's statements about his methods and goals are not actually resolved in the narratives. The following study advances the thesis, however, that Bunyan reduced the conflicts created by the mimetic and didactic principles by developing more effective methods for imitating external actualities and by suggesting or stipulating the significance of narrative material in more oblique or less intrusive ways.

It shows that the development is like the rising of a spring tide through a rocky, labyrinthian estuary: in the midst of varied ebbs and flows, currents and countercurrents, bores and races, the flood current moves inexorably inland. Chapters two and three show that the dominant movements in the development of literal or nonallegorial methods are toward more effective imitation and more subtle or indirect stipulation. Chapter two shows that the most overt manifestations of the didactic principle change, sometimes independently, as the narratives develop. It shows that certain "applications," which appear in all the narratives, gradually change so that they become less inimical to an illusion. It shows, too, that introductory sketches and their stylized extensions gradually become less intrusively didactic in effect and more effective in contributing to an illusion. Chapter three shows that each of the narratives exhibits a fuller realization of the capacity of a scenic method of narration for revealing complex characters effectively, expressing the inner life forcefully, and depicting the drama of social life and manners fully. More important, each narrative, except perhaps *The Holy War,* shows a fuller realization of the capacity of a scenic method of narration for creating and sustaining an illusion. The study shows that Bunyan reduces conflict in developing allegorical techniques as well. Chapter four shows that he does so essentially by making fuller and more systematic use of five oblique ways of stipulating the significance of narrative facts and exploiting temporary obfuscation and, more important, by shifting the imaginative balance so that the dialectical principle becomes dominant in *The Holy War.* Chapter five is a summary of the conclusions reached in this study of five major narratives: *Grace Abounding,* published in 1666; *The Pilgrim's Progress,* 1678; *The Life and Death of Mr. Badman,* 1680; *The Holy War,* 1682; and *The Second Part of The Pilgrim's Progress.*

CHAPTER TWO

REPRESENTATION: DIDACTIC ELEMENTS

Bunyan's critics have long recognized the effects of both the didactic and the mimetic principle in his narratives. They have consistently praised his achievement as an imitation of external actualities. They have commended, especially, the irrepressible vitality of a large gallery of representative characters in both allegorical and nonallegorical narratives. The historian, Charles Firth, said:

> Whatever adventures his pilgrims pass through, they are always flesh and blood Englishmen of the seventeenth century, speaking and acting as English Puritans of their class have acted under the conditions which Bunyan's imagination created.[1]

John Livingston Lowes confessed:

> All at once, to my amazement, I realized this: barring Hardy's rustics, the people whom I heard talking, saw gesturing, felt as almost bodily presences, as they came unsummoned back to memory, were a dozen or so of Bunyan's pilgrims.

And this, despite their "quaint, sometimes outlandish names."[2] In a similar vein, Professor G. B. Harrison insisted that the central figure in *Mr. Badman* was "no painted vice but a very real person."[3] Professor Henri Talon, too, remarked after the appearance of Honest in the *Second Part*:

> This entire passage does not read like an allegory, nor like an old-time story in which the portraits, cracked with age, represent bloodless

figures with stiff gestures, but like a romantic story very near our own time.[4]

They have also praised the settings as authentic reflections of contemporaneous actualities, clear and rich in their concrete realization. Charles Firth assumed that "for the most part he [Bunyan] draws what he has seen with his own eyes" and emphasized the historical accuracy of Bunyan's depiction of the seventeenth-century English countryside.[5] In a similar way, Lowes stressed that a certain:

> setting is not so much a transcript as it is a transformation of reality; as when this or that bit of Bedfordshire landscape all at once *shines*, with that peculiar detached brightness which belongs to familiar objects seen mirrored in a convex glass, or remembered after a vivid dream.[6]

Yet Lowes's emphasis is still, like that of Professor William York Tindall, upon the autobiographical aspects of the work, and, hence, upon the basic authenticity of the settings.[7] Professor Talon, too, at one point in his career, emphasized the accuracy of the settings in *The Pilgrim's Progress* as imitations. He said, "Christian's road was a truly English road, and more especially a truly Bedfordshire road, with its swamps, narrow causeways and deep ditches." This critical awareness of Bunyan's mimetic accomplishment has been great enough, in fact, to create what Professor Talon called an "innocent pastime" for "local archaeologists,"[8] so that the "originals" of many settings in *The Pilgrim's Progress* have been identified.[9]

Previous writers have commented, too, about the effects of the didactic principle. Charles Firth alluded to the prominence of the explicitly didactic element in classifying the *Second Part*. He suggested that Mr. Brisk's courtship of Mercy showed Bunyan as the "forerunner of Hannah More and a whole generation of novelists who sought to combine realistic fiction with moral teachings."[10] The effects of this principle upon particular characters and upon narrative movement has also been pointed out. Professor Talon, for example, said the "central figure [of *Mr. Badman*], who promised to overflow with life ... is stifled by the didactic purpose of the author."[11] And Macaulay described certain passages in *The Pilgrim's Progress* as "most difficult to defend" because Bunyan "puts into the mouth of his pilgrims religious ejaculations and disquisitions, better suited to his own pulpit at Bedford or Reading than to the Enchanted Ground or to the Interpreter's Garden."[12] In a similar way, E. M. W. Tillyard implied that much of *Mr. Badman* was "very dull reading" because it contained the "greatest amount of untrasmuted sermon-material" of all the "major works."[13] Others have played variations upon these themes.[14] The effects of the didactic principle upon the major narratives, in brief, has been recognized and, usually, lamented.

Although previous writers have observed the manifestations of both the didactic and the mimetic principles, they have not pointed out that Bunyan gradually reduced the conflict between them. He did so, essentially, by developing more effective techniques for imitating external actualities and more indirect or subtle ways of suggesting or stipulating the significance of mimetic material.

These dominant movements toward more effective imitation and more subtle didacticism are, of course, intimately related. At times, these two separate movements appear to converge, so that only a necessarily subjective judgment about a specific artistic effect can determine whether a given passage illustrates a further development of one dominant tendency or the other. Yet it would be inaccurate to say that the mimetic evolution, which is examined separately, gradually embodies a vision of actuality in artistic form and leaves behind an inert residue of direct preachments and contrived illustrative material. Undoubtedly, the unchanged residue exists. Vestiges of their didactic origin cling to certain devices Bunyan introduces in even the latest narrative, yet the nature and effect of the manifestations of the didactic principle also change as the narratives develop. They become more subtle or indirect in form; they become less inimical, or more conducive, to the basic illusion necessary to effectual narrative art.

I

Some initial imaginative acceptance of a system of belief that lacks universal appeal is obviously necessary to a reading of Bunyan's narratives.[15] A general demand for at least a temporary concurrence is inherent in the basic structure of each of them; each is, in a sense, a celebration of certain ideals that it illustrates and embodies. *Grace Abounding* affirms the divine participation and human significance of the process of religious conversion it re-creates. *Mr. Badman* is presented as an image of one suffering from divine malediction (pp. 11-13), and the narrative affirms the progressive degradation and eternal perdition attendant upon such a condition. The central metaphors of the allegories, too, are developed essentially as religious assertions about ways of conquering evil or of attaining redemption. The central metaphor of *The Pilgrim's Progress* establishes the nature of the quest and stipulates the exemplary functions of Christian and, later, of Christiana; the narrative affirms the possibility of attaining the predicted goal. The central metaphor of *The Holy City* defines the nature of man in terms of two eternally antagonistic principles, and the narrative asserts the significance and centrality of the struggle between them. An initial acceptance of this basic didactic substratum is as necessary to the reading of Bunyan's narratives as the initial, tentative acceptance of certain latitudinarian ideas are to the reading of Fielding, or of certain evolutionary ideas to the reading of Shaw, or of certain existential ideas to the reading of Sartre. Otherwise, the reader is examining propaganda rather than experiencing literature.

Granted such an initial acceptance, Bunyan's narratives, nevertheless, frequently create a problem of belief in more acute form and, in other ways, distract attention from, or dampen interest in, the complex of images and actions constituting their achieved artistic form. The basic illusion necessary to narrative art is shattered, not only by awkward artistry, but also by direct, specific demands for a concurrence of belief. These appear in the direct characterization, discussed in Section II, and more acutely in passages that may be called collective "applications." Like the passages so labeled in *Gesta Romanorum,* the applications exploit the illustrative capacities of characters and events, suggest an "official" interpretation, thus restricting a reader's own range of judgment, and, sometimes, introduce additional moral instruction and exhortation.[16] Although diverse psychological, ethical, and religious ideas gradually become embodied in artistic form so that applications appear superfluous, applications threaten the illusion at times in all the narratives.

Grace Abounding has prominent didactic characteristics aside from the applications. Professor Tindall has demonstrated that Bunyan molded the amorphous mass of remembered experience into the form of an "enthusiastic autobiography," a form very popular after 1649.[17] Puritan biographies and autobiographies, Professor William Haller emphasizes, conventionally set forth accounts of ministerial experience as examples worthy of imitation.[18] Professor Tindall stresses that writers of sectarian spiritual autobiographies, in particular, normally describe an "irreproachable example for their followers" and, in effect, define sectarian "orthodoxy."[19] Bunyan implies that the experience he describes is exemplary. Addressing his congregation from prison, Bunyan professes to present "a relation of the work of God upon [his] ... own Soul" and to put his readers "in remembrance of what he [God] hath done for their Souls, by reading his work upon [him]" (pp. 1-2). And, of course, the process of religious conversion that he re-creates is exemplary from a sectarian point of view since the young Bunyan experiences effectual calling (p. 36) and turns to the sectarian ministry (p. 83). Nevertheless, the mimetic material is not allowed to stand alone, for the narrator consistently voices applications.

The narrator, who may be referred to as an "older Bunyan" simply as a matter of convenience, is a pervasive presence. He appears as a "reliable narrator" in Professor Wayne C. Booth's sense in that "he speaks for or acts in accordance with the norms of the work (which is to say, the implied author's norms)";[20] he also claims and exercises the right to be an "official" interpreter of the experience he describes. Professor Haller pointed out that, much as Milton published personal confessions as "a kind of certification of the spirit for his right to challenge the prelates and to instruct the parliament and people in their duties and responsibilities," so many sectarian preachers published such an autobiography as a kind of "diploma from the Holy Ghost."[21] In *Grace Abounding* Bunyan makes an explicit, conventional claim to such spiritual authority:

> Truly, I then found upon this account the great God was very Good unto me, for to my remembrance there was not anything that I cried unto God to make known and reveal unto me but he was pleased to do it for me, I mean not one part of the Gospel of the Lord Jesus, but I was orderly led into it.(p. 37)

The narrative itself establishes the sectarian religious authority so claimed, and a mature minister who considers himself more fully enlightened because he had been thus favored in his youth exercises this authority.

Although the mimetic material is presented as exemplary in general, it could, presumably, mislead "weak capacities" (IV, 320) in two respects. On one hand, the young Bunyan was guilty of various doctrinal "errors" (p. 19), and, on the other, the presentation of the process of conversion was sufficiently concrete that it reflected some of the moral ambiguity of "real" experience (p. 85). The officious narrator, committed to the values the young Bunyan is learning to understand, dispels such ambiguity and "error" through varied interpretative commentary. His religious interpretations of experience are consistently implicit in the very terms he selects in describing it, and he consistently "moralizes his song." He freely analyzes and generalizes about the young man's experience: "Onely this, as I said before I will say unto you again, that in general he was pleased to take this course with me, first, to suffer me to be afflicted . . ." (pp. 39-40). He interprets or stipulates the significance of various states of consciousness: "I see it was with me, as it was with *Josephs* brethren..." (p. 68). He moralizes at length about the experience he had described:

> And now to show you something of the advantages that I also gained by this Temptation: and first, By this I was made continually to possess in my Soul a very wonderful sence both of the being and glory of God, and of his beloved Son.

In a long discourse that follows this quotation, the narrator is led far beyond the demands of the immediate situation. He specifies additional benefits: he was no longer "assaulted and tormented with Atheism"; he saw that "the truth and verity of them [the Scriptures] were the Keys of the Kingdom of Heaven"; and he was "greatly beaten off [his] former foolish practice, of putting by the Word of Promise" (pp. 76-77). The narrator emerges, thus, as a religious teacher fearful lest the significance of the experience be misunderstood. He is equally pervasive in other passages so that a mere shift in tenses differentiates his thoughts from the young Bunyan's and evinces his presence as an interpreter. Exploiting the instructional potentialities of narrative material, limiting his readers' freedom of interpretation, the narrator, thus, frequently shatters the basic illusion necessary to effective narrative art through such applications.

A part of the didactic burden borne by the older Bunyan of *Grace Abounding*, of course, does not exist in the allegories because the central metaphors and diverse subordinate devices, which are examined separately in chapter four, fix and define the central values and relationships therein. Aside from the stipulations implicit in the allegorical form of three of them, the fictional narratives contain many applications which are undoubtedly inimical to an illusion. These applications are voiced by the narrators and by certain fictional characters who acquire authority, as the older Bunyan does, from the narrative itself. Though intrusively didactic upon occasion, both the narrators and the authoritative speakers gradually change in the fictional narratives so that they become less inimical to the basic illusion necessary to narrative art.

Certain characters, who derive religious authority from their fictional roles or from their names, assume and exercise such authority in each of the narratives. Early in *The Pilgrim's Progress* Evangelist (pp. 21-24) and the Interpreter (pp. 28-34), who derive authority initially from their names, interpret Christian's experience for him and advise him about his future conduct. Later, Christian, Faithful, and Hopeful, who gain authority from their progress in the pilgrimage, examine their own experience and the experience of others in their discourses. Faithful and Christian discuss the nature of Talkative's "errors" (p. 80), for example, and Christian and Hopeful examine the religious significance of By-ends's (p. 100) and Atheist's (p. 135) conduct in much the same way. Mr. Wiseman consistently exploits occasions both from the story in the background (p. 61) and from the drama in the foreground (pp. 56-57) of *Mr. Badman* to exercise the authority his name gives him; he explains the moral or religious significance of characters and events and discourses at length about them. Many fictional participants of limited, but clearly designated religious authority, such as Lord Understanding (pp. 117-18), and Mr. Conscience (pp. 140-42), share with figures of unrestricted authority, such as Shaddai (pp. 28-29) and Emmanuel (p. 247), the functions of interpreting events and suggesting their significance. The interpretative commentary of characters such as Honest (p. 255), Standfast (p. 301), Valiant-for-Truth (p. 294), and Gaius (p. 263) in the *Second Part* is, perhaps, less unquestionable, yet the narrative clearly establishes the authority used by such speakers as the Interpreter (p. 200), the Shepherds (p. 286), and, most important, the servant of the Holy Ghost, Greatheart himself (pp. 209-11).

These authoritative figures continue to raise the spectre of didactic contrivance and to destroy the illusion when they use other characters as illustrations. The process is usually radically reductive. When Greatheart reduces Mr. By-ends to the status of an illustration in the *Second Part*, for example, all of Mr. By-ends's engaging, though perverse, verbal dexterity evaporates so that he becomes, however briefly, a mere wooden image of prudent hypocrisy (p. 273). And so of others: Wiseman continually uses Mr. Badman in this way, and so the Judge reduces FalsePeace in *The Holy War* (p. 128). Christian and Hopeful reduce the delightful Ignorance in this way (p. 151) and, in fact, press Hopeful's own past into service for its illustrative value (pp. 138-40). The process is not always one of reduction, of course; at times, the illustrative use of a minor figure merely calls attention to the didactic impoverishment of the character's presentation, as it does when Christian and Hopeful discuss their encounter with Atheist (p. 136). Such exploitation raises the spectre of didactic contrivance with special force when the character so used has had no chance to gain autonomy during his appearance, yet few characters, either major or minor, are wholly exempt from service as illustrations.

The authoritative characters continue to threaten the illusion by "pointing the moral" of separate episodes and moralizing at greater length than the occasion appears to demand. Just as the older Bunyan examined and explained at length the religious significance of each phase of his experience in *Grace Abounding* (pp. 76-77), so in the first fictional narrative, Christian points the moral of the encounter with Talkative:

> I told you how it would happen, your words and his lusts could not agree; he had rather leave your company, then reform his life: but he is gone as I said, let him go; the loss is no mans but his own, he has saved us the trouble of going from him . . . [H]e would have been but a blot in our Company: besides, the Apostle says, *From such withdraw thy self*. . . . (pp. 84-85)

In a similar way in the last fictional narrative, when Great-heart had to abandon his charges, he too pointed the moral:

I am at my Lords Commandment. If he shall allot me to be your Guide quite thorough, I will willingly wait upon you; but here you failed at first; for when he bid me come thus far with you, then you should have begged me of him to have gon [sic] quite thorough with you. (p. 220)

Again, just as the older Bunyan was led beyond the demands of the immediate occasion in his discourse (pp. 76-78), so the Evangelist in the first fictional narrative goes well beyond the demands of the immediate occasion in giving Christian a sermon, rather than a simple warning, against Mr. Worldly Wiseman's advice (pp. 22-23). In a similar way, Great-heart seizes upon a narrative occasion to deliver a discourse upon the nature of Christ (pp. 209-12) that is a concise summary of doctrine to which Bunyan himself had devoted much of *Some Gospel Truths Opened* (I, 55-78). Impeding narrative movement, short-circuiting a reader's range of association, the authoritative participants continue to threaten an illusion.

They gradually become less inimical to an illusion in two principal ways. They gradually show greater respect for the confines of the world in which they exist, and they gradually voice fewer discourses without a fairly direct thematic or dramatic sanction.

Many questions of relevance are debatable, of course, but extremes are evident in *The Pilgrim's Progress*. Christian describes Temporary, for example, overtly *in order that* he and Hopeful may "fall upon another profitable question," and the narrative offers no narrative occasion for the long discussion that follows of "the reason of the siddain backsliding of him and such others" (pp. 151-54). Mr. Wiseman and Attentive, of course, indulge in tremendous numbers of such discussions in *Mr. Badman,* yet the matrix of personality lightens the didactic weight of many of them. Wiseman and Attentive, for example, disagree about whether Mr. Badman's father should have given him "Money to set up [business] for himself." During the course of the disagreement, Wiseman discusses the dangerous effects of excessive parental severity, the necessity of parental discipline, and the desirability that parents "carry it lovingly towards their Children, mixing their Mercies with loving Rebukes" (pp. 66-68). The sustained dramatic tension between the speakers, which is examined separately, merely prefigures the dramatic integration realized in *The Holy War*. This integration had proceeded so far that, for example, none of Emmanuel's major addresses (pp. 84, 137, 256) could easily be placed in a different narrative context; each appearance grows out of the earlier narrative situation, and each advances the central plot significantly. And so, to a lesser extent, with the other authoritative figures. In the *Second Part*

Great-heart does, in fact, give a sermon about the nature of Christ (pp. 209-12), as was mentioned, but that is given in answer to a question at the Cross. He seldom talks that long elsewhere without interruption. The Interpreter (p. 200) and the Shepherds (p. 284) teach largely by the Socratic method and are given little opportunity to pursue their topics far beyond the demands of the immediate narrative situation. Untransmuted or irrelevant sermon material, in brief, is rare in the *Second Part.*

The authoritative speakers in the allegories become less inimical to an illusion, too, because they gradually allude to external actuality less directly. Only a few such speakers in *The Pilgrim's Progress* preserve the fiction of the pilgrimage (p. 22); more typical are passages like the following in which Christian and Hopeful sound a bit like "Question" and "Answer" of a moral discourse:[22]

> Chr. *But what was the cause of your carrying of it thus to the first workings of Gods blessed Spirit upon you?*
> *Hope.* The causes were, 1. I was ignorant that this was the work of God upon me. . . . 2. Sin was yet very sweet to my flesh. . . . 3. I could not tell how to part with mine old Companions. . . . 4. The hours in which convictions were upon me, were such troublesome . . . hours that I could not bear, no not so much as the remembrance of them upon my heart.

Or a bit later:

> Chr. *Why, what was it that brought your sins to mind again?*
> *Hope.* Many things, As.
> 1. If I did but meet a good man in the Streets; or,
> 2. If I have heard any read in the Bible; or
> 3. If mine head did begin to Ake; or,
> 4. If I were told that some of my Neighbours were sick. . . . (p. 138)

Speeches alluding directly to external actualities are not quite so inappropriate in the nonallegorical *Mr. Badman,* of course, though many also sound like direct preachments (pp. 97-102). But such is not the case in *The Holy War.*

Authoritative speakers in *The Holy War* respect the confines of their fictional world so completely that much of their commentary merely clarifies stipulations implicit in events (pp. 102, 105) without alluding overtly to external actualities. Allusions to external actuality are very indirect and very subtle in many speeches that function primarily to clarify narrative relationships. The following speech of Emmanuel is typical in that, aside from the appropriately formal style and the compassionate tone, it clearly, but quite obliquely, points beyond the immediate dramatic occasion:

Besides, O my *Mansoul,* thou seest what I have done, and how I have taken thee out of the hands of thine Enemies; unto whom thou hadst deeply revolted from my Father, and by whom thou wast content to be possessed, and also to be destroyed. I came to thee first by my Law, then by my Gospel, to awaken thee, and show thee my Glory. And thou knowest ... how many times thou rebelledst against my Father and me; yet I left thee not ... but ... have waited upon thee, and, after all, accepted of thee, even of my mere grace and favour; and would not suffer thee to be lost, as thou most willingly wouldst have been. I also compassed thee about ... that I might make thee weary of thy ways, and bring down thy heart with molestation to a willingness to close with thy good and happiness. And when I had gotten a complete conquest over thee, I turned it to thy advantage.(p. 247)

The narrative context clearly revitalizes the decayed metaphors as a part of the fiction; at the same time, the figurative language is sufficiently commonplace that a clear stipulatory reference outside the work itself is evident in such phrases as "thine Enemies," "deeply revolted," and "rebelledst against my Father." The speech is one of many in which authoritative commentary points consistently inward and outward only very obliquely indeed. Great-heart shows that he has mastered the art in the *Second Part,* for he recounts Christiana's encounter with "two Ruffians," his own encounters with "Gyant *Bloody-man,* Gyant *Maul,* and Gyant *Slay-good,"* and the rescue of Mr. *Feeble-mind* without direct allusion to any of the relevant external actualities. (pp. 275-76)

The process by which the narrators gradually become less inimical to an illusion is more complicated because, aside from the effects of their stipulatory comments, they affect an illusion in more diverse ways. They continue to be inimical to an illusion in two principal ways. They distract attention from the story to the way it is told by their inconsistency or awkwardness in establishing and maintaining their relationships to the narrative material and to the reader. They also continue to be inimical because they display little artistic detachment about their moral and religious themes.

Quite aside from the effects of their stipulatory comments, the narrators reveal themselves as deeply religious moralists through their narrative and linguistic choices. They pretend to no more neutrality about moral and religious values than does the older Bunyan of *Grace Abounding.* The language of the Dreamer in *The Pilgrim's Progress* consistently implies moral or religious judgments, often by the mere turn of a phrase. He says, for example, that Christian "had not discretion neither to stop his ears, nor to know whence those blasphemies came" (p. 64). His narrative choices in even the most prominent scenes convey a similar impression. The memorable description of Christian's ascent to the Celestial City, for example, ends with the Dreamer's poignant report, "and after that, they shut up the Gates: which when I had seen, I wished myself among them." But the book does not end celebrating the consummation of a Christian ideal; rather, it ends upon a less exalted note. The ignoble end of Ignorance is then depicted, and the Dreamer concludes with an oblique note of warning: "Then I saw that there was a way to Hell, even from the Gates of Heaven, as well as from the City of *Destruction.* So I awoke, and behold it was a Dream" (pp. 162-63). Since the scene is organized so that it emphasizes the sharp contrast between the triumphant and the rejected traveller, the Dreamer's comment merely reinforces the impression, created by his earlier narrative choice, that the narrator is a deeply religious moralist.

Similar implications appear in *The Holy War* through the narrator's choice of agents extending the central metaphor; the language and tone strengthen these implications:

> So when the Town of *Mansoul* had received at the hand of *Emmanuel* their gracious charter, . . . [it was] engraven upon the doors . . . to the end that the Town of *Mansoul,* and all the people thereof . . . might go where they might see what a blessed Freedom their Prince had bestowed upon them, that their joy might be increased in themselves, and their love renewed to their great and good *Emmanuel.* (p. 138)

In a similar way, the narrator of the *Second Part* pretends to little impartiality about questions of value when he decides what aspects of a situation to describe or what adjectives to use in describing it:

> Wherefore the *Pilgrims* grew acquainted with many of the good people of the Town, and did them what service they could. *Mercie* . . . was there an Ornament to her Profession. And to say the truth, for *Grace, Phebe,* and *Martha* they were all of a very good Nature, and did much good in their place. They were also all of them very Fruitful, so that *Christian's* Name, as was said before, was like to live in the World. (p. 277)

And so throughout, the organization of episodes, the evaluations of characters and events, and the general selection and emphasis consistently imply that the narrator is a deeply religious moralist rather than a detached, objective artist.

The narrators gradually become less inimical to an illusion, essentially, because they become less prominent both as distractions and as moralistic *personae* who raise the spectre of didactic contrivance by their mere presence. They become less prominent in this latter sense, perhaps, as indirect results of developments that are examined separately. After the disappearance of the narrator from the opening pages of *Mr. Badman* (p. 18), authoritative fictional characters become more prominent than the narrators as sources of passages that may be classified as applications. So, too, as the scenic method of narration develops, a process examined in chapter three, the narrators become less prominent and, hence, find fewer occasions to effect an illusion. The narrators, thus, contribute to the dominant movements toward effective imitation and unobtrusive didacticism, paradoxically, by doing less. They become less prominent in distracting attention from the story to the way it is told, essentially, by changing the two basic roles they assume.

The narrators of both *The Pilgrim's Progress* and *The Holy War* are composite figures; they are both embryonic omniscient authors and minor figures in the foreground. The narrator of the later work endangers the illusion less frequently than the Dreamer of the earlier one because of changes in both these roles.

The Dreamer is relatively prominent as a "reliable narrator" of a dream vision, a minor figure in the foreground connecting Christian's world to the "real" one. He talks to the figures in the vision upon occasion and freely comments about it (pp. 15, 156). He frequently reminds a reader of his presence as a minor figure who overtly belongs to the reader's world, rather than to Christian's, by the phrase, "Then I saw in my Dream . . ." (pp. 66, 106, 120, 158) and by slight variations like ". . . as I remember my Dream . . ." (p. 53), and "I saw then in my Dream . . ." (p. 63). He insists upon his role in connecting two worlds, too, by such phrases as "No man can imagine unless he has seen and heard as I did . . ." (p. 111). As a minor figure, too, he accepts certain human limitations; he confines himself to the role of a viewer and auditor of a dream vision. He says, for example, "Then he went on, and I heard him sigh bitterly, for . . ." (p. 64). And he speculates about things seen and heard. He says, for example:

> Now I saw in my Dream, that at the end of this Valley lay blood, bones, ashes, and mangled bodies of men, even of Pilgrims that had gone this way formerly: And while I was musing what should be the reason. . . . (p. 65)

Belonging overtly to the reader's world, speculating about the relationship of one world to another, yet suggesting applications by his very phrasing, this minor figure endangers the illusion to the extent that he becomes a separate center of attention in the foreground.

The Dreamer distracts attention from the story to the way it is told by ignoring the human limitations of the minor figure, the spectator, in the foreground and assuming, at unpredictable times, another role. He functions as a knowledgeable, authoritative interpreter in the manner of the older Bunyan in *Grace Abounding*. He often seems quite knowledgeable about the Way and its history. He mentions, for example, "a little ascent, which was cast up on purpose, that Pilgrims might see before them ..." (p. 66). And, more knowledgeably still, he explains that, in the "Country of *Beulah*," the "Sun shineth night and day" and "the shining Ones commonly walked [there], because it was upon the Borders of Heaven" (pp. 154-55). Like the older Bunyan of *Grace Abounding*, too, though less logically, he avails himself of some prerogatives of an omniscient author and raises the spectre of didactic contrivance. For example, he presents Christian's private thoughts, "*O wretched man that I am,* that I should sleep in the day time ..." (p. 44). He also explains the characters' motives, "Yet, could he [Christian] have helped it, he would not have done it ..." (p. 64). Unlike the narrator of *Grace Abounding*, he does not directly establish his religious authority except insofar as he is an aspect of the one privileged to see the vision, yet he clearly exercises such authority and establishes "official" judgments of people and events (pp. 88-89). The Dreamer is thus inimical to an illusion in both his roles because he overtly changes his relationship to the story and to the reader.

Although the narrator of *The Holy War* does not, as Professor Roger Sharrock avers,[23] disappear after the opening paragraph, the minor figure in the foreground is a much less conspicuous presence than his predecessor. He reminds a reader of his existence as a mere auditor and observer by such assertions as "It made me laugh to see how old Mr. *Prejudice* was kicked and tumbled" (p. 61); or "But I never saw *Willbewill* so daunted in all my life" (p. 83); or "But you cannot think, unless you have been there, as I was, what a shout there was in *Emmanuel's* Camp when they saw ..." (p. 93). And he re-establishes his existence as a minor figure from time to time by addressing the reader with a certain conversational informality (pp. 62, 90, 148) and using the first person (p. 161). But he is not conspicuously connecting one world to another; he is in, and about, Mansoul as a reporter in the foreground who is having a bit of trouble getting the story: "But, so far as I could gather by the best information that I could get, all this hubbub came through the words that the *Recorder* said when he told them ..." (p. 98). In contrast to his predecessor in *The Pilgrim's Progress,* he is less inimical to an illusion because he is less overt in interpreting one world to another as well as less prominent as a minor figure.

The omniscient narrator of *The Holy War* is a less distracting presence than his predecessors in the role because he boldly and gracefully assumes many more of his prerogatives than his predecessor. The Dreamer, accepting one of the inherent limits of verisimilitude in the description of a dream, remains in the foreground and describes a dream passing before him. The narrator of *The Holy War*, in contrast, boldly moves through time (pp. 9, 17) and space, now presenting dramatic scenes in heaven (p. 67), later describing sinister scenes in darker regions (p. 172), now implicitly in the midst of a discontented crowd in Mansoul (p. 21), later witnessing a major battle from a great distance (p. 87). And he is more graceful than Mr. Wiseman, his recent predecessor in this respect, in assuming certain of his prerogatives. Mr. Wiseman allowed himself much latitude in reporting the private thoughts of Mrs. Badman and explaining her motivation (p. 77). Upon occasion, however, a reader's attention was called to this violation of the chosen point of view. Attentive once asked, "*Did she talk thus openly?*" Wiseman hastily replied, "No; This she spake but to one or two of her most intimate acquaintance" (p. 150). The narrator of *The Holy War*, in contrast, freely reports private conversations, even of Shaddai and Emmanuel (p. 28), and glides easily into the minds of his characters. He says, for example, "These papers, therefore, were published ... to the no little molestation of the Tyrant *Diabolus*; *for now,* thought he, *I shall be molested, and my habitation will be taken from me.*" And he moves as easily out again. In this case, for example, he simply ends the paragraph and returns to the narrative (p. 29) without awkward apologies.

Bolder as an omniscient narrator, less conspicuous as a minor figure, this narrator creates less distraction than his predecessor by changing his relationship to the story and the reader. He is, further, less inimical to an illusion in both his roles because his most direct textual interpretative suggestions point inward to the text itself rather than outward to external actualities. He suggests an interpretation most directly through concise summaries that end separate phases of the action. Introduced quite unobtrusively (pp. 138, 149-50), these summaries typically cut through the mass of allegorical elaboration and establish the central facts unmistakably:

> And now *Diabolus* thought himself safe. He had taken *Mansoul,* he had ingarrisoned himself therein; he had put down the old Officers, and had set up new ones; he had defaced the image of *Shaddai,* and had set up his own; he had spoiled the old Law Books, and had promoted his own vain lie; he had made him new Magistrates, and set up new Aldermen; he had builded him new Holds, and manned them for himself. And all he did to make himself secure, in case the good *Shaddai,* or his *Son,* should come to make an incursion upon him.(pp. 26-27)

Such clarfiying recapitulations are, perhaps, also less intrusively didactic in effect than comparable ones in *The Pilgrim's Progress* (pp. 28-34) since—with rare exceptions (pp. 171-72)—the narrator creates no awkward narrative occasion to introduce them.

The Dreamer of the *Second Part* is the least conspicuous of the narrators after the departure of Sagacity. Even before his departure, in fact, the two narrators stipulate the significance of relatively few narrative facts. Unlike the narrator of *The Holy War*, the speakers in the foreground introduce no clarifying recapitulations during transitional phases of the action. Despite the threat of Sagacity's name, he and the Dreamer do little adventitious moralizing in Mr. Wiseman's vein. They do, however, constitute a distraction while both are on the scene.

As minor figures conversing in the foreground of the *Second Part* (pp. 175-88), Sagacity and the Dreamer are more notable, perhaps, for their awkwardness as narrative devices than for their didactic intrusiveness.[24] Mr. Sagacity dominates these pages both as a minor figure and as an omniscient author. He is introduced as a minor figure, an "aged Gentleman" who was to go "some part of the way that I [the Dreamer] was travelling" (p. 174), and the Dreamer makes comments about him as a minor figure, saying, for example, the "Old Gentleman [who] ... told me this Story, did himself seem to be greatly affected therewith" (p. 180). Knowing what has happened in the land of the pilgrims since the Dreamer's last visit, Sagacity boldly assumes some of the prerogatives of an omniscient author in describing them. Without awkward apologies, he freely shifts the scene (pp. 184, 185), reports Christiana's private conversation with her sons (p. 180), and allows himself free access to the inner lives of Christiana (p. 177) and Mercy (p. 183). Yet he remains a minor figure like the one in *The Holy War*; he does not interpret one world to another because he is essentially a dweller in the land of the pilgrims. When he is abruptly dismissed—the Dreamer merely asserts, "And now Mr. *Sagacity* left me to Dream out my Dream by my self" (p. 188)—he ceases to distract attention from the vision, and, more important, he allows the Dreamer to recede into the background as a minor figure who belongs to the reader's world though he describes another.

Rarely after the dismissal of Mr. Sagacity does the Dreamer remind a reader of his own presence as a minor figure, a viewer and auditor of a dream vision, by such a phrase as, "Yea, for aught I could perceive, they ..." (p. 297). He becomes primarily a self-effacing, bold, knowledgeable, omniscient narrator thereafter, even assuming to himself knowledge of events that had taken place since the earlier pilgrimage (p. 218). He is so far from apologizing for assuming the prerogatives of an omniscient author that he consistently changes the station point without making even such explanatory remarks as the narrator of *The Holy War* had sometimes made: "Come up, then, to the Mountains, you that love to see military

REPRESENTATION: DIDACTIC ELEMENTS / 39

actions, and behold by both sides how the fatal blow is given . . ." (p. 86). He uses these powers so consistently, boldly, and unobtrusively that he is accepted with an implicit faith. He reports, for example, "Now when *Mercie* was in Bed, she could not sleep for joy, for that now her doubts of missing at last, were removed further from her than ever they were before. So she lay blessing and Praising God who had had such favour for her" (p. 207). His report seems, in context, no more questionable than the similar report of the older Bunyan which it echoes from *Grace Abounding:* "That night was a good night to me, I never had but few better. . . . Christ was a precious Christ to my Soul that night; I could scarce lie in my Bed for joy, and peace, and triumph, thorow Christ" (p. 82). The narrator of the *Second Part* does not moralize about narrative facts but briskly narrates them (p. 297). He becomes, in brief, the least conspicuous of the narrators and the least inimical to an illusion.

II

Bunyan's critics have not mentioned them, but brief homiletic sketches appear in Bunyan's earliest publication, *Some Gospel Truths Opened* (I, 77). These embryonic sketches, and those in *A Few Sighs from Hell* (I, 143), enumerate outward "signs" of various states of the soul and function simply as illustrations. They have four basic parts: brief definitions, enumerations of typical actions, self-revealing speeches, and didactic applications. In *Some Gospel Truths,* for example, Bunyan speaks of "legal righteous men and women" and describes their actions as follows:

[They] go about to establish their own righteousness, as reading, hearing sermons, prayers, public or private, peaceableness with their neighbours, fasting, alms, good works, as they count them, just dealings, abstinence from the grosser pollutions of the world, stricter obedience to the commandments of the first and second table; all which, with many other things, may be comprehended in their own righteousness.(I, 77)

Again, Bunyan speaks of "poor souls that do think to be excused for their ignorance" and allows them to display their attitudes in speech: "Alas, saith one, I am a poor ignorant man, or women; and therefore I hope that the Lord will have mercy upon me" (I, 77). In context, these homiletic sketches illustrate departures from the religious norms of conduct Bunyan is advocating. They function, in fact, much as William Law's descriptions of such figures as Calidus, Fulvius, and Flatus do; in Law's phrase, they illustrate the "folly and madness"[25] of pursuing a course contrary to the recommended one.

The sketches in a second phase are satiric in tone and method. They appear in *The Strait Gate, or The Great Difficulty of Going to Heaven*, which was published ten years after *Grace Abounding*,[26] and two years before *The Pilgrim's Progress*. This pungent series of descriptions of those who "will seek to enter in, and shall not be able" (II, 398-99) make it almost necessary to assume, as many commentators have,[27] that Bunyan had discovered, or rediscovered, the Theophrastan character. Professor Benjamin Boyce says the most popular of the three main kinds of "polemic" characters was a variant of the "Overbury sketch of low types." The "strict form" of that variety, he points out, retains much of the Overburian concentration; it begins with a witty figure, gives a series of "specific suggestive actions and opinions," is arranged so that many sentences begin with "he," contains both a "Jacobean quibble" and a "Senecan seesaw," and ends with a "stinging finale."[28] These characteristics appear in the following sketch from *The Strait Gate:*

> There is yet another professor; and he is for God and for Baal too: . . . his religion alters as fast as his company; he is a frog of Egypt, and can live in the water and out of the water; he can live in religious company, and again as well out. Nothing that is disorderly comes amiss to him; he will hold with the hare, and run with the hound; he carries fire in one hand, and water in the other; he is a very anything but what he should be. This is also one of the many that "will seek to enter in, and shall not be able." (II, 399)

Clearly belonging to the Theophrastan tradition in its rhythm, concentration, organization, and concreteness, the sketch realizes a satiric intent through its witty use of proverbial aphorism, its patterned metaphoric development, its debasing animal imagery, and its controlled tone of wry, amused incredulity. It also offers a better basis than earlier sketches for the creation of a fictional character because it focuses upon a particular kind of person rather than upon a particular quality displayed by a number of people. It is typical of the characters in *The Strait Gate*, however, in that it functions in context just as the homiletic sketches do, as illustrations of departures from the norms of behavior advocated therein.

Direct characterization much like these early Theophrastan characters appear in each of the narratives. They stand out vividly because of their formal pattern, their method of development, and their distinctive stylistic characteristics. In *The Pilgrim's Progress* they describe a spirited group of wayward professors, and the following speech of Mr. Hold-the-World is typical. It exhibits the concentration, the popular aphorism and metaphor, the polished, balanced sentences, and the striking conclusion of a Theophrastan character:

Ai, and hold you there still, good Mr. *By-ends*, for, for my part, I can count him but a fool, that having the liberty to keep what he has, shall be so unwise as to lose it. Let us be wise *as Serpents*, 'tis best to make hay when the Sun shines; you see how the Bee lieth still all winter and bestirs her then only when she can have profit with pleasure. God sends sometimes Rain, and sometimes Sunshine; if they be such fools to go through the first, yet let us be content to take fair weather along with us. . . . And *Job* saies, that a good man *shall lay up gold as dust.*(p. 102)

The norm is still implicit in the name, and no other character comments about the subtle perversions of Christian platitudes involving the busy bee, the wise serpent, and Job's observation about gold.

The sketches in *Mr. Badman* introduce, not minor figures, but separate aspects of the "badness" of the central one. The rigidity of the formal pattern is especially striking in the early pages (pp. 20-48) in which there is an almost mechanical alteration of moral discourse and fictional sketch. The basic pattern, involving the naming or defining of the sin or foible, the enumeration of characteristic acts, the self-revealing speeches, and, in context, the didactic applications, persists, though the sketches lack the polish of those in the earlier masterpiece. Many brief self-revealing speeches and a few longer ones exhibit a striking polish and balance:

I can be religious, and irreligious, I can be anything or nothing; I can swear, and speak against swearing; I can lye and speak against lying; I can drink, wench, be unclean, and defraud, and not be troubled for it. Now I enjoy myself and am Master of mine own wayes, and not they of me. This I have attained with much study, great care, and more pains.(p. 90)

The "Senecan seesaw" and the studied rhetorical flourish, however, are relatively rare in *Mr. Badman*.

Similar abstract, delightful, and artificial sketches introduce a number of minor figures in the final narratives as well. Those of figures such as Mr. Haughty (p. 131) and Mr. Evil-Questioning (pp. 239-41) in the trial scenes of *The Holy War* echo earlier achievements so brilliantly that they have elicited more critical praise than the central figures. Professor Sharrack, for example, commends the trial scenes,[29] and James A. Froude says of them, "Here we have Bunyan at his best. The scene in the court rises to the level of the famous trial of Faithful in Vanity Fair."[30] In the *Second Part* Christiana's refreshingly unregenerate friends attack her and expose themselves (pp. 184-85) with all the vigor of earlier witnesses. So, too, the inimitable Mme. Bubble (pp. 300-02) sparkles as brilliantly as any of her predecessors among the wayward professors satirized in *The Pilgrim's Progress*. Yet the basic parts of the earlier sketches frequently appear in order without interruption. When, for example, Mr. Feeblemind appears, he defines his own nature—"I am a sickly man, as you see . . ."—enumerates typical actions, largely in relation to a symbolic landscape, and brings his speech to a resounding close (pp. 267-68). The rhythm in this latter sketch is less precisely controlled than in the satiric ones, yet the artificiality of the form and the abstractness of the figure are evident.

Delightful in themselves, these sketches prove inimical to an illusion in a fictional context largely because they retain a certain formal rigidity and didactic force. They retain some of their didactic force, not simply because major figures such as Christian and Great-heart discuss characters so introduced as examples, or point the moral of their conditions, but because they are organized and developed as amusing and effective illustrations of typical kinds of people. Moral or religious categories are usually implicit in their definitions. The enumerated actions maintain a sharp focus upon the theme announced by the names, and they themselves exhibit few details irrelevant to their illustrative function before the return to middle "C." The heavily ironic tone further heightens the didactic force of some of them as well. Their retention of the formal pattern and distinctive stylistic characteristics of the Theophrastan form is inimical to an illusion because this artificiality in context distracts attention from the subject to the manner of its presentation. The formal pattern demands, further, an abstract development that, if not inimical to an illusion, is clearly not conducive to one. Some of the sketches in the fictional narratives lose their abstractness, their artificiality, and much of their didactic force, however. The early sketches are analogous to the schemata of the visual artist in these cases.

In *Art and Illusion: A Study in the Psychology of Pictorial Representation*,[31] Professor E. H. Gombrich says an artist creating visual representations of external actuality needs "some starting point, some initial schema."[32] "Every artist," he asserts, "has to know and construct a schema before he can adjust it to the needs of portrayal."[33] "The schema," he explains, ". . . represents the first approximate, loose, category which is gradually tightened to fit the form it is to reproduce."[34] It is a "starting point for corrections, adjustments, and adaptations"[35] during the creative process so that the "correct portrait," for example, "is the end product on a long road through schema and correction."[36] He emphasizes that a "representation is never a replica." Rather, he asserts, the artist's illusion is the product of a long process of "making and matching," of modifying the schemata available within a given tradition by reference to the external actualities being represented.[37]

Whether Bunyan's actual process of composition consisted of "making and matching," of course, cannot be determined,[38] but the sketches are analogous as relatively abstract patterns supplied by tradition. The sketch is analogous, too, in that it serves as a "first approximate, loose category" that he "gradually tightened to fit the form it [was] to reproduce" through evocative details alluding to external actualities. Further, it is analogous in that modifications and extensions of the basic pattern create and sustain an illusion of external actuality. A large gallery of vivid characters introduced by what may be called Bunyan's schemata arouse human interest and take on the iridescent colors of life as tangible creations through modifications and extensions of the initial abstract pattern. When the schemata are developed and extended, they contribute to the dominant movements toward less intrusive didacticism and more effective imitation.

The effects of the modified schemata gradually merge with those of another method of revealing character. In a sense, Bunyan revealed character by adapting these sketches and certain moral discourses to the service of prose fiction. On one hand, he transformed expository dialogues, in which the revelation of character was initially incidental to the presentation of ideas, into a series of dynamic, intense, dramatic scenes which explore moral or religious themes concretely and reveal the natures of complex representative figures. This process will be examined separately in chapter three. On the other, he developed some schemata, in which character *was* the idea, into clearly distinguished, morally unambiguous, representative figures. In the early works, Bunyan adapted the expository dialogues primarily to present major characters like Christian, Faithful, and Hopeful; the sketches, only for minor ones. Later, schemata contribute to the characterization of both major and minor characters, and the stylistic differences in dialogue related to the two separate methods become less notable. Although embryonic sketches continued to appear, some schemata in each of the fictional narratives became more elaborate and more effective as characterization.

In *The Pilgrim's Progress* at least three minor figures, Talkative, By-ends, and Ignorance, benefit miraculously from elaborated schemata. The didactic overtones, the abstractness, and the artificiality of the schemata in *The Pilgrim's Progress* are reduced principally by stylized dialogue, by a partial dispersal of their elements, and by a striking descent to the concrete.

The descent to the concrete enables schemata to suggest the complexity of "real" human experience even though the sharp focus of the Theophrastan form is retained. In the case of Ignorance, the nature of that descent is clear. *The Strait Gate* refers to a "wilfully-ignorant Professor" who is "afraid to know more, for fear of the cross" (II, 399).

In *The Pilgrim's Progress,* Ignorance enters the road to the Celestial City by a "little crooked Lane," rather than by *"the Wicket-gate, that is, at the head of this way."* He rejects Christian's explanation about the "correct" entrance to the Way (pp. 123-24). Later, he rejects the doctrine of justification by faith because "this conceit would loosen the reines of our lust, and tollerate us to live as we list" (p. 148). Again, the "wilfully-ignorant Professor" of *The Strait Gate* was "for the picking and choosing of truth, and loveth not to hazard his all for that worthy name by which he could be called" (II, 399). In *The Pilgrim's Progress,* Ignorance dismisses the suggestion that he should have entered the Way by the "Wicket-gate" on the grounds that "we have, as you see, a fine, pleasant, green Lane, that comes down from our Countrey [of Conceit] the next way into it" (p. 124). Later, he is "picking and choosing" again; he refuses to accept his own absolute unworthiness, saying "I will never believe that my heart is thus bad" (p. 146). He also refuses to "hazard his all"; he rejects the necessity of direct revelation of Christ on the basis that the doctrine is *"the fruit of distracted braines"* (p. 148). It is said of the "wilfully-ignorant Professor" of *The Strait Gate,* "When he is at any time overset by arguments, or awakenings of conscience, he uses to heal all by, I was not brought up in this faith" (II, 399). During Ignorance's initial encounter with Christian, he urges, "Be content to follow the Religion of your Countrey, and I will follow the Religion of mine." He dismisses the "Gate that you talk of," saying, "All the world knows that that is a great way off of our Countrey. I cannot think that any man in all our parts doth so much as know the way to it" (p. 124). Some time later, he interrupts Christian's discourse saying, *"That is your faith, but not mine; yet mine I doubt not, is as good as yours"* (p. 149). And, from a sectarian point of view, of course, Ignorance repeatedly illustrates that he is "wilfully-ignorant" since he avoids the pilgrims (pp. 125, 132), and he says explicitly, *"You go so fast, I cannot keep pace with you; do you go on before, I must stay a while behind"* (p. 149). The generalizations in *The Strait Gate* are superseded by a multiplicity of specific, sensory incidents whose more subtle implications differ though their central function may be merely illustrative.

The temperamental or psychological implications of Ignorance's intellectual commitments are further revealed through the descent to the concrete, too, so that he acquires still greater complexity. The "wilfully-ignorant Professor" of *The Strait Gate* was for the "picking and choosing" of truth, and he was sure the faith he was "brought up in" would suffice (II, 399). In *The Pilgrim's Progress,* Ignorance displays delusive hopes in diverse ways so that a fundamental optimism becomes an inherent aspect of his personality. He says, "I hope all will be well" (p. 124), and reveals this hopefulness graphically as he passes over that final River with "half that difficulty which the other two men met with" through the help of *"Vain-hope* a Ferry-man." It is revealed dramatically in the brief scene by the gate of Heaven before he is "carried ... through the air to the door ... in the side of the Hill" (pp. 162-63). This optimism is revealed, too, through his speech so that it becomes an intrinsic part of the temperament or personality of a particular, authentic character. When Christian asks, for example, *"Come, how do you? how stands it between God and your Soul now?"* Ignorance answers:

> Ignor. I hope well, for I am always full of good motions, that come my mind to comfort me as I walk.
> Chr. *What good motions? pray tell us.*
> Ignor. Why, I think of God and Heaven.
> Chr. *So do the Devils, and damned Souls.*
> Ignor. But I think of them, and desire them.
> Chr. *So do many that are never like to come there:* The Soul of the Sluggard desires and hath nothing.
> Ignor. But I think of them, and leave all for them.
> Chr. *That I doubt, for leaving of all, is an hard matter. ... But why ... art thou perswaded that thou hast left all for God and Heaven?*
> Ignor. My heart tells me so.
> Chr. *The wise man sayes,* he that trusts his own heart is a fool.
> Ignor. That is spoken of an evil heart, but mine is a good one.
> Chr. *But how dost thou prove that?*
> Ignor. It comforts me in the hopes of Heaven. (pp. 144-45)

And so, Christian's relentless pursuit continues, and Ignorance continually refuses to be depressed by deflating doctrines offensive to his optimistic temperament. Such, at least, is the illusion. A quality of personality merely latent in the earlier generalizations has become an intrinsic, coherent part of the effect produced by a vital "round" fictional character.[39]

The rigidity and artificiality of the schemata are softened through a dispersal of the elements. This dispersal gives a Chaucerian appearance of disorder and spontaneity to the passages introducing, for example, a courteous gentleman who was initially evasive about his name:

> Chr. *Pray Sir, what may I call you?* said *Christian.*
> By-ends. I am a Stranger to you, and you to me; if you be going this way, I shall be glad of your Company; if not, I must be content.
> Chr. *This Town of* Fair-speech *said* Christian, *I have heard of it, and, as I remember, they say its a Wealthy place.*
> By-ends. Yes, I will assure you that it is, and I have very many Rich Kindred there.
> Chr. *Pray who are your Kindred there, if a man may be so bold;*
> By-ends. Almost the whole Town; ... And to tell you the Truth. ...
> (pp. 98-99)

The studied formality of By-ends's first speech is softened by brief, colloquial phrases like "Almost the whole Town," and "And to tell you the Truth," which appear throughout the initial discussion. Brief ejaculations and direct vigorous exchanges punctuate the schema so that the self-revelation seems less artificial, though Mr. By-ends himself voices thereafter the other traditional parts of the Theophrastan character in order. The studied rhythm of the schema is modified by the rapid, varied, colloquial rhythm of the dramatic scene in which it is partially subsumed.

The most effective elaborations of the schemata, perhaps, are certain overtly self-revealing speeches. Talkative illustrates the two principle effects of such extensions. He is actually one of many who benefit from the distinctive rhythm of the Theophrastan character. These extensions enable a character introduced by a schema to maintain his identity in the midst of the stylistically undifferentiated flow of discourse. That is to say that as minor figures participate more fully in dramatic scenes, their identity is normally threatened, in a sense, because the movement of ideas becomes as important as the revelation of character. Yet speeches such as the following enable them to preserve it; Talkative is distinguished clearly from Christian and Faithful:

> I will talk of things heavenly, or things earthly; things Moral, or things Evangelical; things Sacred, or things Prophane; things past, or things to come; things forraign, or things at home; things more Essential, or things Circumstantial: provided that all be done to our profit.(p. 77)

The "Senecan seesaw" typical of the polemic character extends the schema and rescues Talkative for better things. He leaves the scene as a fully-realized round character even though he appears and disappears within less than thirteen pages of the book. He grows largely because of a more subtle pattern in some of his speeches.

Lacking the aura of a self-conscious *tour de force* that distinguishes the trial scenes (pp. 96-97), these speeches are, nevertheless, similar because of a distinctive rhythm, suggestive of a specific cast of mind, and a distinctive substance epitomizing an attitude. Yet they are subtle enough to conceal art rather than to call attention to it. They are the distilled essence of a rhetorical device Bunyan had used in earlier treatises.

He used the device as it was described by contemporaneous rhetoricians. John Prideaux says *prosopopoeia*, a scheme which influenced growth of the Theophrastan tradition,[40] occurs "when the person is not there, but brought in upon the stage speaking as if he were present. So a thing that is mute oft-times, is dressed up in a person, and words put in his mouth."[41] John Smith suggests further that it occurs "when in our speech, what thing soever, which is not a person, is Metaphorically brought and represented as a person" and comments that "by this figure God, Angels and men, dead, or alive, the Heavens, Earth, Sea, etc. are brought in speaking, hearing, etc."[42] In addition to "God, angels and men, dead, or alive," abstract concepts such as "Wisdom" and moral types such as "A Harlot" were also so presented.[43] Bunyan wrote such speeches for Christ in *Some Gospel Truths Opened* (I, 70) and in *Sighs from Hell*, for God, for the rich man of the parable, and for the eternally damned (I, 151, 166). Bunyan does not simply capture the sound of the living voice, or maintain an appropriate tone, but suggests the mood and nature of the speaker through modulations of tone and rhythm. The eternally damned, for example, exhibit both anger and explosive force:

> Many a time was I admonished, desired, entreated, beseeched, threatened, forewarned of what I now suffer; but alas! I was ignorant, self-conceited, surly, obstinate, and rebellious. Many a time the preachers told me, hell would be my portion, the devil would wreck his malice on me.... But he had as good have preached to the stock, to the post, to the stones I trod on; his words rang in mine ears, but I kept them from my heart.... The Scriptures, thought I, what are they? A dead letter, a little ink and paper, of three or four shillings price.(I, 166)

The rhythm heightens the almost palpable sense of reality and intimates as much about the speaker, perhaps, as the words themselves.

Talkative's speech also has a distinctive cadence or sentence pattern that obliquely and amusingly reinforces the schema. True to his name, Talkative speaks in round and full oratorical sentences, sentences with a certain ease and amplitude; however, he often ends each of them with "etc." or its equivalent. This telling phrase suggests that the sound, rather than the meaning, of the word beguiles him, that he passes to another aspect of the subject when no further *words* suggest themselves:

> To talk of such things is most profitable, for by so doing, a Man may get a knowledge of many things; as of the vanity of earthly things, and the benefit of things above: (thus in general) but more particularly, By this a man may learn the necessity of the New-Birth, the insufficiency of our works, the need of Christs righteousness, etc. Besides, by this a man may learn by *Talk*, what it is to repent, to pray, to suffer, or the like: by this also a Man may learn what are the great promises and consolations of the Gospel, to his own comfort. Further, by this a Man may learn to refute false opinions, to vindicate the truth, and also to instruct the ignorant.(p. 76)

The distinctive cadence, the distinctive pattern, of the sentence creates the illusion that a distinct, individual character speaks. In a similar way, the precise diction and short, incisive sentences of Mr. By-ends suggest the assurance of a "practical" man who has mastered the law of expediency by which he lives (p. 99). And, upon occasion, the rhythm and substance of Ignorance's speech suggest the youthful thoughtlessness of one who does not really know what he is to say until he has said it: "I take my pleasure in walking alone, even more a great deal then in Company, unless I like it the better" (p. 144).

The schemata introducing separate aspects of the character of Mr. Badman, in contrast, contain few such stylized extensions, but the dispersal of their elements, begun in *The Pilgrim's Progress,* becomes even more notable after the opening pages of *Mr. Badman.* The most significant developments in *Mr. Badman,* however, are that a new kind of schema unifies diverse elements, a new emphasis is placed upon the growth of a character through time, and a remarkable visual clarity is attained through a further descent to the concrete. This latter development is, perhaps, the most prominent of the ways in which the schemata become more effective as direct characterization.

Collectively the schemata give a fuller picture of the everyday life and manners of the common people in *Mr. Badman* than those in earlier works. They contain multitudes of what Bunyan calls "outward signs" (p. 130) or "symptoms" (p. 129) of various states of the soul, and the appearance and, especially, the gestures of the central figure attain a remarkable visual clarity. A few such descriptions, to be sure, are little more than general catalogues of such "signs" with a few especially effective participles and adverbs:

> *Heart pride* is discovered by a stretched-out Neck, and by mincing as they go. For the wicked, the Proud, have a *proud* Neck, a *proud* Foot, a *proud* Tongue, by which this their going is exalted. This is that which makes them look scornfully, speak ruggedly, and carry it huffingly among their Neighbours.(p. 129)

More typical of *Mr. Badman,* however, are less-stylized, concrete, precise descriptions of gestures and actions without a trace of didactic impoverishment. Wiseman, for example, describes young Badman's reaction to a parental reprimand:

> How! why like to a Thief that is found. He would stand gloating, and hanging down his head in a sullen, pouching manner; (a body might read, as we use to say, the picture of Ill-luck in his face,) and when his Father did demand his answer to such questions concerning his Villany, he would grumble and mutter at him, and that should be all he could get.(p. 25)

Or again, such "signs," which "render" a scene fully, appear in a description of young Badman at church:

> This ungodly young man . . . had these wicked ways to hinder himself of hearing, let the Preacher thunder never so loud. 1. His way was . . . to sit down in some corner, and then to fall fast asleep. 2. Or else to fix his adulterous eyes upon some beautiful Object that was in the place, and so all Sermon-while, therewith to be feeding of his fleshly lusts. 3. Or, if he could get near to some that he observed would fit his humour, he would be whispering, giggling, and playing with them, till such time as Sermon was done.(p. 44)

Precise participles such as "gloating" or "pouching," and others such as "giggling" convey an almost palpable sense of the sensory quality of the scene. Profuse series of such precise, visual details about Mr. Badman in a great variety of commonplace situations—even the methods he uses to cheat his customers are described in detail (pp. 108-10)—constantly suggest much about his social environment. Lowes was talking of *The Pilgrim's Progress* when he said, "Direct vision, with the power of evoking it in us, is the gift of few, and among these are the greatest. Bunyan has it, and it is with his unswerving intensity of vision that we see."[44] Yet such profuse amassing of precise, suggestive "signs" surely makes the observation even more applicable to *Mr. Badman.*

The schemata in *Mr. Badman* strengthen the imitation of external actualities, most notably, perhaps, by emphasizing the growth through time of a character as they had not done in *The Pilgrim's Progress*. The doomed professors of *The Pilgrim's Progress* were essentially as static as Homer's Achilles or Thackeray's Captain William Dobbin. This is evident in the case of Mr. By-ends, for example; even his creator's generalizations about him, however introduced, do not change. Bunyan wrote of a "temporizing Latitudinarian" in *The Strait Gate,* "His religion is always like the times, turning this way and that way, like the cock on the steeple" (II, 399); Mr. By-ends admits, "We never strive against Wind and Tide"; and Mr. Great-heart remarked of Mr. By-ends in the *Second Part,* "He had his *Mode* of Religion for every fresh occasion. . . . He would turn and change from Opinion to Opinion" (p. 273). Or, again, the temperamental optimism of Ignorance surprises one in a convincing way as he passes through Death (p. 162), yet the dominant impression is that a reader's knowledge, rather than Ignorance's character, changes. Even Christian, though he attains notable complexity, reveals only superficial changes; he does not outgrow his self-righteousness or his pride, for example. One of Bunyan's most sympathetic critics, John Kelman, admits that the parallel between "the pilgrimage and the life of man" is maintained "not by any means with minute accuracy."[45] Progressive revelation, rather than growth or change, is central in *The Pilgrim's Progress*.

In contrast, Mr. Badman is a central character, and there is a minute accuracy in the depiction of his changes. The schemata introduce successive phases of his development as an undutiful son (p. 22), a bad apprentice (p. 51), an imprudent merchant (p. 69), a religious hypocrite (p. 71), a larcenous bankrupt (p. 94), a rapacious tradesman (p. 107), and so forth through a virtual "anatomy" of sins until he dies an unrepentant sinner (p. 163). A conception of external probabilities apparently determines the order of appearance of the schemata. Mr. Wiseman implies that he describes the aspects of the central character's "badness" in the order that such traits typically "make a difference betwixt one and another," between a Christian and a Badman. Mr. Wiseman's principle is clear when he explains why he discusses Mr. Badman's pride when he does:

> I might at first have begun with Mr. *Badmans Pride*, only I think it is not the *Pride* in Infancy that begins to make a difference betwixt one and another, as did, and do those wherewith I began my relation of his life, therefore I passed it over, but now, since he had no more consideration of himself . . . but to be proud when come to years; I have taken the occasion of this place to make mention of his pride. (p. 127)

The stages in the "progress" are clearly, almost analytically, defined.

The growth of Mr. Badman is further emphasized through narrative transitions establishing causal relationships between successive stages. For example, Wiseman describes three "evil companions" the young Mr. Badman acquired: "One of them was chiefly given to Uncleanness, another to Drunkenness, and the third to Purloining or stealing" (p. 46). He then describes Mr. Badman's promiscuity and drunkenness. He turns to the fact that Badman "would pilfer and steal from his Master" on the basis that, being "but an Apprentice," Badman needed money "to follow this practice, for drunkenness" (pp. 50-51). Of course, such causal relationships do not always exist (p. 123), yet they unify many successive stages of that development so that occasions for renewed plunges into the "real," the concrete, the commonplace, seem to grow out of the continuing narrative of Badman's growth.

Further movement toward mimetic effectiveness is evident when Wiseman voices a new kind of schema in *Mr. Badman*. This schema may be called a "portrait" since it relates many facets of his nature.[46] Late in the book, Wiseman says, "But what need I thus talk of the particular actions, or rather the prodigious sins of Mr. Badman, when his whole life, and all his actions, went, as it were, to the making up one massy body of

REPRESENTATION: DIDACTIC ELEMENTS / 51

sin?" He then summarizes Badman's characteristic actions in failing to honor God for his "mercies," in attributing God's "mercies" to his own "wit, labour, care, industry, cunning, or the like," in attributing his misfortunes either to chance or to his wife's religion, in ignoring or denying the "authority, harmony and wisdom of the Scriptures," and in mocking and slandering his religious wife and her friends. He concludes:

> He was an *angry, wrathful, envious* man, a man that knew not what meekness or gentleness meant, nor did he desire to learn. His temper was to be surly, huffie, and rugged, and worse; and he so gave way to his temper, as to this, that it brought him to be furious and outrageous in all things, especially against goodness itself, and against other things, too, when he was displeased.... Mr. *Badman* was as malicious and envious a man as commonly you can hear of.(pp. 135-38)

Relationships among separate aspects of Mr. Badman's character, merely implicit elsewhere, become explicit in this analysis of his basic intellectual position, his moral nature, and his temperament. This composite portrait is more richly suggestive of the complexity of "real" badmen than any previous schema.

The stages of growth are defined even more precisely in *The Holy War* than in *Mr. Badman,* though the central figure, an Everyman representing the Elect, does not appear as a character at all. Without participating in the further descent to the concrete that gave mimetic effectiveness to their predecessors, the schemata of *The Holy War* also bring together or unify many diverse elements as the portrait of Mr. Badman does. They do so, however, in a quite different way. The schemata of *The Holy War* constitute a new synthesis rather than a further realization of their mimetic capacities; their extensions are typically abstract lateral movements rather than further descents to the concrete. Sensuous immediacy and representative fullness, in brief, are less evident than a new consistency in serving two separate functions.

Aside from a few mythological figures, whose significance is determined by conventions outside the work of art, the central characters in *The Holy War* represent inner forces or faculties of the soul. These figures are not simply subcharacters like Shame, who projects an aspect of a specific conflict in *The Pilgrim's Progress;* they remain on the scene as significant agents of the central metaphor. They do not typically reveal the nature of that force symbolically as, for example, Spenser's Errour or Milton's Sin or Death do. Rather, they function in two separate ways involving two different points of reference. First, they are agents extending a metaphor. They are meaningful, neither as symbolic "statements," nor as imitations of inner experience, nor as instruments of meditations, but primarily as extensions of a dominant metaphor which itself alludes to an external actuality. As agents, they are as completely dependent upon the initial analogy as are the separate legs of Donne's stiff twin compasses in "A Valediction: Forbidding Mourning." Second, they function as fictional types and, hence, are meaningful in direct relation to the external actualities they imitate. They are typically both personifications of the forces in a psychomachia and, at the same time, fictional types like those drawn in the earlier narratives.

Lord Willbewill is more fully developed as a fictional type than many central characters in *The Holy War,* yet he is typical in that he is introduced as both an agent in a dialectical process and as a fictional type. Both the "Carnel will" and a wilful man appear in the schema introducing him after the Fall:

> This *Willbewill* was as highborn as any man in *Mansoul,* and was as much, if not more, a free holder than many of them were; besides, if I remember my tale aright, he had some priviledge peculiar to himself in the famous Town of *Mansoul.* Now, together with these, he was a man of great strength, resolution, and courage, nor in his occasion could any turn him away. But I say, whether he was proud of his estate, priviledges, strength or what (but sure it was pride of something), he scorns now to be a slave in *Mansoul*; and therefore resolves to bear office under *Diabolus.* . . . And, headstrong man that he was! thus he began. . . . (pp. 21-22)

Bunyan's phrase is suggestive. He says, "*together with* these [privileges 'peculiar to himself'], he was a man of great strength, resolution, and courage." The "priviledge peculiar to himself" is an attribute of the will, rather than of a wilful man. It is explained more fully later when the narrator reports, ". . . nor could anything now be done, but at his will and pleasure, throughout the Town of *Mansoul*" (pp. 21-22). The courage, resolution, and pride referred to in the schema, on the other hand, are attributes of a compatible type and have no necessary relationship to the will as such. The schema clearly differs from those examined earlier in that it has a dual, rather than a single, conceptual basis.

Both the fictional type and the agent introduced by the schema develop through dialogue and action. Lord Willbewill, for example, as a headstrong wilful man, rapidly changes many customs in *Mansoul* after he accepts office under Diabolus (pp. 22-24), and he characteristically speaks in "big and ruffling words" (p. 42). There is, in fact, a certain Moloch-like abruptness and explosiveness in some of his speeches:

> *Gentlemen, we have heard your demands, and the noise of your threats, and have heard the sound of your summons; but we fear not your*

force, we regard not your threats, but will still abide as you found us. And we command you, that in three days' time you cease to appear in those parts, or you shall know what it is once to dare offer to rouse the Lion Diabolus when asleep in his Town of Mansoul.(p. 49)

At the same time, his function as an agent, rather than as a headstrong wilful man, explains, for example, why he needed "one Mr. *Mind* for his Clerk, a man to speak on every way like his Master." His nature as the "Carnel will" explains why he "would neither endure to see him [Mr. Recorder, the Conscience], nor to hear the words of his mouth; he would shut his eyes when he saw him, and stop his ears when he heard him speak" (pp. 22-23). And so throughout, the schemata of central figures like Lord Willbewill extend in the midst of constantly shifting points of reference—to the central metaphor and to external actuality—so that, though happy correspondences exist between the attributes of a person and of a concept, the moral type is less fully and freely developed than those in the earlier narratives.

Although the central figures lack the mimetic fullness of figures such as Ignorance and Talkative, their abstractness is clearly not didactic impoverishment. On the contrary, it is evidence of a new effectiveness in serving two functions simultaneously; it is a product of the dual conceptual basis of the characters' schemata and the consistency with which action is extending metaphor as well as character. This remarkable fusion does not appear again in the final narrative, the *Second Part,* for the elements of the schemata make, perhaps, their most effective mimetic contribution as direct characterization therein. They do so because self-revealing speeches heighten the complexity of several major figures in thematically focused scenes; schemata are greatly elaborated and extended to characterize several major figures; and elaborate yet informal schemata introducing major figures are largely subsumed in dramatic scenes.

The elaborate schemata introducing such complex figures as Honest (p. 247) or Mercy (p. 185) or even Standfast (p. 299) or Valiant-for-Truth (p. 289) create an effect of spontaneous disorder yet clearly establish the nature of the figure. The pilgrims, for example, precipitate a dramatic scene when, finding Honest sleeping under a tree, they awaken him. Within less than two pages, in the midst of a dramatic scene, Honest has defined his nature—"Not Honesty in the *Abstract,* but *Honest* is my Name"—provided a partial analysis of it—he comes from the "Town of *Stupidity*" which "lieth about four Degrees beyond the City of Destruction"—displayed his nature partially when he "stands upon his guard," and uttered at least two speeches which function primarily to reveal that nature. In one of these speeches he answers Great-heart's hypothetical question about what he would have done had he been beset by those who "did rob *Little-faith* of his money":

Done! Why I would a fought as long as breath had been in me; and had I so done, I am sure you could never have given me the worst on't, for a *Christian* can never be overcome, unless he shall yield of himself.

In the other, he explains how one of his capacity was able to become a pilgrim:

Yes, we lie more off from the Sun, and so are more Cold and Sensless; but was a Man in a Mountain of Ice, yet if the Sun of Righteousness will arise upon him, his frozen Heart shall feel a Thaw; and thus it hath been with me.(pp. 246-48)

Honest's nature as a plain, ungifted, honest man, made resolute by his religion, has been vividly established, and the separate elements have been subsumed in a rapidly moving dramatic scene.

The schemata introducing several complex figures are greatly elaborated and widely dispersed. Honest, for example, participates in countless discussions and adventures after his first appearance in the dramatic scene. The striking finale of the schema on Honest, as of several pilgrims, appears at the river, Death (pp. 305-09). He receives a summons; unlike the others, he makes no will because he takes his honesty with him; and he departs:

Now the *River* at that time overflowed the Banks in some places. But Mr. *Honest* in his Life time had spoken to one *Good-conscience* to meet him there, the which he also did, and lent him his Hand, and so helped him over. The last Words of Mr. *Honest* were, *Grace Reigns.* So he left the World.(p. 309)

The finale bringing the schema to a resounding close is not unlike that which earlier concluded the short, unexpanded schema of Mr. Feeblemind:

This I have resolved on, to wit, to *run* when I can, to *go* when I cannot *run,* and to *creep* when I cannot *go.* As to the main, I thank him that loves me, I am fixed; my way is before me, my Mind is beyond the *River* that has no Bridg, tho I am as you see, but of *feeble Mind.*(p. 268)

The artificiality has largely disappeared, yet the similarity to the earlier form seems evident. The schemata of several central figures have been thus extended and elaborated far beyond anything promised by the earlier ones. Characters such as Mercy, Standfast, Christiana, and Honest gain at least part of their complexity from such elaborations.

The self-revealing speeches of major figures in the *Second Part* are more subtle than those in earlier works largely because of their dramatic contexts. They appear in scenes isolated by hints of artificiality: a theme, rather than a conflict, gives them a sharp focus; the speakers talk largely of themselves; and their speeches have carefully modulated, if not individualizing, rhythm. Shortly after Great-heart gave an account of Mr. Fearing, for example, appears a scene focused by the theme, religious fears. The theme is explored through contrasting responses:

> Hon. *He was a very zealous man, as one may see by what Relation you have given of him. Difficulties, Lyons, or Vanity-Fair, he feared not at all: 'Twas only Sin, Death and Hell, that was to him a Terror;* because he had some doubts about his Interest in that Celestial Country.
>
> * * *
>
> Christiana. *Then said* Christiana, *This Relation of Mr.* Fearing *has done me good. I thought no body had been like me, but I see there was some Semblance 'twixt this good man and I, only we differed in two things. His Troubles were so great they brake out, but mine I kept within. His also lay so hard upon him, they made him that he could not knock at the Houses provided for Entertainment; but my Trouble was always such, as made me knock the lowder.*
>
> Mer. If I might also speak my Heart, I must say that something of him has also dwelt in me. For I have ever been more afraid of the Lake and the loss of a place in *Paradise,* then I have been of the loss of other things. Oh, thought I, may I have the Happiness to have a Habitation *there,* 'tis enough, though I part with all the World to win it.
>
> Mat. *Then said* Mathew, *Fear was one thing that made me think that I was far from having that within me that accompanies Salvation, but if it was so with such a good man as he, why may it not also go well with me?*
>
> Jam. No fears, no Grace, said *James.* Though there is not always Grace where there is the fear of Hell; yet to be sure there is no Grace where there is no fear of God.
>
> Greath. *Well said,* James, *thou hast hit the Mark, for fear of God is the beginning of Wisdom; and to be sure they that want the* beginning, *have neither* middle *nor* end.(pp. 253-55)

The theme is explored concretely, and several central characters reveal themselves without placing themselves on display.

The simultaneous exploration of the theme makes the self-revelation relatively subtle, and the juxtaposition of the speeches makes the revelation more precise. Honest and Great-heart show characteristic objectivity, yet their speeches establish a clear contrast between the experienced ordinary men and the experienced extraordinary men. Honest contributes a sensible, straightforward, and rather obvious generalization; Great-heart makes a forceful, precise, emphatic assertion about the *significance* of religious fears. The phrasing suggests that his vision has been earned. The boys, too, are relatively objective, yet their speeches imply a clear contrast.

Matthew's scarcely-articulate, scrupulous, tentative efforts to relate genuine inner experience to established doctrine contrast sharply with James's characteristic precocious facility in reducing the question to a pertinent copy-book maxim. Both Mercy and Christiana exhibit characteristically subjective responses, yet their speeches contrast the youthful innocence and aspiration of Mercy to the mature discrimination and perception of Christiana. Christiana's acute awareness of the incongruity between inner conditions and outward "signs" is also evident. Although these speeches lack the overt self-revelation of those of the wayward professors, they are more subtle and, therefore, more effective in revealing character because the central theme itself commands attention and because they are supplemented by effective dramatic contrasts. Such scenes as this contribute to the vital complexity of several major characters in the *Second Part*.

CHAPTER THREE

MIMETIC DEVELOPMENT

I

The mimetic principle is manifest in a characteristically dramatic way in a moral dialogue appearing in Bunyan's first published work, *Some Gospel Truths Opened*. Brief, lively exchanges punctuate the highly colloquial rhythm of the prose and transform "Question" and "Answer" momentarily into characters in a drama:

> Quest. But did this Man rise again from the dead, that very man, with that very body wherewith he was crucified? for you do seem, as I conceive, to hold forth so much by these your expressions.
> Ans. Why do you doubt of it?
> Quest. Do you believe it?
> Ans. Yes, by the grace of the Lord Jesus Christ, for he hath enabled me so to do.
> Ques. And can you prove it by the Scripture?
> Ans. Yes.
> Quest. How?
> Ans. First, from that scripture in Luke....[1]

Brief exchanges of this kind, suggestive of a lively, intense conversation, often quicken the sense of immediacy created by the colloquial rhythm and invite a reader to determine whether self-consistent characters lie behind the separate utterances. The conflict of ideas is very close to becoming a conflict of personalities.

Adapted to the service of narrative art, losing much of its didactic weight, such dialogue became a flexible medium for the artistic exploration of significant themes, the depiction of subtle interactions of characters, and the revelation of complex fictional characters. It is the speeches of such characters as Honest and Great-heart that arouse human interest and heighten the sense of probability necessary to sustain an illusion. It is the speeches of Christian and Faithful that make them memorable: their speeches reveal a self-consistent, coherent group of values in the speaker, reveal motives compatible with the nature of their quest, and, at times, suggest the ambiguities, or even the mysteries, of their unique, individual experience. It is in fully realized dramatic scenes that characters such as Christian and Gaius impress themselves upon the memory, either struggling with the Giant Despair or presiding over the dinner table. Bunyan developed the mimetic potentialities of narrative material most memorably through such dialogue and scenes. The dominant movement toward more effective imitation in the development of his narrative art, therefore, is evident in the fact that he gradually transformed the relatively straightforward narrative method of *Grace Abounding* into a dominantly scenic method of narration.

Each of the narratives, of course, shows a different kind of emphasis. *Grace Abounding*, published in 1666, and *The Pilgrim's Progress*, 1678, concentrate upon the inner drama and convey the vicissitudes and intensities of the process of religious conversion. *The Holy War*, 1682, is essentially an elaborate, analytical, allegorical exploration of some of the same areas. *The Pilgrim's Progress, Mr. Badman*, 1680, and the *Second Part*, 1684, show a progressively greater emphasis upon the outer drama of social life and manner. The *Second Part*, is, perhaps, Bunyan's fullest anticipation of the novel of manners of a later era.

A consistent formal development underlies these changes in emphasis. In formal terms, this transformation involves four major changes: a reduction in the proportion of undramatized narrative and expository material, an enlargement and refinement in the development of separate scenes, a closer integration of successive scenes, and a fuller exploitation of three mimetic capabilities of dialogue. These potentialities are the power of Bunyan's dialogue to suggest immediacy and spontaneity, to externalize inner conflicts effectively, and to convey a vivid, precise impression of the character of both major and minor speakers primarily by *what* they say. Other methods discussed in relation to the schemata doubtless have their effects, yet these qualities of the dialogue are largely responsible for the fact that Christiana, Mercy, Honest, Great-heart, and, perhaps, Matthew and James, are more fully realized fictional characters than many of their predecessors. Changes in these four major areas did not by any means proceed at a uniform pace; Bunyan is now gaining, now losing ground. Each of the narratives, nevertheless, exhibits a fuller realization of the capacity of a scenic method of narration to create and sustain that basic illusion necessary to effective narrative art.

Evidence of such a movement in *Grace Abounding* appears in the facts that the style exhibits the qualities characteristic of Bunyan's best dialogue, the character of one central figure is revealed in an essentially dramatic way, certain interior monologues and dialogues attain the force of action in the dramatic present, some mimetic potentialities of the dialogue are realized, and six highly-effective dramatic scenes re-create portions of the outer life of the young Bunyan.

Although *Grace Abounding* contains less dialogue than the later narratives, the style has the distinctive qualities that were to appear in Bunyan's best dialogue. Despite the abundance of biblical symbols, metaphors, rhythms, echoes, and allusions, which Professor Henri A. Talon has analyzed,[2] and despite the profusion of imagery drawn from the commonplace things and events of everyday life, the dominant impression is of a simple, unadorned "natural" way of speaking. This impression of rapidity, spontaneity, and immediacy is conveyed by the powerful verbs, the simple, concrete, colloquial diction, the absence of adjectives, the frequency of verbs, the uncomplicated syntax, the absence of elaborate schemes and tropes, and, above all, by the colloquial rhythm and movement of the prose:

> The Law, doth belong to and lay hold of all men as they come into the World.(p. 85)
>
> My conscience now was sore, and would smart at every touch: I could not now tell how to speak my words, for fear I should mis-place them. (pp. 26-27)
>
> These things would so break and confound my Spirit, that I could not tell what to do, I thought, at times, they would have broke my wits, and still, to aggravate my misery, that would run in my mind.... (p. 46)
>
> Now was my soul greatly pinched between these two considerations, *Live I must not, Die I dare not:* now I sunk and fell in my Spirit.(p. 80)

Such colloquial vigor, which is rare in the dialogue of "serious" seventeenth-century fiction,[3] becomes characteristic in the dialogue of the later narratives. It will be evident that this aura of unpremeditated informality and spontaneity contributes greatly to the illusion in Bunyan's best known scenes.

The character of one central figure, the young Bunyan, is revealed in an essentially dramatic way so that he acquires the coherence of a complex fictional character without the aid of static characterization.

The narrator, the older Bunyan, analyzes, interprets, and even stipulates the significance of the experience he describes. Yet his comments are so consistently focused upon the religious or doctrinal, rather than the human, significance of experience that few of them may be classified as explicit, unifying, character analysis. The young Bunyan depicted in the narrative, however he may be related to the "real" Bunyan,[4] nevertheless escapes the sprawling incoherence of the actual experience from which he was born.[5] He does so largely because the narrative is a highly selective account of religious conversion.

Although both the inward and outward vicissitudes of the central figures are intimated along the way, the focus throughout is upon the inner life, the central drama of conflicting opinions, sentiments, and emotions. So much so, in fact, that the narrator ignores the probability that many ideas and arguments actually come to the young Bunyan from other people, or from books. He writes, for example, "After this, that other doubt did come with strength upon me, *But how if the day of grace should be past and gone?*" (p. 22). Or, again, he mentions that the young Bunyan was "much troubled to know whether the Lord Jesus was both Man as well as God, and God as well as Man" (p. 38). Even though these traditional questions[6] could have reached the young Bunyan in a number of ways, the narrator does not distract attention from the central conflicts to explain how. This is to say that, as Professor G. B. Harrison points out, Bunyan "suppressed and minimized much that he had received from men and women."[7] Just as St. Augustine frequently used indefinite expressions in his *Confessions*, even when he could obviously have given precise details, so that he does not distract attention from "the really important thing—the working of Providence,"[8] so Bunyan intensifies the central drama by omitting mundane outward events.

The account concentrates upon moments of heightened tension and describes them in climactic order. A reader sees one central character briefly as a child with a sensitive conscience (p. 6), as a young married man turning with superstitious veneration to the Anglican Church (pp. 9-10); a reader sees, then, the central character's gradual awareness of God's disapproval and growing shame for his sins (p. 11), his outward reformation and preliminary study of the Bible (p. 13), his recognition of the joy of grace in women at Bedford (p. 14), his denial of old "carnal" friends (p. 16), his systematic study of the Bible (p. 21), and then, the first of a series of major sources of pain, his doubts as to whether he is of the Elect (p. 22). And so, through each stage of conversion, a reader sees the haunting fears and mounting resolution, the alternating despair and hope; he sees the growth of a more susceptible conscience and senses a gradual heightening of the tension, as the character gropes his way through each painful stage, now feeling the love of Christ "as hot as fire" (p. 41), now fearing the full "terrours of the Law" (p. 85). A reader is led to the climactic moment when the central figure in the narrative says he can "scarce lie in my Bed for joy, and peace, and triumph, thorow Christ" (p. 83). Thereafter, he senses decreasing tension: he sees the central figure resisting the temptation to blaspheme in the pulpit (p. 90), avoiding the "common Salutation of a women" (p. 94), parting with his "Wife and poor Children" (p. 98), and, often, admiring the "Wisdom of God" (p. 94). The basic progression is psychological, rather than rhetorical, of course, and the concentration upon crucial moments both suggests the pulsations and intensities of the process of conversion and enhances the coherence of the central figure.

Nothing is recollected in tranquility in *Grace Abounding*; the facade of quiet that obscures spiritual struggle in the poetry of George Herbert is simply missing. Rather, there is a Donnian intensity because the picture of the young Bunyan, like an Impressionistic painting, is created by countless separate, bold, vibrant, colorful strokes. The separate vivid impressions evoke an imaginative response, scarcely restricted by the narrator's stipulations, so that the depiction has a problematic value, or in Professor Talon's phrase, a "general value,"[9] not limited by the sectarian context. The successive impressions suggest the movement, rhythm, and intensity of spiritual struggle and, at the same time, imply the existence of a dynamic, self-consistent central figure. It is, essentially, the concrete particularity of the rendering of the inner life that gives the young Bunyan the immediate, dramatic impact of a major fictional character. The inner life is "rendered" with an almost palpable solidity through interior monologues, interior dialogues, and sensuous descriptions.

Both literal and figurative descriptions express the sensory and emotional aspects of inner experience. The diction in these descriptions is largely perceptive and sensory, rather than conceptual and abstract, and the analogies are typically both imaginative and illuminating. The physical effects of fear are powerfully suggested, for example, by the report, "I felt also such a clogging and heat at my stomach by reason of this my terrour, that I was, especially at some times, as if my breastbone would have split in sunder" (p. 50). Sensations and emotions aroused by thought are communicated forcefully through imaginative analogies such as: "And truly I did now feel myself to sink into a gulf, as an house whose foundation is destroyed" (p. 62). And, such is the unified sensibility depicted, states of consciousness are fully conveyed by more extensive analogies:

I did liken myself in this condition unto the case of some child that was fallen into a Mill-pit, who though it could make some shift to scrable and spraul in the water, yet because it could find neither hold for hand nor foot, therefore at last it must die in that condition.(p. 62)

In contrast to the imagery of *The Holy War*, such imagery is extended far enough to embody the emotion but not so far as to leave it behind in *Grace Abounding*. It is primarily the "metaphysical" impression that the body felt the soul's terrors, perhaps, that gives the picture of internal struggle the "terrible immediacy" that John Livingston Lowes commended.[10]

Interior monologues and dialogues convey the dynamic flux of the inner life so that it strikes the mind with the force of action in the dramatic present. The monologue frequently attains an almost breathless suspense and intensity; it re-creates the surge of ideas and the interfusion of thought and emotion by the very rapidity and apparent spontaneity of the report:

Just as I was about to speak, this thought came into my minde, *But go under yonder Hedge, and pray first, that God would make you able:* but when I had concluded to pray, this came hot upon me, That if I prayed and came again and tried to do it, and yet did nothing notwithstanding, then be sure I had no Faith, but was a Cast-away and lost. (p. 19)

Separate ideas burst upon this movement of mind with the force of physical facts. The narrator sometimes merely reports something like, "I have been violently assaulted with thoughts of blasphemy" (p. 90); more often, he *makes* the assault violent by describing the emotional impact of the idea: "Those words did sound suddenly within me, *He is able*: but me thought this word *able*, was spoke so loud unto me, it shewed such a *great* word, it seemed to be writ in *great* letters" (p. 64). He dramatizes the conflict of ideas, merely implying the emotion, by placing contrasting currents of thought in rapid juxtaposition; he reports, for example:

The wicked suggestion [was] still running in my mind, *Sell him, sell him, sell him, sell him,* as fast as a man could speak; against which also in my mind, as at other times, I answered No, no, not for thousands.(p. 43)

The dominant tone is that of objective drama, rather than of either subjective didacticism or sentimental indulgence, because the movement of mind is re-created directly and the conflicts of ideas are "rendered" dramatically.

The incipient drama becomes overt at crucial moments, for the narrator transforms the interior monologue into an interior dialogue, or even into embryonic scenes. Some ideas are introduced in the form of direct quotations by an unidentified speaker: "I was as if I heard it thus expounded to me; Sinner, thou thinkest that because of thy sins and infirmities I cannot save thy Soul..." (p. 80). At other times the "as if" disappears and a "tempter" says, "Your sin is unpardonable" (p. 63), or "Satan" does "greatly labour to pull this promise" from him (p. 67), and the internal struggle is fully dramatized as Bunyan attributes mordant, chilling dialogue to the devil:

> Well, I will watch and take what heed I can: Though you do, said Satan, I shall be too hard for you, I will cool you insensibly, by degrees, by little and little: what care I, saith he, though I be seven years in chilling your heart, if I can do it at last; continual rocking will lull a crying Child asleep: I will ply it close, but I will have my end accomplished: though you be burning hot at present, yet, if I can pull you from this fire, I shall have you cold before it be long.(p. 35)

Quite literally, the antagonist is Satan. Conflicting ideas and impulses are, thus, dramatized through embryonic scenes which both imply the motives and values of one participant and stipulate the nature of the other.

Grace Abounding, thus, clearly realizes some of the mimetic potentialities of dialogue since the interior monologues and dialogues partially externalize inner conflicts, create an effect of immediacy and spontaneity, and convey a vivid impression of the young Bunyan. But the further power of dialogue to generate coherent, self-consistent, palpable minor characters is not realized in *Grace Abounding.*

Figures from the outward environment of the young Bunyan are seldom allowed to intrude in the drama of the "Lord's... dealings" (p. 79) with him, and those who do appear usually do so only through indirect discourse (p. 55). The few minor figures who *are* allowed to speak for themselves make only promising beginnings. For example, the narrator speaks of one Harry, a "young man of our Town," who was "a most wicked Creature for cursing and swearing, and whoring." He adds:

> I met him in a certain Lane, and asked him how he did; he after his old swearing and mad way, answered, he was well. *But* Harry, said I, *why do you swear and curse thus? What will become of you if you die in this condition?* He answered me in a great chafe, *What would the devil do for company if it were not for such as I am?* (p. 16)

Harry's speech certainly has some of the force and vigor of the satanic one, yet he does not reappear. He is developed no further.

Figures who externalize the inner life of the young Bunyan, in a similar way, appear as promising beginnings rather than as realizations of the capacity of the dialogue to create clearly-defined, self-consistent, minor characters. Reports of religious experience in the Bible and elsewhere had established a mythology and a conventional rhetoric that "employed dreams, visions, voices, and supernatural terrors, admonitions and interventions of all sorts" as early as the time of St. Augustine,[11] and Bunyan used these conventions in describing spiritual struggle in the early treatises. In *Some Gospel Truths Opened*, for example, he presented man's soul quite literally as a field of battle and described the whole process of conversion by reference to the separate acts of Christ and the devil (I, 46-48). *Grace Abounding* illustrates the beginnings of the process of differentiation.

A pervasive satanic agency is expressed through both the devil of *Some Gospel Truths Opened* and the Tempter of *Grace Abounding*. Both these figures vaguely suggest Milton's Satan ignominiously hissing forbidden thoughts into the ear of the sleeping Eve rather than the heroic figure who urged his followers never to submit or yield. Both figures are extremely clever, subtle, and cunning sophists when they are allowed to speak for themselves, yet neither acquires specific form as a coherent fictional character.

The devil is described as a "merciless butcherer of men," who "lieth in wait" with "strategems or subtle temptations," makes "his delusions take place in the hearts of poor creatures" and labors to make one "fall short of eternal life" (I, 46). His motives are explained and his diabolical sophistry is exemplified through numerous specific "strategems," but the very diversity of his activities prevents him from achieving fictional unity. Bunyan says, for example, the devil tries "to keep thee in love with thy sins and pleasures knowing that he is sure of thee if he can but bewitch thee to live and die in them" (I, 46). At another point Satan "labours to render the doctrine of the Lord Jesus ... very odius and low" (I, 48); or, again, he pretends to lead professors "up into some higher light, mysteries, revelations of the Spirit" (I, 48). The implications are protean.

Unlike the devil of *Some Gospel Truth's Opened*, who was "very busy with his doctrines and ministers" in the outward world (I, 81) as well as "exceeding subtle and expert" in creating mental delusions (I, 48), the Tempter of *Grace Abounding* displays his subtlety and cunning primarily as an inner voice offering diverse temptations:

The Tempter came in with this delusion, That there was no way for

me to know I had Faith, but by trying to work some miracle.(p. 18)
Then would the Tempter so provoke me to desire to sin that [unpardonable] sin, that I was as if I could not, must not.... (p. 33)
Sometimes also the Tempter would make me believe I had consented to it [abandoning Christ], then should I be as tortured on a Rack for whole dayes together.(p. 42)
The Tempter suggesting thus, *For if these things should indeed be true, yet to believe otherwise, would yield you ease for the present. If you must perish, never torment yourself so much beforehand, drive the thoughts of damning out of your mind, by possessing your mind with some such conclusions that* Atheists, *and* Ranters *use to help themselves withal.*(p. 49)
Which when the Tempter perceived, he strongly suggested to me, That I ought not to pray to God.... (p. 54)

Although his sphere of his activity is, thus, more restricted than the devil's, he does not emerge as a clearly-defined, self-consistent actor in the drama because he tries to persuade the young Bunyan to *all kinds* of un-Baptist action and because the coherent pattern underlying his appearances is not in himself, but in the young Bunyan. Despite the power of some of his separate speeches, he fades away between them so that he lacks definition and autonomy. The dialogue in *Grace Abounding* externalizes inner conflicts without generating concrete, effective minor characters.

Further dramatic achievements appear in "A Relation of the Imprisonment of Mr. John Bunyan," which Professor Roger Sharrock suggests "must have been written in prison immediately after the events" and which is usually reprinted with *Grace Abounding*.[12] Six highly effective embryonic scenes re-create portions of the outer life of the young Bunyan. They are vivid, sharply focused by conflict, and effectively varied in tempo. The method Bunyan used in reconstructing these scenes is suggested by a parenthetical comment. He says, "Then came the Justice and Mr. Foster to me again (we had a little discourse about preaching, but because the method of it is out of my mind, I pass it)" (p. 112). There is no reason to doubt the essential accuracy of his reports. The events in one of them appear in climactic order, and less intense moments are either summarized or presented through indirect discourse. Moments of heightened tension that reveal characters as well as issues are treated in fuller detail:

Chest. My Lord, said Justice *Chester*, he is a pestilent fellow, there is not such a fellow in the country again.
Twis. What, will your husband leave preaching? If he will do so, then send for him.

> *Wom.* My Lord, said she, he dares not leave preaching, as long as he can speak.
> *Twis.* See here, what should we talk any more about such a fellow? Must he do what he lists? He is a breaker of the peace.
>
> * * *
>
> *Hales.* Hast thou four children? said Judge *Hales*; thou art but a young woman to have four children.
> *Wom.* My Lord, said she, I am but mother-in-law to them....
> *Hales.* Whereat, he looked very soberly on the matter, said, Alas poor woman!
> *Twis.* But Judge *Twisdon* told her, that she made poverty her cloak. (pp. 127-28)

Aside from the short, blunt sentences revealing Judge Twisdon's anger, the scene exhibits subtle use of such external minutiae as often differentiates one character and another in fiction. The matter, tone, and style of speeches of Justices Hales, Twisdon, and Chester sustain sharp dramatic contrasts among the speakers so that the scene displays much of the dramatic facility that came to fruition in *The Pilgrim's Progress*.

II

In contrast to the literal account of religious conversion in *Grace Abounding*, Bunyan presents in *The Pilgrim's Progress* a fictional story of spiritual adventure involving, in Lowe's words, "a road, and a dangerous journey, and at the end a shining city paved with gold."[13] *The Pilgrim's Progress* conveys a much fuller and richer experience than in *Grace Abounding*. It clearly has a greater social range than the spiritual autobiography. Unlike *Piers Plowman*, *The Pilgrim's Progress* does not, of course, attack corruption or expose multiple political, social, economic, and ecclesiastical abuses, yet it reflects many of the conditions of contemporaneous rural society and castigates a number of representative religious offenders. The allegory also presents a greater variety of spiritual experience than *Grace Abounding*. Professor Roger Sharrock's study of the formative influence of the "beliefs and spiritual experiences recorded in his autobiogarphy" upon *The Pilgrim's Progress* demonstrates that Christian's experience was much like the formed experience seen in *Grace Abounding*,[14] yet Christian is but one of three contrasting major figures whose inner life is explored in *The Pilgrim's Progress*. While the study of varieties of religious experience remains central, in brief, the fictional narrative explores both the inner and outer aspects of spiritual adventure more extensively than the earlier one.

MIMETIC DEVELOPMENT / 67

In doing so, *The Pilgrim's Progress* exhibits seven major dramatic developments. The narrative develops largely through dramatic scenes; many effective scenes achieve a form that magnifies their immediate dramatic impact; and three major characters are revealed primarily by dramatic means in both allegorical and mimetic scenes. The allegorical scenes exhibit self-consistent minor figures and explore the conflicts of major ones primarily through dialogue; the mimetic ones exploit sustained and subtle dramatic contrasts effectively.

The explorations of both the inner and outer aspects of spiritual experience in *The Pilgrim's Progress* are largely dramatic in form. The extended central metaphor, the pursuit of Salvation is an arduous journey, creates a series of settings wherein intangible forces assume material form. This field of action, is at once, an imitation of the "real" world perceived by the senses, an allegorical expression of a religious system of values, and an allegorical representation of states of consciousness usually perceptible only to the inward eye. Minor characters, who usually impede the advance of the protagonists, represent forces from the outward world and, more important, materialize equally intangible ideas and attitudes. Or, in other terms, the process of differentiation illustrated by *Grace Abounding* has proceeded a pace so that many separate figures have superseded the angelic and diabolic ones of the earlier treatises. The devil of *Some Gospel Truths Opened*, for example, adumbrates many such figures. Like Mr. Worldly-Wiseman, he appears "with a fair show in the flesh, yet denying the Lord, and refusing to be justified by the blood of Jesus" (I, 81). Like Shame, he "labours to render the doctrine of the Lord Jesus... very odius and low" (I, 48), and like Atheist, he would invite one to "dispute with him" (I, 51). Like Flatterer, he appears to professors "under the name of Christ... with a fair show in the flesh of outward holiness"; he appears "like an angel of light" rather than "in his black colours" (I, 81). Basic elements of drama largely implicit in *Grace Abounding*, in brief, assume material form in *The Pilgrim's Progress*. Crucial conflicts in the lives of Christian and, to a lesser extent, of Faithful and Hopeful, are rendered in intense dramatic scenes; less decisive moments are occupied largely by the central characters' discussions with each other. The narrative method is thus largely a scenic one, and relatively few passages lack a dramatic aspect.

Many memorable scenes in *The Pilgrim's Progress* realize distinctively dramatic potentialities merely latent in *Grace Abounding*. The scenes depicting Faithful's encounters with the old Adam and Moses (pp. 69-71), Faithful's trial at Vanity Fair (pp. 92-97), Christian and Hopeful's encounters with such figures as By-ends (pp. 98-100), Atheist (pp. 135-36), and Ignorance (pp. 144-49), create an immediate dramatic impact unprecedented in Bunyan's work. The formal sources of their power are illustrated by the scene in which Christian encounters Apollyon in the Valley of Humiliation. The scene is focused by a sharp conflict, for, in narrative terms, Apollyon blocks the road Christian is determined to follow. The action develops so that tension gradually increases until a climactic moment resolves it. The pattern is familiar from earlier romances: hostilities begin with a "flyting," develop through three episodes of increasing severity, and end with the hero's triumph. A similar pattern is evident quite frequently in, for example, Richard Johnson's *The Seven Champions of Christendom*.[15] As in Johnson's account of St. George's fabled fight with the dragon, the hero needs, and receives, supernatural aid, though, as in Spenser's better-known account, the aid is overtly religious rather than magical.[16] Within this general pattern, the tempo is effectively varied in a simple and direct way. Apollyon says during the "flyting," for example:

> *Thou has done in this, according to the Proverb, changed a bad for a worse: but it is ordinary for those that have professed themselves his Servants, after a while to give him the slip, and return again to me: do thou so too, and all shall be well.*(p. 57)

During the conflict, his speech is no less "natural" but moves more rapidly. At one point he exclaims, *"I am sure of thee now"* (p. 59). Although the trappings of romance are more prominent than in many memorable scenes, this scene is typical, in brief, in that it exhibits a sharp focus, sustained tension, a climactic order of events, "natural" dialogue, and an effectively varied tempo.

Further development of dramatic method is evident, too, in that *The Pilgrim's Progress* develops three major, complex, fictional characters primarily by dramatic means. Christian, Faithful, and Hopeful owe relatively little to static characterization or to overtly illustrative action. They are neither distinguished by characteristic "turns" of speech nor introduced by schemata, though elements of them appear in both Faithful (pp. 67-74) and Hopeful's (pp. 137-44) accounts of their earlier adventures. Several of the episodes in these accounts, particularly that of Faithful, are similar to the enumerated actions in the sketches since they lack individualizing detail and, hence, seem simply illustrative. Christian, too, is characterized by illustrative action from time to time. Typical of these overtly illustrative actions, which are summarized by a moral in context, is an incident that occurred when Christian asked Faithful to wait for him:

Faithful answered, *No,* I am upon my life, and the Avenger of Blood is behind me. At this Christian was somewhat moved, and putting to all his strength, he quickly got up with *Faithful,* and did also overrun him, so the *last was first.* Then did *Christian* vain-gloriously smile, because he had gotten the start of his Brother: but not taking good heed to his feet, he suddenly stumbled and fell, and could not rise again, until *Faithful* came up to help him.

The specific moral in context, that pilgrims should "go lovingly together" (p. 66), seems central; the revelation of the same pride Christian exhibited in fighting Apollyon seems incidental.

The central figures do benefit *indirectly* from the elements of the extended schemata insofar as they are the vehicles of that commentary. Christian, for example, reveals as much about himself as he does about Pliable in saying:

> I have said the truth of *Pliable,* and if I should also say all the truth of my self, it will appear there is no betterment 'twixt him and my self. 'Tis true, he went back to his own house, but I also turned aside to go the way of death.(p. 26)

Christian in particular benefits, too, from speeches which are somewhat similar to both the self-revealing speeches of the minor figures and the interior monologues of *Grace Abounding:*

> Thus therefore he now went on, bewailing his sinful sleep, saying, *O wretched Man that I am,* that I should sleep in the day time! that I should sleep in the midst of difficulty! that I should so indulge the flesh, as to use that rest for ease to my flesh, which the Lord ... hath erected only for the relief of the spirits of Pilgrims.(p. 44)

Nevertheless, compared to figures like Talkative, Ignorance, and Hold-the-World, the central figures owe little to the diverse methods Bunyan used in presenting the wayward professors. The central figures are revealed primarily by dramatic means.

The motives and values, fears and hopes, and most of all, the inner conflicts of the major figures are revealed in dramatic scenes which themselves exhibit further dramatic developments. Although the racy colloquial tone and rhythm of the dialogue obscures the distinction at times, these scenes may be classified as either basically mimetic or basically allegorical. The mimetic scenes allude directly to external actuality; the allegorical ones, indirectly. Most scenes, of course, contain both direct and indirect allusions to external actuality; many separate narrative facts in both kinds of scenes make dual allusions. Nevertheless, a basic functional distinction exists between the two kinds of scenes in *The Pilgrim's Progress*. The mimetic scenes reveal the central figures' motives and values through their interactions with minor representative figures and their discussions with each other. The allegorical scenes, in contrast, externalize the major figures' inner conflicts through interactions with minor figures who represent both supernatural agents and their own thoughts, sentiments, and emotions. The allegorical scenes may be examined first since they exhibit, perhaps, the most notable dramatic developments.

The allegorical scenes reveal coherent, self-consistent minor figures primarily through dialogue. Like the Tempter of *Grace Abounding*, these figures clarify the nature of inner conflicts, but unlike the Tempter, they do not fade into relatively abstract symbols of evil between separate conflicts. In a sense, the Tempter is superseded by many minor figures who make a brief appearance, serve their function in the psychomachia, and then disappear. They make a vivid impression because, just as many Puritan preachers were instructed to use *prosopopoeia* to present variously "Gods, angels and men, dead or alive," abstract concepts, and moral "types,"[17] their creator gave them a local habitation and a name. They attain memorable self-consistency during their brief appearances. Their arguments are limited by the dramatic situation, and these arguments imply a coherent group of related values.

When Shame attacks Faithful in the Valley of Humiliation, for example, his "action" is mostly in the form of a clever argument:

> He said it was a piteful, low, sneaking business for a man to mind Religion; he said that a tender conscience was an unmanly thing, and that for Man to watch over his words and ways, so as to tye up himself from that hectoring liberty, that the brave spirits of the times accustom themselves unto, would make him the Ridicule of the times. He objected also, that but few of the Mighty, Rich, or Wise were ever of my opinion ... that it was a *shame* to sit whining and mourning under a Sermon, and a *shame* to come sighing and groaning home.(pp. 72-73)

Shame here acquires sufficient force and concreteness that he readily finds a place beside such figures as Messrs By-ends and Hold-the-World even though comments *about* him are limited. Faithful merely reports, "But indeed this *Shame* was a bold Villian; I could scarce shake him out of my company; yea, he would be haunting of me, and continually whispering me in the ear, with some one or other of infirmities that attend Religion" (pp. 73-74). Shame is one of many minor figures who reveals yet this unique monster produces a lasting impression primarily through the "flyting" rather than through either an awesome presence or an ominous or symbolic appearance. In the initial verbal skirmish, Apollyon reveals the pride he represents, not merely through the authorial reference to his "disdainful countenance," but dramatically through his claim to be "Prince and God" of all the country, as though he were Satan himself rather than a subordinate fallen angel. He reveals dramatically the kind of pride he represents by arguing from his own nature, "There is no Prince that will thus lightly lose his Subjects," and, more important, by adding, "But since thou complainest of thy service and wages, be content to go back, what our Country will afford, I do here promise to give thee." He reveals dramatically, too, the weaknesses in Christian that gave him particular force by summarizing Christian's earlier "infirmities" and adding, "When thou talkest of thy Journey, and of what thou has heard, and seen, thou art inwardly desirous of vain-glory in all thou sayest or doest." And in all of his arguments he reveals his descent from the cunning, subtle Tempter of *Grace Abounding*, for he is a sophist of no mean ability:

> Thou knowest that for the most part, his Servants come to an ill end, because they are transgressors against me, and my ways: How many of them have been put to shameful deaths! and besides, thou countest his service better than mine, whereas he never came yet from the place where he is, to deliver any that served him out of our hands: but as for me, how many times, as all the World very well knows, have I delivered, wither by power or fraud, those what have faithfully served me, from him and his, though taken by them; and so I will deliver thee.(pp. 56-58)

His appeals are more diverse than those of Shame, more dramatic than those of Lucifera: he forcefully reveals the complexity of an individual internal conflict primarily through the rapid verbal interactions in the flyting. His dialogue gives him his distinctive character and impact as well as exploring a complicated conflict dramatically.

The basically mimetic scenes extend the social range of the narrative through a series of encounters with representative wayward pilgrims such as Talkative and Ignorance. These encounters obviously exploit more sustained dramatic contrasts than did the trial scenes appended to *Grace Abounding*, and they do so in a less rudimentary way than the passages treating such pairs of figures as Pliable and Obstinate, Formalist and Hypocrisy. Yet the contrasts between the major figures and the doomed professors are the sharp and clear ones demanded by satiric art. Beyond the fact that dramatic contrasts are sustained more fully in *The*

Pilgrim's Progress, the more significant dramatic development is that relatively subtle contrasts are also sustained.

These subtle contrasts are evident, for example, in the reports of Faithful and Hopeful's journeys through the countryside Christian had recently traversed (pp. 67-74; 136-44) and, perhaps more memorably, in the trial scene at Vanity Fair. This latter scene attains a powerful dramatic immediacy, objectivity, and concentration largely through the contrasts among four figures who reveal both their ideas and their characters through speech. Envy, Superstition, and Pickthank attain a surprising complexity, without the aid of interpretative commentary, through a few short speeches as they accuse Faithful; Faithful's answer to those charges gains much of its impact through the contrast with them. Envy is typical of the minor figures:

> Then stood forth *Envy*, and said to this effect; My Lord, I have known this man a long time, and will attest upon my Oath before this honourable Bench, That he is—
> *Judge.* Hold, give him his Oath: So they sware him. Then he said, My Lord, this man ... is one of the vilest men in our Countrey; He neither regardeth Prince nor People, Law nor Custom; but doth all that he can to possess all men with certain of his disloyal notions, which he in the general calls Principles of Faith and Holiness. And in particular, I heard him once my self affirm, *That Christianity, and the Customs of our Town of Vanity, were Diametrically opposite, and could not be reconciled.* By which saying, my Lord, he doth at once, not only condemn all our laudable doings, but us in the doing of them.
> *Judg.* Then did the Judge say to him, Hast thou any more to say?
> *Envy.* My Lord, I could say much more, only I would not be tedious to the Court. Yet if need be ... I will enlarge my Testimony against him.... (pp. 93-94)

Despite his name, Envy seems a fully-realized fictional type, rather than a simple personification, because of the eagerness to condemn Faithful which leads him to begin his harangue before he is sworn, the vehemence of his tone, the malicious hatred implicit in the ingenious nature of his testimony, and, most significant, the logically-irrelevant pretense to self-restraint in his expressed fear lest he be "tedious to the Court." Yet the author does not describe him, analyze him, or introduce commentary of any kind about him.

Beyond the stipulated "meanings" in the names of Faithful's accusors, they acquire dramatic definition by contrast as successive speakers reveal themselves—also by dialogue—and contribute to the dramatic impact of Faithful's reply:

Faith. *May I speak a few words in my own defence?*
Judg. Sirrah, Sirrah, thou deservest to live no longer, but to be slain immediately upon the place; yet that all men may see our gentleness towards thee, let us hear what thou hast to say.
Faith. 1. I say then in answer to what Mr. *Envy* hath spoken, I never said ought but this, *That what Rule, or Laws, or Custom, or People, were flat against the Word of God, are diametrically opposite to Christianity.* If I have said a miss in this, convince me of my errour, and I am ready here before you to make my recantation.
2. As to the second, to wit, Mr. *Superstition,* and his charge against me, I said only this, *That in the worship of God there is required a divine Faith; but there can be no divine Faith, without a divine Revelation of the will of God: therefore whatever is thrust into the worship of God, that is not agreeable to divine Revelation, cannot be done but by an humane Faith, which Faith will not profit to Eternal Life.*
3. As to what Mr. *Pickthank* hath said, I say, (avoiding terms, as that I am said to rail, and the like) That the Prince of this Town, with all the Rablement His Attendants, by this Gentleman named, are more fit for a being in Hell, then in this Town and Countrey; *and so the Lord have mercy upon me.*
Then the Judge called to the Jury.... (p. 95)

Dramatic contrasts to the earlier speakers enhance the effect of Faithful's speech so that his disdain for human frailty and pettiness, his contempt for wordly values, his independence, his resolution, his courage, his indomitable will, and, in short, his truly heroic stature are forcefully conveyed in a scene remarkable for its dramatic immediacy and force. The scene does not, to be sure, create the effect of a group of characters interacting—as do some scenes in the *Second Part*—yet the implicit contrasts to the characters behind the ideas to which Faithful responds give the scene a powerful cumulative effect.

The mimetic aspects of *The Pilgrim's Progress* are developed largely by dramatic means, then, in that it has a largely scenic narrative method and presents many memorable scenes with a sharp focus, sustained tension, a climactic order of events, "natural" dialogue, and an effectively varied tempo. Further, the character of three complex, major figures— and some minor ones—is revealed primarily by dramatic means through two kinds of scenes. In the allegorical scenes, many self-consistent, coherent, minor fictional characters reveal themselves primarily by dialogue, and the great psychological complexity of the major figures' inner conflicts are objectified and explored. In the mimetic scenes, sharp dramatic contrasts are sustained and some relatively subtle ones appear so that a few scenes have potent dramatic immediacy, objectivity, and concentration.

III

The dominant movement toward more effective imitation is sustained through two significant dramatic developments in *Mr. Badman.* Bunyan created a complex, fully-realized feminine character primarily through dialogue in the central story, and he sustained character differentiation between the two central figures in the foreground despite the tremendous burden of exposition and narration they bore. The extended moral discourse between the teller of the story and the listener may be examined first.

The speakers are, in a sense, direct descendants of the pilgrims, Wiseman of Christian, Attentive of Hopeful, and they would seem to be in serious danger of disintegrating into mere expository devices. The discussions in the foreground of *Mr. Badman* are much like the long moral discourses that constitute the chief dramatic weakness of *The Pilgrim's Progress.* Faithful says at one point *"Let us spend our time in discoursing of things that are profitable"* (p. 75), and, as has been mentioned, the major figures engage in numerous religious and moral discussions that impede narrative movement and almost dispense with the fiction of the journey. Faithful and Christian discuss at length the religious significance of Talkative's condition, for example, and they cite pertinent biblical texts to support their assertions (pp. 79-80). Again, Hopeful and Christian engage in a long doctrinal discussion about Atheist after his departure (pp. 135-36). These discussions usually allude directly to external actuality. And so throughout, abstract themes were pursued at the expense of character differentiation so that the central figures suggested the "Question" and "Answer" of the earlier treatises.

The danger of a similar disintegration would seem to be even greater in *Mr. Badman.* Neither Wiseman nor Attentive benefit from direct characterization or analysis; their dialogue is undistinguished by individualizing rhythms or "turns" of speech. Both suffer as distinct personalities from their creator's occasional lapses.[24] In contrast to the four figures Arthur Dent used in *The Plaine-Man's Pathway to Heaven,*[25] the two speakers do not even reveal sharply contrasting values through their speech. Wiseman himself calls attention to this latter fact when he says, "Many other things might be added, but between persons so well agreed as you and I are, these may suffice at present" (p. 21). Although the speakers give themselves personal histories, these are neither extensive nor very illuminating. Attentive did not know Mr. Badman, and he shows himself simply as a generous father in the one incident from his own past which is discussed (p. 66). Wiseman claims personal knowledge of many episodes in Mr. Badman's career (p. 22), but he reports no encounters with the anti-hero, his father, his wife, or his companions which reveal his own character as a minor participant. He merely alludes to, but does not develop, aspects of his own past which are similar to that of his creator.[26] Most important, in striking contrast to Christian and Hopeful, the speakers define themselves through no memorable action; the two moralistic, gossipy old gentlemen simply sit under a tree and examine the career of the notorious Mr. Badman who had recently died. Only the dialogue takes place in the dramatic present, and the dialogue is between speakers who share many interests and values.

Despite these diverse dangers, the speakers do not disintegrate into mere rhetorical or expository instruments. On the contrary, Wiseman and Attentive generate continued interest and become distinct, lively participants in a drama. They command attention, and even grow, as the dialogue unfolds because of subtle, changing tensions between them. This tension, which both focuses their differences and gives rise to many subtle exchanges, springs from two basic sources. The first of these is inherent in the narrative situation itself; the second is in the personalities of the speakers.

Since *Mr. Badman* is in part, as Professor Tindall points out, an "elaboration of the judgment tale,"[27] the manner of Mr. Badman's death is a matter of some importance, and Attentive's curiosity about this matter is aroused early in the dialogue. Wiseman says he is sure Badman has "gone to hell" because of his *"wicked* life, and *fearful* death, especially since the Manner of his death was so corresponding with his life" (p. 19). To Attentive's prompt questions about this latter point, Wiseman answers, "First, we will begin with his Life, and then proceed to his Death: Because a relation of the first may the more affect you, when you shall hear of the second" (p. 20). Thereafter Wiseman proves adamant in his refusal to divulge this information, and the fearfully-peaceful deathbed scene is not described until the closing pages (p. 155). However this heavy-handed use of suspense may affect a reader,[28] it has notable effects upon Attentive.

Shortly after Wiseman's initial refusal, Attentive urges, *"Be as brief as you can, for I long to hear the manner of his death"* (p. 20). Subsequent, continual reiterations and variations of this request imply Attentive's mounting impatience, *"Well, sir, now I have heard enough of Mr.* Badman's *naughtiness, pray now proceed to his Death"* (p. 126). Some imply merely his restiveness: *"But pray let us return again to Mr.* Badman *and his companions"* (p. 53). And a few his resignation: *"But pray, do it* [discuss his other adventures] *with as much brevity as you can"* (p. 106). At other times, he is apparently torn between his desire to rush to the end and his fascination with a provocative current theme, and, in some cases, he finally delays the final revelation himself (pp. 31, 74).

Attentive's fluctuating avidity and discontent and Wiseman's bland refusals create occasion for many subtle exchanges. Being a captive audience and knowing that he is so, Attentive allows irony to tinge his resignation when he says, *"If you please, let us return again to Mr.* Badman *himself, if you have any more to say of him."* Wiseman, seemingly unaware of the ironic undercurrent, as imperturbable now as he had been in the face of other signs of impatience, answers "More! we have yet scarce thoroughly begun" (p. 88). It seems a matter of policy with Wiseman, in fact, to be insensitive; he shows no awareness, for example, of the wry humor of Attentive's statement:

> *Certainly, malice and envy flow from pride and arrogancy, and they again from ignorance, and ignorance from the* Devil. *And I thought, that since you spoke of the pride of Mr.* Badman *before, we should have something of these before we have done.*(p. 138)

And so throughout, Wiseman's refusal gives rise to amusing byplay that defines dramatically the conflicting attitudes of the speakers.

The second source of tension is essentially a matter of personalities. Attentive himself is adept in the art of "godly conversation" and clearly attempts to distinguish himself. He too can readily quote a pertinent biblical text (p. 22); upon occasion, he proudly announces the text the moment after Wiseman has mentioned the subject (p. 32). He too has been "an ear-and eye-witness" to pertinent examples of divine judgements, and he relates them with practiced facility (p. 41). He too is resourceful in tracing the development of one sin from another (p. 44), and he is always alive to, as Wiseman is alive to, the moral and psychological implications of outward events:

> Atten. *This was an ill beginning indeed, and argueth that he began to harden himself in sin betimes. For a lye cannot be knowingly told and stood in, (and I perceive that this was his manner of way in Lying) but he must as it were force his own heart unto it. Yea, he must make his heart hard, and bold to doe it. Yea, he must be arrived to an exceeding pitch of wickedness....* (p. 21)

And he seems as eager as Wiseman to see *"if by the Scripture we can make it* [this conclusion] *good"* (p. 159). At times his eagerness to contribute, to be a brisk talker in religious matters, is especially evident when he appears to turn the course of discussion so that he may do so:

> Atten. *But was he not afraid of the Judgments of God, that did fly about at that time?*
> Wise. He regarded not the Judgment nor Mercy of God, for had he

at all done that, he could not have done as he did. But what judgments do you mean?
Atten. *Such Judgments, that if Mr.* Badman *himself had taken but sober notice of, they might have made him a hung down his ears.*
Wise. Why, have you heard of any such persons that the Judgments of God have overtaken?
Atten. *Yes, and so, I believe, have you too, though you make so strange about it.*
Wise. I have so indeed, to my astonishment and wonder.
Atten. *Pray, therefore, if you please, tell me what it is, as to this, that you know; and then, perhaps, I may also say something to you of the same.* (pp. 85-86)

"Look," the neophyte implies with a complacent smile, "I too have something to say." And so throughout, the religious conversationalist who would shine in the pages of Arthur Dent's work[29] refuses to accept the inferiority implicit in silence and strives to be something more than attentive.

In contrast, Wiseman is, as his name implies, armed at all points for such discussions, and he shows a Johnsonian disregard for Attentive's self-esteem, though Attentive is often tossed and gored along the way. He readily indulges Attentive's insatiable curiosity but has little patience with ignorance or error. Attentive says, for example, *"But I wonder since Curseing and Swearing are such evils in the eyes of God, that he doth not make some Examples to others, for their committing such wickedness."* Attentive could well have found Wiseman's answer a crushing one: "Alas! so he has, a thousand times twice told, as may be easily gathered by any observing people in every Age and Countrey" (p. 37). Wiseman insistently dominates the situation and freely reprimands Attentive when he detects signs of careless listening. At one point Attentive asks, *"But what was that other Villian addicted to, I mean, young* Badmans *third companion?"* Wiseman answers, "Uncleanness; I told you before, but it seems you forgot" (p. 52). On a similar occasion, Wiseman answers "How he carried it! why, he did as they. I intimated so much before" (p. 48). He is more caustic when he detects an unimaginative response. Attentive exclaims, *"Well, this* Badman *was a sad wretch."* Wiseman answers "Thus you have often said before. But now we are in discourse of this, give me leave a little to goe on" (pp. 115-16). And Wiseman consistently asserts his prerogatives in the interest of accuracy. For example, Attentive says, *"It is a fearful thing for Youth to be trained up in a way of Cursing and Swearing."* Wiseman replies, "Trained up in them! that I cannot say Mr. *Badman* was, for his father hath oft-times in my hearing, bewailed the badness of his Children, and of this naughty Boy in particular" (p. 40). This is not to say that either Wiseman or Attentive is, in the Johnsonian sense, simply talking for victory, but it is clear that Attentive is a bit nettled to find himself, in effect, anticipating the part of Goldsmith, and that Wiseman will endure no usurpations of the prerogatives of age and wisdom.

This competitive situation alters as the dialogue progresses. Early in the discussion, Attentive ventures to disagree with Wiseman; he suggests that Badman's father should have been less generous to his son, that he should not have given him money to begin his own business, and he debates with Wiseman about the proper relationship of the father and the son. About a thousand words later, Attentive says, *"Well I yield. But pray let us return again to Mr. Badman"* (p. 68). After that, he seldom disagrees directly. Thereafter, he seems more eager to learn than to talk, or even to lapse into an admiring apprenticeship, for he interrupts more often to ask questions (pp. 74, 123) than to voice objections or additions. He commends his preceptor and teacher upon occasion (p. 134), and is generous in acknowledging his debt upon parting: *"I also thank you for your freedom of me, in granting of me your reply to all my questions"* (p. 179).

Nevertheless, the two central sources of conflict are continually operative so that Wiseman's bland "Of his Dying, as I told you, I will give you a Relation anon" (p. 30) and the implicit competitiveness of the speakers are continual sources of tension. A series of subtle dramatic contrasts arising from these sources sustain the central differences between two similar but distinct personalities interacting in the foreground.

The principal dramatic development in the central story appears in the revelation of an important, fully-realized feminine character primarily through dialogue. Her deepest emotions are externalized without the aid of allegorical settings, actions, or personifications. The first Mrs. Badman is treated by the speakers in the foreground initially as an illustration of the dangers of an imprudent marriage (pp. 78-79), yet she speaks for herself frequently enough to become the first complex feminine character in Bunyan's narratives. Typically, if she and her husband appear in the same scene, his speeches are summarized; hers, quoted directly (pp. 150-52). Although these speeches are not distinguished by a characteristic cadence or "turn" of speech, they convey a unified cumulative impression. She evinces in an early speech a certain uncompromising, youthful, self-righteousness which is reminiscent—despite its Baptist color—of Antigone or, perhaps, of Cordelia, and which becomes central: "You are commanded to love me, as you love your own body, and so do I love you; but I tell you true, I prefer my Soul before all the world, and its Salvation I will seek" (p. 85). As she emerges more fully, it becomes evident that she lacks the solid good sense of Christiana, the wit and charm of Mercy, and, perhaps, the clear definition of both, yet she shares the religious fervor of her successors. She is consistently punctilious and conspicuously feminine in her range of interests and her point of view. These qualities are particularly evident in a long interior monologue (pp. 149-50) and, especially, in some of her longer speeches:

> And, ah children, said she, will it not be dreadful to you, if we only shall meet at the day of Judgment, and then part again, and never see each other more? And with that she wept, the Children (also) wept; so she held on her discourse: Children, said she, I am going from you, I am going to Jesus Christ, and with him there is neither sorrow, nor sighing, nor pain, nor tears, nor death. (p. 151)
>
> Said she, "God knows, and thou shalt know, that I have been a loving, faithful Wife unto thee; my prayers have been many for thee; and as for all the abuses that I have received at thy hand, those I freely and heartily forgive, and still shall pray for thy conversion, even as long as I breathe in this world. But husband, I am going thither, where no bad man shall come, and if thou dost not convert, thou wilt never see me more with comfort; let not my plain words offend thee: I am thy dying wife, and of my faithfulness to thee, would leave this Exhortation with thee: Break off thy sins, fly to God for mercy while mercies gate stands open; remember, that the day is coming, when thou, though now lusty and well, must lye at the gates of death, as I do: and what wilt thou then do, if thou shalt be found with a naked soul, to meet with the Cherubims and their flaming swords? Yea, what wilt thou then do, if Death and Hell shall come to visit thee, and thou in thy sins, and under the Curse of the Law?" (pp. 150-51)

This latter speech, her final exhortation to her husband, exhibits, not only the fullness of her creator's imaginative realization of her situation, but the characteristic blend of Puritan theology and matronly tenderness, of conjugal regard and Puritan self-righteousness, that had become characteristic of Mrs. Badman.

Mrs. Badman is depicted with sufficient fullness to serve an important dramatic function as a foil by anticipation. In contrast to the death of Mr. Badman, her death is presented as exemplary in that she exhibits joyful anticipation of her future home, continued urgent concern for the souls of the husband and children she leaves behind, and even a certain eagerness to use the emotional authority her situation gives her to encourage her family's reformation. She exhibits "many signs of her salvation" and dies with "a soul full of Grace, a heart full of comfort" (pp. 149-53). The elaborate, almost ritualistic, preparation for death establishes a norm in light of which Mr. Badman's ignoble end (p. 157) is to be seen. The pathos of virtue in distress is turned to the service of piety by the speaker rather than simply by the narrator.

IV

Representative critics have found *The Holy War* lacking in the elemental human interest often held necessary to the highest dramatic effects.[30] Paul Elmer More, for example, finds *The Holy War* the "least human of his books."[31] Charles Firth avers that the work "lacks the human interest" of *The Pilgrim's Progress* and that "the characters remain abstractions throughout, with the exception of some of the wicked who make a brief appearance on the stage only to be hung or knocked on the head by the virtuous abstractions."[32] Other critics share the views of More and Firth.[33]

It would seem, therefore, that no significant new achievements were to be seen in *The Holy War*. The few scenes which have elicited critical praise are simply echoes of past achievements. Professor Sharrock and James A. Froude lavish praise upon the trial scenes.[34] These scenes (pp. 119-38; 238-43) are written in a rich, comic, satiric vein; they exhibit a racy, colloquial style, amusingly sharp contrasts, a few extended schemata (pp. 121, 125-26), and rapid dramatic interactions much like those which enlivened both the pilgrim's encounters with wayward Christians and the dialogue of Wiseman and Attentive. It would seem so, further, because the design of the allegory has all of the labyrinthian intricacy of a medieval tapestry; it exhibits an elaborate, systematic fusion of the method of character drawing developed from the homiletic sketches, the "method" of implying the nature of the speaker primarily by *what* he says, and of diverse methods of both concealing and revealing stipulated truths emphatically. The mimetic elements are but a small part of this design.

Nevertheless, because of the more extensive and systematic application of principles and methods developed in earlier narratives, *The Holy War* exhibits four significant dramatic developments. Many long, elaborate, formal scenes appear. Speeches consistently convey a fuller impression of the scenes through their overt relevance to the narrative situation. Effective dramatic contrasts are consistently sustained. At least a dozen complex central figures consistently speak "in character" in complicated ways through countless scenes and episodes. Some of these changes, to be sure, are more significant as anticipations than as achievements insofar as dramatic effects are concerned, yet they clearly illustrate a further realization of dramatic potentialities.

Many long, elaborate, formal scenes, unprecedented in Bunyan's narratives, appear in *The Holy War*. In these scenes, alternate courses of action are debated (pp. 215-18), crucial decisions are formally announced (pp. 246-52), and crucial conflicts are explored through a series of formal orations and rebuttals (pp. 44-49). The separate speeches are more reminiscent of popular contemporaneous romances[35] than of Bunyan's earlier narratives since rapidity of movement is sacrificed to rhetorical effectiveness (pp. 215-18). Incidental interactions of characters are less evident than the detailed, formal marshalling of arguments. At one point, for example, Mr. Incredulity systematically summarizes and answers the abstract arguments of each of his four opponents point by point before he allows the scene to move again by voicing his vehement defiance (pp. 47-49). The spontaneity of utterance suggested by the style of earlier speeches is less evident than long, rotund sentences exhibiting elaborate parallel structure, balance, antithesis, and, occasionally, alliteration:

> *O ye inhabitants of the Town of Mansoul, when I heard your Trumpet sound for a Parley with us, I can truly say I was glad; but when you said you were willing to submit yourselves to our King and Lord, then I was yet more glad; but when, by your silly provisoes and foolish cavils, you laid the stumbling-block of your inquity before your own faces, then was my gladness turned into sorrows, and my hopeful beginnings of your return, into languishing fainting fears.*(p. 56)

The formality of the style is echoed in the way the stage is set and the conflict is resolved, usually in the final address. Although they scarcely attain epic dignity,[36] these scenes are orderly, systematic, logical culminations of the "flytings" depicted in the earlier allegory.

The speeches in even the most elaborate scenes consistently attain greater direct, specific relevance to the narrative situation than was common in earlier narratives. In *The Pilgrim's Progress,* many of the major characters' doctrinal discussions, for example, contain only incidental, if any, direct allusions to the immediate dramatic situations (pp. 137-40). Taken by itself, even the speech of Shame (pp. 72-73), which was discussed earlier, could easily have been placed in the streets of the City of Destruction. Mrs. Badman's speeches, which were also examined earlier, are somewhat unusual in *Mr. Badman* because they gain force and relevance from the explicit allusions to her imminent death. The fuller imaginative realization created by such allusions is consistently maintained in the speeches in *The Holy War.* Even in Captain Execution's long, highly figurative speech on the theme of the "fruitless Bough," a theme Bunyan himself had developed in *The Barren Fig-Tree* (II, 257-58), the Captain's closing exhortation appears in pertinent narrative terms: "Thy sin has brought this Army to thy Walls, and shall it bring it in judgement to do *execution* into thy Town?" (p. 47). Again, as Diabolus addresses Emmanuel from the walls of Mansoul:

> *Wherefore art thou come to torment me, and to cast me out of my possession? This Town of* Mansoul *... is mine, and that by a twofold*

> *Right.* 1. *It is mine by right of Conquest; I won it in the open field* . . . 2. *This Town of* Mansoul *is mine also by their Subjection. They have opened the Gates of their Town unto me* . . . (p. 72)

And so throughout. Although many speakers lack the common humanity to give their utterances notable dramatic impact, their speeches consistently give a fuller impression of the scene and the dramatic situation than was common in the earlier dialogue.

Effective dramatic contrasts are consistently sustained through these long, elaborate scenes and, of course, through many shorter ones. In the formal scenes, the consistency is, perhaps, more notable than the dramatic effectiveness because the contrasts are simple products of the author's consistency in developing arguments through characters who say what they are. Whereas Christian, Hopeful, and Faithful are sometimes hurried by the rush of ideas into pursuing a theme at the expense of character differentiation, the speakers in *The Holy War* are more circumspect. They represent specific aspects of the theme and confine themselves accordingly. At one point, for example, Captains Boanerges, Conviction, Judgment, and Execution deliver orations before Mansoul. Although all four speakers allude to the same narrative situation, each speech consistently emphasizes one central theme: Boanerges announces their reasons for besieging the city, Captain Conviction attempts to convince them of their sinful state, Captain Judgment threatens them with the judgment by the law, and Captain Execution, of course, emphasizes the threat of execution (pp. 43-47). The arguments and the figures who voice them, however, too often remain a few feet above the stage.

Less abstract dramatic contrasts sustained through informal scenes, on the other hand, are very precise, subtle, and effective. The most subtle of these, perhaps, involve figures representing attitudes. Such contrasts appear during the exchanges between Mr. Carnal-Security and Mr. Godly-Fear at the feast when the latter awakens Mansoul to the fact that Emmanuel had departed (pp. 154-57). The passage is too long to quote, but a few of these contrasts are summarized in one of Mr. Carnal-Security's speeches:

> Fie! fie! Mr. *Godly Fear,* fie! will you never shake off your *timorousness*? Are you afraid of being Sparrow-blasted? Who hath hurt you? Behold, I am on your side; only you are for doubting, and I am for being confident. . . . Why . . . do you now, to your shame, and our trouble, break out into such passionate, melancholy language, when you should eat and drink, and be merry? (p. 155)

These sustained dramatic contrasts between the attitudes that caused the backsliding and the one that ended it are more effective than those in the formal scene involving Boanerges because the rapidity and informality of the dialogue give it a mimetic coloration, the attitudes represented are relatively concrete, and the speakers illustrate the human implications of the attitudes they represent through hints of personality. Although the degrees of dramatic effectiveness, thus, vary, such contrasts are sustained with great consistency in *The Holy War*.

Unlike earlier narratives, *The Holy War* exhibits at least a dozen complex central figures who consistently speak "in character" through many scenes and episodes. Among these major figures, Shaddai, Emmanuel, and Diabolus are unusual in that they reveal themselves primarily through dialogue; the Lord High Secretary, who represents the third Member of the Trinity, is unusual in that he speaks only by report, though he dwells in Mansoul. In contrast, figures like Lord Willbewill, Lord Understanding, Mr. Godly-Fear, and Mr. Incredulity do not reveal their "natures" only, or even primarily, through dialogue. On the contrary, they are products of a complex fusion of the diverse methods used in earlier narratives: they are introduced by schemata, developed through dialogue and action, and defined along the way by additional methods yet to be discussed. They represent a significant dramatic development, nevertheless, because they consistently speak "in character" in a complicated way and because, in contrast to Wiseman and Attentive of *Mr. Badman,* there are not simply two, but many, of them.

These figures speak "in character" in a different sense than earlier ones. Minor representative figures like Talkative and Ignorance in *The Pilgrim's Progress* spoke "in character" in that their speech was compatible with the schemata introducing them. Minor figures like Shame and Apollyon, who were not introduced by schemata, spoke "in character" in that their dialogue itself implied a self-consistent, coherent group of related values in the speakers. The nature of the specific inner conflicts they externalized actually defined and focused their characters. In contrast, the central figures in *The Holy War* speak "in character" both in relation to their schemata and as participants in separate inner conflicts. As was mentioned, the schemata introducing these central figures have a dual conceptual basis so that such a figure may speak "in character" either as a faculty, or attitude, or force involved in an inner struggle, or as a compatible moral type, or as both. Upon occasion, too, he may speak as a representation of specific contemporaneous persons or events.[37] Speaking "in character" in this more inclusive sense, many figures like Lord Willbewill, Lord Understanding, Captain Conviction, and Mr. Conscience define their "natures" as precisely as did minor figures in *The Pilgrim's Progress,* who left the arena after a scene or two, and as consistently as did Wiseman and Attentive.

Typical of these figures is Mr. Conscience. The schema introduces him as both a complex faculty of the soul and a compatible fictional type. The appositeness of the image and the idea is maintained since the attributes of the concept of the moral type correspond, yet Mr. Conscience clearly maintains both a direct and an indirect relationship to external actuality. He consistently speaks "in character" in relation to both aspects of his nature through many separate episodes and conflicts.

As a complex faculty of the soul he was capable of being "pleased with many of the Giant [Diabolus's] Laws and service," but incapable of escaping his own innate knowledge of God and of the moral law.[38] When the "dread of his [Shaddai's] Law was upon him," Conscience also had the power, to "make the whole town of *Mansoul* shake with his voice." He could not be reduced "wholly" to the service of Diabolus (p. 19). Although he became unreliable under Diabolus's concerted attack, "every outcry of Mr. *Recorder* against the sin of *Mansoul* [continued to be] ... the voice of God in him to them" (p. 20). Later, after the Scriptures were "published in all the corners of the Kingdom of *Universe*" (p. 29) and the forces representing the Law besieged Mansoul, the "old Gentleman, too, ... also began to talk aloud, and his words were not to the Town of *Mansoul* as if they were *great claps of thunder*" (p. 54). After the Prince entered the city, "Whoever came to him, or discoursed with him [Mr. Conscience, the Recorder], nothing would he talk of, tell them, or hear, but that Death and Destruction now attended *Mansoul*" (p. 89). After the "general pardon," (p. 106), which represents the new covenant of grace historically and, in regard to the individual soul, effectual calling, his domain is clearly prescribed by Emmanuel himself. Mr. Conscience is to confine himself "to the teaching of Moral Virtues, to Civil and Natural Duties," except for such "high and supernatural Mysteries" as he learns "at the mouth of the Lord High *Secretary*," who represents the Holy Ghost (pp. 140-42). And, thereafter, he consistently observes these limitations (pp. 154, 181, 192). After Mr. Godly-Fear makes him aware of Emmanuel's departure, he spreads the alarm and gives a sermon full of "power and authority" (p. 157). He recedes into the background during the early stages of sanctification, but he consistently speaks as a complex faculty of the soul through successive, varied circumstances.

Mr. Conscience, who functions as the Recorder and, later, as the Subordinate-Preacher in narrative terms, is also introduced and consistently developed as a fictional type. In the schema he is an old man of "courage and faithfulness to speak truth on every occasion" with "a tongue as bravely hung, as he had a head filled with judgment." Though impelled to speak frightening truths during occasional "terrible fits," he seems susceptible to evil counsels, and "when he was merry, [would] unsay and deny what he in his fits had affirmed" (pp. 19-20). Yet he felt great remorse for his own weakness after the coming of Emmanuel (p. 89), and he gracefully accepted his own limitations after he had experienced effectual calling (pp. 141-42). After Mr. Godly-Fear made him aware of the backsliding of his followers, he publicly acknowledged his own responsibility:

Unhappy man that I am! that I should do so wicked a thing! That I, a Preacher! whom the Prince did set up to teach to Mansoul *his Law, should myself live senseless and sottishly here, and be one of the first found in transgression! This transgression also fell within my precincts: I should have cried out against the wickedness; but I let* Mansoul *lie wallowing in it, until it had driven* Emmanuel *from its borders!* (p. 158).

He bestirs himself to mitigate the effects of his weakness. And, playing an active part in a few subsequent events, he begins to talk himself alive. Deferential to Mr. Godly-Fear (p. 159), glad to be of use, quick to spread the word of Mr. Prywell's discoveries as "Chief Preacher in Mansoul" while the Lord Secretary is ill at ease (p. 181), eager to deliver Mansoul's messages to the Lord Secretary (p. 192), Mr. Conscience becomes more prominent as a mimetic creation—a weak, fallible, human old man with an unassailable basic integrity under stress, and a real need of divine aid—as his functions as a complex faculty of the soul becomes less prominent. Although he is not developed with the concrete particularity that could individualize a fictional character, his "nature" as a type is consistently displayed through his dialogue and action under diverse circumstances. Mr. Conscience is but one of many who illustrate remarkable consistency in the precise revelation of two aspects of a speakers' nature through varied scenes and episodes.

A further development of the scenic method of narration is evident, then, in the long, fully-developed scenes, the fuller integration of the speeches into the dramatic situation, the effective dramatic contrasts consistently sustained through many scenes, and the large number of complex figures who consistently speak in character through diverse scenes and episodes. These developments are largely products of a fuller and more systematic exploitation of methods which had been used in the earlier narratives. This same consistency may well have weakened the immediate dramatic impact of the allegory since it is also manifest in the ponderous formality, the intricate design, the allusive complexity, the vast proliferation of allegorical devices, and the continuing emphasis upon the abstract, rather than the concrete, nature of the speakers in *The Holy War.* Such is not the case in the *Second Part,* for the mimetic potentialities of such dramatic methods are fully realized therein.

V

The dramatic facility developed in the earlier narratives is manifest at every turn in the depiction of the inexhaustible diversity of social life and manners in the *Second Part*, Bunyan's fullest realization of the mimetic potentialities of narrative materials. The distinctively dramatic nature of this final achievement is evident in a number of ways. The narrative movement occurs in dramatic scenes with remarkable consistency. Among many highly effective scenes are some elaborate ones which create an effect, unprecedented in Bunyan's narratives, of a series of interactions among a group of characters. At least six fully-realized, complex, varied characters reveal themselves through a series of sharply-focused, rapidly moving, progressive scenes. Dramatic contrasts among the central figures are sustained in their speeches under diverse circumstances so that they seem both self-consistent and complex. The inner life is externalized primarily through lively, effective dialogue in mimetic, rather than allegorical, scenes. Scenes treating both the inner and the outer lives of the central figures give unprecedented prominence to human emotions, sentiments, and relationships so that, in a sense, the *Second Part* is the most fully human of Bunyan's works; it is certainly the most dramatic.

The scenic method is so fully developed that much of the work could readily be adapted for theatrical performance. The schemata are largely subsumed in the dialogue, and the settings are given relatively little attention. Transitional passages are unencumbered by allegorical elaborations like those in *The Holy War*. In quantitative terms, in fact, the *Second Part* contains very little expository, descriptive, and narrative material. In the first ten pages after Christiana's appearance, for example, there are six scenes, each of which involves from two to four speakers. The speeches contain sufficient expository material that there are no expository paragraphs within the scenes. The transitions between separate scenes consist of from two to four sentences (pp. 178-88). In contrast, eight embryonic scenes appear in the first ten pages after Christian's appearance in *The Pilgrim's Progress*. Some of these scenes are rather suggested than developed: three involve one speaker, five involve two. One short expository paragraph appears within the fifth scene; Help expounds background material to the Dreamer for over a page in the middle of the sixth scene. About three-quarters of a page of narrative and descriptive material appears between the fourth and fifth scenes (pp. 8-18). These facts are typical. The narrative moves more rapidly in the earlier masterpiece; it evolves more consistently through fully developed dramatic scenes in the *Second Part*.

Highly effective scenes, exhibiting a racy colloquial style, effective,

MIMETIC DEVELOPMENT / 89

subtle contrasts, rapid interactions of characters, and notable concentration and force, abound in the *Second Part.* Among these are a number of long scenes which create the effect—unprecedented in earlier narratives— of a series of interactions among a group of speakers (pp. 253-58; 258-64; 274-77). Bunyan had actually managed dialogues between only two speakers in *The Pilgrim's Progress.* When Talkative joined Faithful and Christian, for example, Faithful talked to Talkative, then separately to Christian, then separately to Talkative (pp. 75-84). Again, when By-ends joined Christian and Hopeful, only Christian talked to By-ends; then he talked to Hopeful *about* By-ends (pp. 98-101). The "Shepherds" whom the pilgrims met in "Immanuel's Land" had four names, but they spoke with only one voice, first with Christian (pp. 119-21), then with Hopeful (pp. 122-23).[39] Several figures spoke in succession in the elaborate scenes of *The Holy War,* but these scenes were marked by an outward formality, or even a certain rhetorical rigidity, so that the effect of rapid, spontaneous, interactions of a series of speakers was attained, if at all, only briefly.

In the *Second Part,* in contrast, the speeches are often rapid, spontaneous, and colloquial in tone, and the speakers seem to speak in a "natural" order. At one point, for example, Great-heart and Honest had been talking of the errors of the Ranters, and Christiana said, "There are strange Opinions in the World. I know one said 'twas time enough to repent when they came to die" (p. 257). Both Great-heart and Honest discussed this idea until another speaker brought a warning about two characters who threatened further trouble ahead. Great-heart speculated about who they could be briefly before Christiana, not eager for further adventure, said that she wished they could find an "Inn for her self and her Children." Honest then suggested that they visit the house of Gaius (pp. 257-58). The scene seems to develop through personal associations and dramatic interactions so that the scene suggests some of the incongruity of "real" experience and produces the effect of a group of people talking spontaneously together.

Christiana and Mercy, Great-heart and Honest, and, to a lesser extent, Matthew and James reveal themselves as complex and notably self-consistent fictional characters through countless dramatic utterances. The central contrasts among them appeared in a scene (pp. 254-55) which was discussed in chapter two. These central contrasts are sustained through diverse scenes so that these varied characters seem both self-consistent and complex. The central distinctions between these speakers do not vanish in the midst of their discourses, though their utterances are not consistently distinguished by characteristic cadences or "turns" of speech. Such individuality as they attain through specific episodes or incidents is not lost in the rush of ideas in subsequent scenes; rather, it is preserved through a few central, sustained contrasts.

It was said that the central contrast between Great-heart and Honest was one between the experienced ordinary man and the experienced extraordinary man since Honest contributed a sensible, straightforward, and rather obvious generalization; Great-heart, a forceful, precise, emphatic assertion about the religious significance of the subject (pp. 254-55). This contrast is evident in many other passages. The superior knowledge and penetration of Great-heart are evident when Honest presents a general summary of certain doctrines and Great-heart voices a precise, forceful repudiation (pp. 256-58); or again, when Honest asks about the interpretation of a biblical passage and Great-heart delivers a subtle and astute disquisition about it (p. 266). The sensible generalities of Honest contrast to the sagacious observations of Great-heart when both men discuss Faithful and Christian (pp. 271-72) and, most notably, when both men are asked about their journey. Honest generalizes at large about "way-fairing men" and concludes, "But for the most part we find it true, that has been talked of, of old, *A good Man must suffer Trouble*" (p. 275). He refers the question *"What Rubs have you met withal?"* to Great-heart, who enumerates three and then gives a specific account, in just the right tone, of the slaying of Slay-good (pp. 275-76).

Similar sustained contrasts in the speeches of the boys enable them to be both self-consistent and complex. It was said in chapter two of this study that Matthew's scarcely-articulate, scrupulous, tentative efforts to relate genuine inner experience to established doctrine contrasted sharply with James' precocious facility in reducing the question to a pertinent copy-book maxim. A similar contrast appears when Prudence catechizes the children. James answers with a precocious facility and assurance which suggests that he probably does not understand the answers he gives:

> Pru. *Good Boy. And canst thou tell who saves thee?*
> Jam. God the Father, God the Son, and God the Holy-Ghost.
> Pru. *Good Boy still. But how doth God the Father save thee?*
> Jam. By his Grace.
> Pru. *How doth God the Son save thee?*
> Jam. By his Righteousness, Death, and Blood, and Life.
> Pru. *And how doth God the Holy Ghost save thee?*
> Jam. By his *Illumination,* by his *Renovation,* and by his *Preservation.*

There is less glibness in Matthew's answer to a more difficult question (pp. 224-26). He displays his conscientious, hesitant, serious, devout character more fully in the midst of another discussion:

> When you all have thought what you please, I think God has been wonderful good unto us, both in bringing us out of this Valley, and in delivering us out of the hand of this Enemy; for my part I see no reason why we should distrust our God any more, since he has now, and in such a place as this, given us such testimony of his love as this. (p. 246)

He displays similar characteristics elsewhere (p. 261), just as James evinces the same superficial, youthful, facility in voicing the accepted sectarian answers in other passages (pp. 216, 220).

It was said in chapter two, too, that, in the scene discussed earlier (pp. 254-55), the subjective feminine responses were contrasted to the objective masculine ones and that the youthful innocence and aspiration of Mercy were contrasted to the mature discrimination and perception of Christiana. These women are by no means soft and effusive, yet both freely engage in frank and unreserved discussions of personal emotions in other scenes (pp. 212, 222-23). The youthful innocence and aspiration of Mercy are evident in the scene at the Gate; Christiana's comments in this scene are notably judicious and acute (pp. 189-90). Christiana's mature penetration and insight are evident, too, during the tour of the Significant Rooms, and her reaction contrasts conspicuously to Mercy's admission, "Sir, I see nothing." (p. 200). Other scenes also display both Mercy's naiveté and aspiration (pp. 197, 206) and Christiana's alert sagacity (pp. 192, 298-99).

Although relatively few of these characters' speeches seem overtly self-revealing, their speeches contribute greatly to their complexity through their very diversity and self-consistency. If the characters attain individuality through some of their speeches or actions, they do not lose it by becoming media for the presentation of ideas. These sustained contrasts prevent the characters from losing their individuality in the movement of ideas and made them seem both self-consistent and complex.

The inner life is externalized primarily through dialogue rather than by allegorical means in the *Second Part*. The journey, to be sure, is an allegorical one, yet the power of the central metaphor to give separate narrative facts dual or multiple points of reference is in abeyance during much of the narrative. The settings function only in relatively minor ways to reveal the travellers' states of consciousness. There are a few minor figures such as the Reliever (p. 195) and Secret (p. 179) who externalize spiritual struggle allegorically, but most of the minor figures are developed simply as fictional types. The schemata introducing characters such as Messrs Stand-fast (p. 299), Valiant-for-Truth (p. 289), Feeble-mind (pp. 267-68) and Honest, (pp. 246-48) have no dual conceptual basis. Honest insisted upon the pertinent distinction when he said, "Not Honesty in the *Abstract*, but *Honest* is my Name" (p. 247). The figures who join the pilgrims along the way are both introduced and developed, not as abstract ideas, or as figures in a psychomachia, but simply as representative types who reveal themselves through dialogue and action. Even the three crucial moments in the lives of Christiana and Mercy which are described in symbolic form are not developed as parts of the allegorical journey. They are reported as visions or dreams, and the characters' responses to them are revealed dramatically. Christiana's two dreams are described by Mr. Sagacity (pp. 178-79), and her responses to them are revealed in subsequent discussions with Mercy (p. 197) and the Interpreter (p. 205). Mercy's dream is known only through her conversation about it with Christiana (p. 223). Great-heart's encounter with Maul, in contrast, is developed as a part of the allegorical journey, yet his response to that encounter is externalized, not during the scene, but only in a subsequent, sociable discussion with Christiana (p. 246). The motives and values of the characters are externalized primarily in mimetic scenes.

Scenes treating both the inner and outer lives of the central figures give unprecedented prominence to human emotions, sentiments, and relationships. These characters are less dominated by a religious vision of attainable perfection than their predecessors. Christian, Faithful, and Hopeful continually sought to formulate the doctrinal implications of their experience and to test those formulations by reference to pertinent biblical texts (pp. 79, 195, 149). In contrast, Christiana and Mercy show relatively little interest in doctrine as such; they show much greater interest in the human response to experience. Characteristically, Christian once asked Hopeful, "But tell me particularly what effect this had upon your spirit?" (p. 143). Christiana, on the other hand, asks Great-heart, *"But was you not afraid, good Sir, when you see him* [Maul] *come with his Club?"* (p. 246). That is, how did you *feel* about it? Great-heart himself is one of the few characters who—upon rare occasions—discusses doctrines and related biblical texts (pp. 256, 266). The sentiments and emotions externalized through dialogue are still concerned with relationship of the human to the divine, but not exclusively so:

> Chris. *Little did I think once, that when my Husband went on Pilgrimage I should ever a followed.*
> Mercie. And you as little thought of lying in his Bed, and in his Chamber to Rest, as you do now.
> Chris. *And much less did I even think of seeing his Face with Comfort, and of Worshipping the Lord the King with him, and yet now I believe I shall.*
> Mercie. Hark, don't you hear a Noise?
> *Christiana.* Yes, 'tis as I believe a Noise of Musick, for joy that we are here.
> *Mer.* Wonderful! Musick in the House, Musick in the Heart, and Musick also in Heaven, for joy that we are here,(p. 222)

Many scenes focus, in this way, less exclusively upon the divine "personality" and more fully upon specific human emotions, sentiments, and relationships. The *Second Part* is literally the most fully human of Bunyan's works; it is certainly the most dramatic.

CHAPTER FOUR

ALLEGORICAL DEVELOPMENT

John Tullock, whose general opinion of *The Holy War* is fairly typical, says:

> It neither seizes upon the imagination nor touches the heart as the story of Christian does. Singularly ingenious, elaborate, and coherent in its illustrations and characters, it is almost as great a marvel, but is not nearly so felicitous nor exquisite a product of genius.[1]

Beyond such general contrasts, critical opinion of *The Holy War*[2] has varied largely with the individual critic's appreciation of allegorical ingenuity or dexterity. Professor Henri Talon, who has little praise for the intellectual virtuosity of the work, says that his "whole criticism" of *The Holy War* "may be summed up in one sentence by Edward Dowden who said that ... it was 'an allegory rather manufactured than inspired.'"[3] Macaulay, who emphasizes the artistic difficulties involved in the allegorical method, on the other hand, says that, if *The Pilgrim's Progress* did not exist, *The Holy War* "would be the best allegory that ever was written."[4] G. B. Harrison, who also emphasizes the greatness of the difficulty overcome, speaks of *The Holy War* as "a most elaborate and ingenious allegory," and asserts that it is "for that very reason less successful as an appeal to conscience than *The Pilgrim's Progress*, because the reader is compelled all the time to admire the astonishing ingenuity of the author." Nevertheless, Harrison asserts that, judged as a "work of art," *The Holy War* is "the greatest English allegory."[5] Those who praise Bunyan's mastery of allegorical methods and devices, thus, tend to commend *The Holy War* more highly than others do.

This critical spectrum reflects the fact that *The Holy War* exhibits the fullest, the most elaborate and systematic, exploitation of the allegorical methods Bunyan had used in *The Pilgrim's Progress*. Although the *Second Part* was the last of the major narratives to be published, this second pilgrimage reveals a further resolution of conflicts, not through a further development of allegorical technique, but through the further shift of emphasis to dramatic form that was examined earlier. As will be shown, the *Second Part* actually creates relatively few distinctively allegorical effects. The most significant allegorical developments first became apparent in *The Holy War*. The two central contrasts between *The Holy War* and *The Pilgrim's Progress* reveal the nature of these central developments.

The first of these contrasts is that five basic methods of stipulating the significance of narrative facts and of exploiting purposeful obscurity are used more fully and systematically in *The Holy War*. Section IV will show that embryonic personifications, topographical names, emblematic elements, allusive symbols, and related Biblical allusions facilitate a resolution of conflicts in that, at the sacrifice of some of their impact, they stipulate in more oblique or less intrusive ways in *The Holy War*. The second of these central contrasts involves a more meaningful resolution of these conflicts between two allegorical principles.

The "mimetic" or "very natural" principle and the "dialectical" one are two separate, but related, allegorical principles that Bunyan himself applied when he interpreted Biblical passages allegorically.[6] As was mentioned earlier, the mimetic principle demands primarily that an image or action be level with the norm of common experience so that its abstract significance appear to arise from the "natural properties" of the expressive forms; it implies an ideal of mimetic fullness and concreteness in the development of images and actions. The dialectical principle, on the other hand, demands primarily that a metaphor extend logically so that a precise series of point by point correlations appears between narrative facts and abstract ideas. It demands that each image or event in the concrete pattern "fitly" suit "each particular" in the abstract one, and it implies an ideal of precision and economy in the development of separate episodes.

Conflict exists because the mimetic principle is essentially a centrifugal force in Bunyan's allegories; the dialectical one, a centripetal one. The mimetic principle leads toward the creation of a narrative differing from other mimetic fiction only because of its metaphoric basis. The dialectical principle, in contrast, leads toward the creation of a self-contained, almost diagrammatic, verbal entity, a closed dynamic system of abstract, precisely-defined, relationships. Both aesthetic and pedagogical qualities of a narrative are affected when one or the other of these principles is dominant.

When the mimetic principle is dominant, a passage may achieve evocative concrete realization. It may awaken an imaginative response that is only partially or intermittently restricted or controlled by the dialectical pattern within the work itself. Characters and actions in such passages allude directly to external actualities and, hence, may reflect some of the moral or religious ambiguity of external actualities. Metaphors may be "opened up" so fully when the mimetic principle is dominant that the source of coherence in a given passage may appear to reside in some actuality outside the work rather than in the metaphor. When the dialectical principle is dominant, on the other hand, a passage typically demands an analytical response and focuses attention upon the changing relationships of images and actions within a more or less closed dynamic system. The power of separate characters and actions to allude independently to external actualities is restricted so that the passage may function as a unit making an unequivocal assertion *about* external actualities. At one extreme, then, are narrative facts which are level with the norm of common experience and, perhaps, ambiguous; at the other, are narrative facts abstracted from the norm, patterned dialectically, and, when understood, unequivocal. Between these extremes appear most of the narrative facts in Bunyan's allegories. They appear to function mimetically, or simply independently, and, so, invite comparison to external actuality and, at the same time, challenge an awakened ingenuity because the narrative has a metaphorical basis, for analogies are, as Professor Fletcher pointed out, by nature inexhaustible.[7]

The most prominent contrast between *The Pilgrim's Progress* and *The Holy War* involves the imaginative balance maintained between these basic principles. The salient development in Bunyan's allegories may be described in terms of these separate, but related, principles. Section I will show that the allegorical potentialities of "very natural" images and actions are realized in *The Pilgrim's Progress*. Section II will show that the allegorical potentialities of "very natural" images and actions are exploited somewhat less extensively in the *Second Part*. Section III will show that the imaginative balance has shifted so that mimetic fullness is sacrificed to dialectical consistency in *The Holy War*. Essentially, it will be clear that Bunyan transformed a method of giving unique, imaginative expression to the inner and outward aspects of spiritual adventure and, at the same time, of partially controlling a reader's interpretation of that experience, into an elaborate, systematic, formal method of expressing an analysis and interpretation of spiritual processes, obliquely and precisely. The resolution of conflicts is achieved partially through the fuller use of the devices examined in Section IV and partially through the shift in imaginative balance that makes the dialectical, rather than the mimetic, principle dominant in *The Holy War*.

I

The homiletic sketches and expository dialogues had evolved far enough in *The Pilgrim's Progress* that, as has been mentioned, a brilliant gallery of minor figures displayed themselves, the narrative moved largely through dramatic scenes, some of which exhibited notable concentration and force, and three major, complex, fictional characters revealed themselves primarily by dramatic means. These "very natural" images and actions contribute to the dominance of the mimetic principle in *The Pilgrim's Progress*. An examination of the allegorical aspects of *The Pilgrim's Progress*, in fact, will show that the mimetic and sensuous fullness of the characters and actions, itself evidence of the dominance of the mimetic principle, facilitates additional powerful allegorical effects as well. The allegorical potentialities of "very natural" images and actions are realized in *The Pilgrim's Progress*.

The dominance of the mimetic principle is evident in the fact that the central characters, and especially Christian, rather than the central metaphor, dominate the narrative. This is so primarily because of the appositeness and flexibility of the central metaphor itself. In arguing that *The Pilgrim's Progress* was superior to *The Holy War* primarily because of the central image, C. S. Lewis described the basis of the radical appositeness of that analogy:

> The journey has its ups and downs, its pleasant resting places enjoyed for a night and then abandoned, its unexpected meetings, its rumours of danger ahead, and, above all, the sense of its goal, at first far distant and dimly heard of, but growing nearer at every turn of the road. Now this represents far more truly than any combat in a *champ clos* the perennial strangeness, the adventurousness and the sinuous forward movement of the inner life.[8]

The central metaphor allows fluctuations in the rhythm and intensity of the spiritual process, rather than the logic of an extended metaphor, to determine the basic tempo of the narrative. That forward movement is neither rigid nor ritualistic.

Moreover, the central metaphor allows great variety in form, for it required little more than that Christian, Faithful, and Hopeful fulfill the metaphor by moving along the Way. Professor Fletcher generalizes:

> Surprise diminishes as the analogy is extended, because we see more and more clearly the meaning of the hidden tenor. In most cases allegories proceed toward clarity, away from obscurity, even though they maintain a pose of enigma up to the very end.[9]

In *The Pilgrim's Progress,* however, surprise does not diminish and purposeful obscurity does not evaporate as the narrative develops, for the central analogy proves compatible with disparate elements. It is not exhausted as the narrative unfolds, but expanded through myriad, diversified, subordinate analogies. These analogies and other devices continually introduce surprise, variety, and even obscurity during the exploration of separate phases of the spiritual life. The central metaphor imposes neither strict logical patterns nor insurmountable logical barriers to the use of a great variety of forms in the extension and elaboration of the central metaphor.

The central characters appear to dominate the narrative because of this conspicuous appositeness and compatibility. The pulsations of the inner life appear to determine the rhythm of the narrative movement, and the coherence of a spiritual process appears to lie behind the varied forms of successive episodes. Despite a Dantesque richness and variety, the essential continuity and coherence of the narrative, thus, clearly spring from the characters rather than from the central metaphor.

The dominance of the mimetic principle is further evident in that the allegory gives a unique depiction of both inner and outer aspects of the life of spiritual adventure. It does so primarily through the dramatic allegorical and mimetic scenes which were examined earlier. As has been shown, these central characters establish themselves firmly as mimetic creations through the direct allusions to external actualities in their speeches and through the plausibility of their interactions; being capable of folly and error, and being free, even to wander from the Way (p. 118), these central figures attain such autonomy as fictional characters may readily acquire so that, outwardly, they appear "very natural," or level with the norm of common experience, in the mimetic scenes. Their inward conflicts, in all their complexity and intensity, are dramatized in allegorical scenes such as those depicting Faithful's encounter with Shame, or Christian's struggle with Apollyon. Christian, Faithful, and Hopeful, thus, become memorable as coherent, self-consistent fictional characters. The allegorical revelations supplement and confirm those of the mimetic scenes and episodes so that *The Pilgrim's Progress* gives an incomparable picture of the progress of religious conversion and spiritual growth largely through the dramatic scenes which were examined in chapter three of this study.

The settings augment the incomparable picture of the central characters' spiritual development. These settings in *The Pilgrim's Progress* demand a more detailed exploration. Robert Southey suggested that a reader could see Bunyan's evocative descriptions "more satisfactorily to himself because the outline only of the picture is presented to him, and the author having made no attempt to fill up the details, every reader supplies them according to the measure and scope of his own intellectual and imaginative powers.[10]

Subsequent critics, perhaps because of this paucity of detail, have devoted relatively little space to Bunyan's settings. Those who have commented about them have generally emphasized either their "realism" or their "unreality." Charles Firth, the historian, for example, dwells upon the historical accuracy of Bunyan's depiction of the seventeenth-century English countryside,[11] and a number of critics have speculated about possible "originals" of the settings of *The Pilgrim's Progress.*[12] Others, concerned particularly with the allegorical masterpiece, emphasize the "unreality" of the settings. Macaulay, for example, speaks of the "charm" of the book that "gratified the imagination of the reader with all the action and scenery of a fairy tale."[13] Harold Golden consistently emphasizes the similarities of the settings to those in earlier romances or describes them as romantically-perceived Biblical ones.[14] Many, less extreme than Golder, have emphasized the "unreal," or even emblematic,[15] elements of the settings. Many commentators have recognized that the fusion of "realistic," "romantic," and "dream-like" elements in the settings were tempered by a basic figurative necessity, yet the functional aspects of the settings have received relatively little attention.

Considering the settings of *The Pilgrim's Progress* separately, Professor Talon recently said that he had earlier been in error in emphasizing the "realism of the background," and he focuses new attention upon their significance:

> It is a dream land which rises from the very first sentence of the book. Mingled and blending into one another, we find, making a new and individual landscape, the worlds of the Bible and of the folktales dear to the author, pictures of his native country and of the Holy land, all dominated by the features of that inner landscape where his conversion takes place, where his salvation is decided, and where, in short, the lot for his whole life is cast.

He further concludes that the land of the pilgrims is "a projection" of Bunyan's "inward landscape and the manifestation in space of his sense of values. Mountains, plains, and sloughs have a meaning at once psychological, religious, and axiological." Professor Talon, thus, gives due emphasis to the "feature of ... the inner landscape"[16] and considers the settings as functional rhetorical structures. However, he considers the significance of those settings largely in relation to the author rather than to other elements in the work itself. Considered in relation to other elements of the narrative, the settings not only contribute to the immediate impact of certain scenes but also facilitate the unique revelation of the inner and outer aspects of the spiritual life.

Although varying degrees of concrete, sensuous development and varying amounts of symbolic and verbal identification appear in separate settings, there are basically only two kinds of settings in *The Pilgrim's Progress*. These settings, which are unified by the central image, the Way, may be called "psychic" if they extend a subordinate analogy and objectify or express states of consciousness, or state of the soul, so fully as to become evocative symbols of them. They may be called "representative" if they allude directly to external actualities and preserve the illusion that the figurative journey is also a "real" one through a tangible, contemporaneous, countryside.

The representative settings deepen the illusion and extend the social range of the narrative in *The Pilgrim's Progress*. The mimetic norm, which sustains the illusion, is established much as it had been in *Grace Abounding*.

Events in the spiritual autobiography appear firmly rooted in time and space because of incidental descriptive details in narrative passages, imagery drawn from commonplace objects and events, and detailed descriptions of the settings of crucial events. The incidental details are frequent and specific as the narrator reports, "I was travelling into the Countrey" (p. 36), or "I sat by the fire in my house" (p. 36), or "getting out of my Bed, I went moping into the field" (p. 43), or "about ten or eleven a Clock one day, as I was walking under a Hedge..." (p. 44). The comparisons are precise and graphic as the narrator says, for example, "Down I fell, as a Bird that is shot from the top of a Tree, into great guilt" (p. 43), or "My sin, when compared to the Blood of Christ, was no more to it, than this little clot or stone before me, is to this vast and wide field that here I see" (p. 44). The crucial episodes include enough concrete detail to give the scene depth or dimension:

> But the same day, as I was in the midst of a game of Cat, and having struck it one blow from the hole; just as I was about to strike it the second time, a voice did suddenly dart from Heaven into my Soul.... I was put to an exceeding maze; wherefore, leaving my Cat upon the ground, I looked up to Heaven, and was as if I had ... seen the Lord Jesus looking down upon me, as being very hotly displeased with me.... I felt my heart sink in despair.... Thus I stood in the midst of my play, before all that then were present, but yet I told them nothing: but, I say, I having made this conclusion, I returned desperately to my sport again.(pp. 10-11)

Although the settings do not consistently contribute to the depth or "density" in *Grace Abounding*, they do firmly establish the social milieu

ALLEGORICAL DEVELOPMENT / 101

as a limitation upon the characters' actions, and they impart vividness and credibility to countless separate episodes.

Incidental descriptive details and comparisons in *The Pilgrim's Progress* function in a similar way—except, of course, that one element of the analogies is usually silent—for they also establish a mimetic norm within the work and contribute to sustain an illusion. Doubting Castle, for example, has many prototypes in the romances,[17] and the episode could well have become one of the most bizarre or "romantic" in the pilgrimage. Yet the Dreamer falls immediately to the discussion of the most prosaic kind of detail, writing,

> The *Giant* therefore drove them before him, and put them into his Castle, into a very dark Dungeon, nasty and stinking to the spirit of these two men; Here then they lay, from *Wednesday* morning till *Saturday* night, without one bit of bread, or drop of drink, or any light, or any to ask how they did.(p. 114)

The familiar details give the episode a mimetic coloration or atmosphere compatible with the mimetic norm sustained through the dialogues so that the episode seems "very natural," or level with the norm of common experience. The vivid sensuous details persuade a reader to accept the story. The dual meanings of the bread, drink, and light and the comment upon days in which doubts might be most appalling, as well as, finally, the implicit promise that such doubts might be dispelled on Sunday— these familiar and commonplace objects and events, though they have become symbolic, clearly sustain such an illusion. The details in such representative settings do not, of course, consistently have dual points of reference in this way.

One notable representative setting in *The Pilgrim's Progress* develops the "very natural" aspects of the central metaphor in a strikingly abstract way. Kelman exaggerates but little when he says, "Almost all the worldliness and folly which a Christian has to meet with in a lifetime is concentrated in the streets and building of this [Vanity] Fair."[18] The suggestions of universality are quite overt:

> And as in other Fairs of less moment, there are the several Rows and Streets under their proper names, where such and such Wares are vended: So here likewise, you have the proper Places, Rows, Streets, (*viz.* Countreys, and Kingdoms) where the Wares of this Fair are soonest to be found: Here is the *Britain* Row, the *French* Row, the *Italian* Row, the *Spanish* Row, the *German* Row, where several sorts of Vanities are to be sold. But as in other *fairs*, some one Commodity is as the chief of all the *fair*, so the Ware of *Rome* and her Merchandize is greatly promoted in *this fair*.(pp. 88-89)

The setting extends the social range of the narrative despite its abstractness, perhaps because it is supported by the mention of incidental concrete detail such as "then were they remanded to the Cage again," or "they put them in, and made their feet fast in the Stocks" (p. 92). These incidental direct allusions to external actuality support the mimetic norm implicit in the dramatic development of the episode. The setting also anticipates those of *The Holy War* in its abstractness.

The "psychic" settings such as the Valley of the Shadow of Death (pp. 62-63), the Slough of Despond (pp. 14-15), or the Plain of Ease (p. 106), in contrast, express states of consciousness, or states of the soul, so fully as to become evocative symbols of them. These settings consist basically of five parts: imaginative analogies between states of consciousness and outward situations, sensuous expansions of such analogies, allusive symbols, dialectical extensions of such analogies, and stipulatory names. These five elements had appeared separately in *Grace Abounding* and other early works.

Imaginative analogies like these underlying the "psychic" settings of *The Pilgrim's Progress* appeared frequently in the earlier works. They are related to a method of Biblical exegesis, honored especially among the Quakers, which was based on the assumption that, in Professor William Haller's words, "the temptation of Adam and all that followed thereupon was a picture of what happened within the individual soul" as well as a record of historical events.[19] Bunyan voiced such an analogy when, for example, he equated the words "And darkness was upon the face of the deep" with the "heart of man before conversion" in *An Exposition of the First Ten Chapters of Genesis* (III, 373). He used such analogies frequently in *Grace Abounding*. He did so, for example, when he wrote, "I did liken myself in this condition unto the case of some Child that was fallen into a Mill-pit, who though it could make some shift to scrable and spraul in the water, yet because it could find neither hold for hand nor foot . . ." (p. 62). This, and other analogies (p. 32), materialize primarily sensations or emotions, rather than conceptions, by setting forth outward situations that would induce such inward responses.

Grace Abounding contains examples of both sensuous expansions of such analogies and allusive symbols that identify or illustrate the principle through which the state of consciousness is to be interpreted. Bunyan gives, for example, two successive versions of the same episode. In the midst of a literal account of his encounter with "three or four poor women sitting at a door in the Sun," Bunyan defines tentatively his response to them. He says that he felt that they were "far above" him and that "they were to . . . [him] as if they had found a new world, as if they were people that dwelt alone, and were not to be reckoned among their

Neighbors" (pp. 14-15). This response is then described as a "kind of Vision":

> I saw as if they were set on the Sunny side of some high Mountain, there refreshing themselves with the pleasant beams of the Sun, while I was shivering and shrinking in the cold, afflicted with frost, snow, and dark clouds; methought also betwixt me and them I saw a wall that did compass about this Mountain; now, thorow this wall my Soul did greatly desire to pass, concluding that if I could, I would goe even into the very midst of them, and there also comfort myself with the heat of their Sun.(p. 19)

The sensuous expansions of the analogy, the phrases "shivering and shrinking in the cold, afflicted with frost, snow, and dark clouds," exploit the appositeness of the analogy to express the emotion more fully. The allusive symbol, the "little door-way," introduces the conceptual terms in which the state of consciousness is to be interpreted. When he explains the significance of the "kind of Vision," Bunyan alluded to Matt. 7:14, a passage he had explicated in *The Strait Gate,* to justify the identification of the door with Christ, and in *The Strait Gate* itself he had further justified this identification by allusion to Acts 14:27, "I am the door..." (II, 378). He had also used the gate earlier as an allusive symbol when he explicated the description of the new Jerusalem in Revelations in *The Holy City* (I, 295-96). The sensuous expansions, thus, render the state of consciousness more fully, and the allusive symbol clarifies the theological significance of the situation.

Dialectical extensions and stipulatory names that conflate imagery and its interpretation are adumbrated, rather than illustrated, in *Grace Abounding*. A dialectical extension is an abstract, logical, usually fanciful, elaboration of an analogy that appears to state related conceptions obliquely rather than to materialize sensations or emotions. Some analogies in the spiritual autobiography, to be sure, appear to be compatible logical extensions, rather than sensory expansions, of analogies, yet they lack stipulatory names to conflate them:

> Thus... was my Soul, like a broken Vessel, driven, as with Winds, and tossed sometimes head-long into dispair; sometimes upon the Covenant of works, and sometimes to wish that the new Covenant, and the conditions thereof, might... be turned another way, and changed. But in all these, I was but as those that jostle against the Rocks; more broken, scattered, and rent.(p. 58)

The introduction of stipulatory names such as "Rock of Dispair" and "Rock of the Old Covenant" in this passage would conflate the imagery and its interpretation in the manner used in *The Pilgrim's Progress*. Only the *materials* for such a conflation, however, appear—in a few cases—in the spiritual autobiography. The description of the "kind of Vision" of the "poor women" who sat on "the Sunny side of some high Mountain," for example, is actually explained point by point: "The Mountain signified the Church of the living God; the Sun that shone thereon; the comfortable shining of his mercifull face on them that were therein..." (p. 20). The stipulatory names, however, do not appear, so that *The Pilgrim's Progress* is the first of Bunyan's narratives in which the conflation appears in the settings.

These five separate parts are fused in the "psychic" settings of *The Pilgrim's Progress*. Typically, the basic, underlying analogies express sensations or emotions, rather than conceptions; the analogies are expanded through sensuous detail; the dialectical extensions are limited in number and extent; the stipulatory names conflate imagery and interpretation; and the allusive symbols, though few, advance the explication of the setting. Fairly typical in these respects is the Slough of Despond, which expands an analogy Bunyan himself had voiced in *Grace Abounding*. "I found myself as on a miry bog, that shook if I did but stir" (p. 27):

> Now I saw in my Dream, that just as they had ended this talk, they drew near to a very *Miry Slough* that was in the midst of the Plain, and they being heedless, did both fall suddenly into the bogg. The name of the Slow was *Dispond*. There therefore they wallowed for a time, being grieviously bedaubed with the dirt; And *Christian*, because of the burden that was on his back, began to sink in the Mire.... [Later, Christian] was left to tumble in the Slow of *Dispond* alone; but still he endeavoured to struggle to that side of the Slow, that was still further from his own House ... but could not get out, because of the burden that was upon his back.(pp. 14-15)

The sensory elaborations which exploit the appositeness of the analogy in this passage are more notable than the dialectical extensions in the subsequent one, for the image of the Slough is not extended to disguise statement when Help explains the existence of the "Miry Slough." Essentially, Help reverts to literal statement:

> And he said unto me, this *Miry slow*, is such a place as cannot be mended: It is the descent whither the scum and filth that attends conviction for sin doth continually run, and therefore is it called the *Slough of Dispond*: for still as the sinner is awakened about his lost condition, there ariseth in his soul many fears, and doubts, and discouraging apprehensions, which all of them get together, and settle in this place: And this is the reason of the badness of this ground.(p. 15)

The passage is typical, too, in that the stipulatory names, Slough of Despond, Christian, and Help conflate the imagery and its interpretation without contributing to fanciful extensions, and in that only one allusive symbol appears. The burden on Christian's back had been established earlier (p. 8) as an allusive symbol by a marginal allusion to Psalms 38:4, "For mine iniquities are gone over mine head: as an heavy burden they are too heavy for me." Such symbols are, as will be shown, more rare in *The Pilgrim's Progress* than in *The Holy War.*

Because of their sensuous fullness, on one hand, and their relative paucity of stipulatory names, allusive symbols, and fanciful dialectical extensions, on the other, the psychic settings contribute greatly to a unique realization of the inner life during a process of spiritual growth in *The Pilgrim's Progress.* Again and again, a series of evocative images such as the following summon up a complex of sensations and emotions by objectifying secret anxieties, doubts, and fears:

> The path way was here so dark, that oft times when he lift up his foot to set forward, he knew not where, or upon what he should set it next.... And ever and anon the flame and smoke would come out in such abundance, with sparks and hideous noises ... that he was forced to put up his Sword, and betake himself to another weapon called *All-prayer....* [A]lso he heard doleful voices, and rushings too and fro, so that sometimes he thought he should be torn in pieces, or trodden down like mire in the Streets.(pp. 62-63)

The "official" significance of the state of consciousness is suggested clearly enough by the image of the way and the stipulatory name, "All-prayer," but these stipulations are neither so precise nor so narrowly doctrinal, surely, that they either introduce a serious problem of belief or appreciably inhibit imaginative expansions of meaning. Moreover, a relatively small part of the imagery illustrates the principle through which the state of consciousness is to be interpreted. In a sense, the emotion— dolorous, poignant, or exuberant—is crystallized by the image rather than rationalized away by it. The dynamic intensity of conflict dramatized in the allegorical scenes is, thus, supplemented by uniquely expressive psychic settings that become evocative symbols of many states of consciousness.

The settings, thus, contribute greatly to the impact of the narrative and to the revelation of an incomparable picture of inner and outward aspects of the spiritual life. Together with the dramatic scenes which were examined separately, they constitute an important part of the material that "opens up" both the central and diverse subordinate analogies in *The Pilgrim's Progress.* The "very natural" potentialities of the central analogy are developed in the mimetic scenes, the representative settings, and the episodes that appear level with the norm of common experience; the "very natural" potentialities of subordinate analogies—which are compatible with, but not necessarily connected with, the central analogy—are developed in allegorical scenes that dramatize inner conflicts, in "psychic" settings, and in certain actions that seem, in Professor Fletcher's phrase, "magically based."[20] As has been mentioned, the very concrete particularity of some of this development endows the images and actions with moral and religious ambiguity and suggests imaginative expansions of meanings unrestricted by stipulatory devices. This mimetic fullness and concreteness also lend force and authority to additional, significant allegorical effects.[21]

The mimetic fullness of the central figures, and of Christian in particular, greatly amplifies the effect of their functions as embodiments of ideas. The central metaphor implies a coherent Christian system of belief and places the fictional journey in that larger ideological context so that certain images and events derive emotive power primarily from the conceptions they convey. Many passages are, thus, saturated with an otherworldly glow or radiant with suggestions of infinitude because the relationship of Christian to the antecedent conceptual scheme is especially prominent. The meaning condensed and concentrated in the picture of Christian's headlong flight from the City of Destruction, for example, appears to be derived primarily from the larger context by way of the metaphor:

> So I saw in my Dream, that the Man began to run; Now he had not run far from his own door, but his Wife and Children perceiving it, began to cry after him to return: but the Man put his fingers in his Ears, and ran on crying, Life, Life, Eternal Life: so he looked not behind him, but fled towards the middle of the Plain.(p. 10)

Similar intimations of the overwhelming significance of events hover about later passages as well, but they are there reinforced by the independent weight or authority Christian has acquired as a robust, fully-developed, human character. Christian surely transcends the merely human role in which he has become familiar, for example, during the ascent to the Celestial City and, so, creates the nearest approach to the sublime in *The Pilgrim's Progress:*

> Now I saw in my Dream, that these two men went in at the Gate; and loe, as they entered, they were transfigured, and they had Raiment put on that shone like Gold. There was also that met them with Harps and Crowns, and gave them to them.... Then I heard in my Dream,

that all the Bells in the City Rang again for joy; and that it was said unto them, *Enter ye into the joy of your Lord*.(pp. 161-62)

The mimetic fullness clearly enhances the effect of the conception and is enhanced by it because the agent and the human characters are one. As the mimetic fullness deepens some effects created by the central metaphor's function in relating the fictional journey to a system of belief *outside* the work of art, so it heightens or intensifies some effects created by the central metaphor's function in establishing relationships *within* the work of art. In a sense, the "heights and depths in grace, and love, and mercy" mentioned in *Grace Abounding* (p. 78) are transformed into geographical heights and depths, and the pilgrims' progress from the first conviction of sin to the final glorification is marked off by the places between the City of Destruction and the Celestial City. Stipulating, thus, the basic relationship between the dominant unifying image, the Way, and the central agents, the central metaphor establishes the two basic levels upon which the narrative is to move. At the same time, it establishes the outward form within which the discontinuous interplay between them is to take place. Even though the allegory moves, as it were, underground during many episodes, the metaphor creates a pervasive sense of teleologically ordered movement and lends a subtle sense of inevitability to the forward movement of the chief agents. This sense of inevitability, a product of a reader's awareness of the central characters as agents, gains notable emotive force through a mimetic fullness that aggrandizes the human significance of the foreknown, predestined end. This sense of the inevitability of the final fulfillment is undoubtedly strongest when the relationship of the character to the metaphor is especially prominent, as it is, for example, when the protagonists pass through Vanity Fair (pp. 88-97) or approach the river, Death (pp. 156-57), yet such prominence merely heightens an awareness that is a continuing part of the experience of the allegory.

II

The *Second Part,* as was shown, is conspicuously more dramatic in form than the earlier masterpiece. The dramatic revelations of sectarian life and manners among the group of pilgrims who are strolling toward the Celestial City together appear largely in mimetic, rather than allegorical, scenes so that the central metaphor is held in abeyance during a great many passages. This emphasis upon the social, rather than the spiritual, aspects of experience is also evident in the development of subordinate analogies, for, as will be shown, relatively few "psychic" settings appear in the *Second Part*. Although several complex major characters are developed as "very natural" ones, in brief, the allegorical potentialities of "very natural" images and actions are exploited less extensively in the *Second Part* than in the earlier masterpiece. This lack of exploitation is most evident in relation to the characters and the settings.

The central characters are revealed so fully as mimetic creations, glowing with vitality, and neglected so far as agents extending a metaphor that figurative counterpoints are relatively rare in the *Second Part*. The separate patterns, mimetic and dialectical, are so far separated in one case, at least, that actual incongruity appears between the qualities of the agent and those of the character. Mercy, as was mentioned earlier, becomes a complex "round" character, a charming young Puritan maiden whom Bunyan himself cites as an exemplary figure (p. 172), kind, generous, merciful, and not at all prudish. She is shown (p. 227) performing at least two of the six—or seven—acts of Mercy traditionally attributed to personifications of mercy in literature and the visual arts,[22] and as a personification of mercy, she is asked to pronounce upon the plight of Simple, Sloth, and Presumption. Mercy does so with a vengeance:

> *No, no, let them hang and their Names Rot, and their Crimes live for ever against them; I think it a high favour that they were hanged afore we came hither, who knows else what they might a done to such poor Women as we are?* (p. 214)

Even though the character exemplifying and personifying God's mercy may be obliged theologically to condemn such crimes as those of Simple, Sloth, and Presumption, the utterance is completely out of character for the charming person who had revealed herself through countless mimetic scenes and episodes. It is as though Dante had introduced a "natural symbol" like Ciacco, the Hog, among the wrathful or the heretics. The mimetic fullness is great enough, in fact, that the dialectical or abstract patterns discernible in such passages as this are themselves incongruent. The *Second Part* does not exhibit such precise, economical balancing of mimetic and dialectical elements as had appeared in *The Holy War*.

Both the readers' memories and Puritan psychology restricted the settings of the *Second Part* to some extent because all members of the Elect were expected to reach a conviction of sin, to experience an effectual calling, the immediate effects of which was their justification in God's eyes and the beginning of their regeneration, to experience gradual sanctification, and, ultimately, to experience a glorification that would not be completed until after death. The positions of such settings as the City of Destruction, or the Enchanted Grounds, therefore, could not have been changed radically when the Dreamer returned to describe the journey of a new group of pilgrims. The settings of the *Second Part* realize some of their allegorical potentialities, however, because the Dreamer introduced some modifications in them.

The settings contribute to the later pilgrimage because of modifications in the landscape itself, in the route of particular persons, and in the extent to which changes in the weather are used. As thunder and rain expressed the remorse of Christian and Hopeful (p. 112) and "Sun-shine weather" affected the "fits" of the Giant Despair in *The Pilgrim's Progress* (p. 115), so weather appropriate to "the Summer-time" expressed the reactions of Christiana (p. 237), Mercy (p. 239), and Mr. Fearing (p. 252) to the Valley of Humiliation in the *Second Part*. The weather externalizes inner states of consciousness, and variations in the routes of individual pilgrims define their natures, more frequently in the *Second Part* than in the earlier masterpiece. Despite a few "new" obstacles in the *Second Part*, mostly animate, such as Maul and Slay-good, the landscape offers fewer impediments than that of the earlier masterpiece. Christiana, for example, neither encounters Mr. Worldly-Wiseman nor deviates toward the Village of Morality; she does not meet Timorous, Mistrust, Mr. By-ends, or Flatterer; she does not explore By-Path Meadow, but stays safely on the Way while the Giant Despair and Diffidence are killed and Doubting Castle is destroyed. *"Chains, Posts,* and a *Ditch"* prevent her from being lost as were Formality and Hypocrisy (p. 215). The settings, thus, perform some of the functions of those of the earlier masterpiece largely because of the fuller use of the weather, the extensive modifications in the landscape itself, and variations in the routes of separate pilgrims.

The settings in the *Second Part* realize some of their allegorical potentialities, too, because they function as fixed points of known significance in the dramatic revelation of character. The Slough of Despond illustrates the tendency here because it is one of the settings that function this way in both parts of *The Pilgrim's Progress*. Christian's struggle in the Slough (pp. 14-16) was a memorable experience; Faithful's reported avoidance of the Slough (p. 68) revealed him as an unimaginative person just as the avoidance of the House Beautiful (p. 71) revealed him as an independent one. In the *Second Part,* Messrs Fearing, Feeble-mind, and a great many others revealed themselves through allusion to the verbal fixed point, the setting of previously fixed meaning. It is said, of Mr. Fearing:

> Well, after he had layn at the *Slow of Dispond* a great while, as I had told you; one sunshine Morning, I do not know how, he ventured, and so got over. . . . He had, I think, a *Slow of Dispond* in his Mind, a *Slow* that he carried every where with him, or else he could never have been as he was. So he came up to the Gate . . . that stands at the head of

this way, and there also he stood a good while before he would adventure to knock. When the Gate was opened he would give back, [sic] and give place to others, and say that he was not worthy.... There the poor man would stand shaking and shrinking,(pp. 249-50)

The action in relation to a verbal sign of fixed significance has come perilously close to degenerating into a species of disguised statement, as the reference to the "*Slow of Dispond* in his Mind" clearly is. Although some of these settings exist as abstract or verbal entities, rather than as concrete, sensory ones, as evocative symbols, they clearly contribute to the allegorical revelation of the natures of the characters who react, or are defined, in relation to them.

Relatively few powerful allegorical potentialities of the settings are realized in the *Second Part* because they lack the concrete particularity of those in the earlier masterpiece. Only one setting, the Enchanted Ground, as William Hale White points out,[23] is described more fully than in the earlier masterpiece. And only this one setting (pp. 295-99) functions as a "psychic" setting in the old manner, an evocative symbol of a state of consciousness. The other settings in the *Second Part* do not externalize states of consciousness, or concentrate meanings, or crystallize emotions as did those in *The Pilgrim's Progress,* for the places mentioned in the earlier scenes, both mimetic and allegorical, are merely *named* in the *Second Part.* To be sure, the Dreamer occasionally refers the reader to "the first part of these Records" (p. 197) for additional information about places along the way, but he does not describe them anew so that they heighten the impact of the narrative.

Since it does not exploit the allegorical potentialities of "very natural" settings, characters, or events as fully as the earlier masterpiece, the *Second Part,* thus, does not represent a further stage in Bunyan's allegorical development, however admirable it may be as a triumph of dramatic art. The major effort in the application of allegorical method is manifest, instead, in *The Holy War.*

III

The Holy War is undoubtedly the fullest expression of Bunyan's genius for allegorical expression, for the imaginative balance has shifted so that mimetic fullness is sacrificed to dialectical precision and consistency. The immediate impact, the dramatic emphasis, the splendid chiaroscuro, and even the sense of the mystery of the commonplace are lost in the midst of the rationalistic, dialectical refinement. This shift is evident in the fact that the central metaphor dominates the narrative structure, the

ALLEGORICAL DEVELOPMENT / 111

character development, and the settings. This shift is also strikingly evident in the development of separate episodes.

Only a few isolated passages in the two parts of *The Pilgrim's Progress* exhibit an economic fusion of mimetic and dialectical elements. These passages of allegory by simple personification approximate the ideal implicit in Bunyan's admiring comment in *The Resurrection of the Dead*. He said that a Biblical passage, which he interpreted allegorically, was "very natural, and fitly suiteth each particular" (I, 346). Such passages typically develop on a point by point basis, exhibit a rapid alteration of points of reference, move alternately or simultaneously upon two levels, suggest inward changes through outward action, and exhibit a relative paucity of mimetic detail. Little-faith, a "good man" who "dwelt in the town of Sincere," for example, was "going on a Pilgrimage," frequently begging the help of others and making "dolefull and bitter complaints." He suffered an attack of faintheartedness, mistrust, and guilt:

> Now there happened at that time, to come down the *Lane* . . . three Sturdy Rogues; and their names were *Faint-Heart, Mistrust,* and *Guilt,* (three Brothers) and they espying *Little-faith* . . . came galloping up with speed: Now the good man was just awaked from his sleep, and was getting up to go on his Journey. So they came all up to him, and with threatning Language bid him *stand*. At this *Little-faith* look'd as white as a clout, and had neither power to *fight*, nor *flie*. Then said *Faint-heart*, Deliver thy Purse; but he making no haste to do it, (for he was loth to lose his Money) *Mistrust* ran up to him, and thrusting his hand into his Pocket, pull'd out thence a bag of Silver. Then he cried out, Thieves, thieves. With that *Guilt* with a great Club that was in his hand, strook *Little-Faith* on the head, and with that blow fell'd him flat to the ground, where he lay bleeding as one that would bleed to death. All this while the Thieves stood by. But at last, they hearing that some were upon the Road, and fearing lest it should be one *Great-grace* . . . they betook themselves to their heels, and left this good man to shift for himself. Now after a while, *Little-faith* came to himself, and getting up, made shift to scrabble on his way. (pp. 125-26)

The names prevent the spiritual theme from disappearing into alien fact and invite a reader to pursue further parallels—to see, for example, that the literal bleeding suggests the figurative loss of life-giving faith—as two levels unfold alternately or simultaneously. Although the passage does not create the sublime effects which are possible in the allegorical mode, it clearly offers a reader the minor joys of penetrating temporary obfuscation and perceiving the appropriateness of the vehicle. Minimal detail about the "natural" man beset by robbers appears; Little-faith is neither developed so fully that he becomes a center of separate interest as a person nor neglected so far that he becomes a mere counter in a dialectical process.

Such passages, however, are rare. More typical of both parts of *The Pilgrim's Progress* are passages in which one "level" is frequently held in abeyance during extensive mimetic episodes. The central, abstract, spiritual process is held in abeyance, for example, while Talkative displays himself in the long dramatic scenes which were examined earlier. More important, the central metaphor is "opened up" so fully in many passages that the figurative or abstract patterns themselves are somewhat nebulous or obscure.

Bunyan himself apparently judged in this way the episode involving, for example, Timorous and Mistrust. Their names could be taken for moral labels like Talkative's, and they could be interpreted simply as kinds of doomed professors who, fleeing from the lions, attempting to persuade Christian to join them in flight, enhance a reader's awareness of Christian's courage. Bunyan, however, clarifies their allegorical significance by adding a marginal note in the second edition: "Christian *shakes off fear*" (p. 43) and by specifying in the *Second Part* that Timorous and Mistrust were burned through the tongue *"for endeavouring to hinder* Christian *in his Journey"* (p. 218). He does not, of course, so emphasize the figurative significance of many such episodes.

The mimetic aspects of the images and actions are developed so fully in some passages of *The Pilgrim's Progress* that the allegorical one becomes, not merely obscure, but positively problematic. When, for example, Christian and Hopeful encounter the engaging Ignorance, who comes from the Country of Conceit (p. 123), they make a few vain attempts to advise him, decide that he needs time to think about their advice, and walk ahead of him. It is not until four pages later that Hopeful shows his ignorance of the value of the soul and suffers a severe reprimand from Christian; it is not for six additional pages that Flatterer beguiles Christian and Hopeful through their vanity, or conceit, and ignorance (p. 133). Is there an allegorical exploration of a subjective phenomenon in the original encounter? Or is there an oblique statement about the infectious nature of Ignorance behind this episode? Again, the pilgrims, encountering Atheist, treat him with scorn; it is not until the following page that Hopeful feels an almost irresistible urge to go to sleep—almost invariably a spiritual phenomenon in Bunyan's allegories—on the Enchanted Ground (p. 136). Again, Mr. By-ends is also scornfully dismissed from the pilgrim's company. In the first edition, it is on the following page that Hopeful proposes that they accept Demas's invitation to go out of the Way to see the silver mine; in the second edition, it is six pages later that this possible effect of Mr. By-ends upon Hopeful shows itself (p. 108). And so, in many cases, the extensive mimetic development makes the metaphoric statement about the inner life obscure, if not problematic.

ALLEGORICAL DEVELOPMENT / 113

In striking contrast, mimetic development is almost invariably severely restricted in *The Holy War*. Isolated passages, to be sure, contain a few sensory details that allude directly to contemporaneous actualities and serve no discernible allegorical purpose. Many of the details of the wars of Mansoul, as has often been pointed out,[24] are developed as imitations of contemporary actualities, and a few of the illuminating reflections of contemporary problems, manners, and customs that had aroused much interest in *Mr. Badman* (pp. 84-85) have their counterparts in *The Holy War* (pp. 168, 217). So, too, there are counterparts to the amusing realistic episodes that enliven the journey of Christiana, Mercy, and Great-heart. There is, for example, the delightful scene in *The Holy War* (pp. 115-16) referred to by G. B. Harrison as "an admirable picture of the awestruck countrymen at his first state banquet."[25] But, on the whole, there is very little adventitious mimetic detail in the narrative passages of *The Holy War*.

There is typically so little that simultaneously unfolding narrative and figurative patterns are, in effect, conflated by names or marginal notations so that point by point movement is prominent and, usually, unequivocal, though temporary obfuscation may exist. Typical is a part of the narrative treating two themes: the inability of evil to silence conscience and the value of conscience to the Elect. After Diabolus had aroused the men of Mansoul against Mr. Conscious, he was "preserved in being amongst them" because "his House was as strong as a Castle, and stood hard by a stronghold of the Town. Moreover, if at any time any of the crew or rabble [identified in the margin as "ill thoughts"] attempted to make him away, he could pull up the sluices ["of fears"] and let in such floods as would drown all round about him" (p. 21). Later, when the Prince's forces broke open Ear-gate, they found that "from *Ear-gate* the Street was straight even to the House of Mr. *Recorder*" (p. 87). Although Bunyan had forgotten to release Mr. Conscience from the prison in which Diabolus had placed him (p. 62), they found the old gentleman at home. They demanded possession of his house for the use of their noble Prince because "the *Recorder's* House was a place of much convenience for *Emmanuel*, not only because it was near the Castle [the heart] and strong, but also because it was large, and fronted the Castle, the Den where now *Diabolus* was" (p. 88). Each detail works in two ways, even to the pun upon "fronted," so that a reader may find point by point correlations consistently.

The shift in imaginative balance is evident, not merely in the development of separate episodes, but, also in the fact that the central metaphor dominates the narrative. And this happens despite the increased thematic complexity. Using a time-honored central image so popular that it was in the air he breathed,[26] Bunyan undertook to present in *The Holy War* the process of conversion in the individual soul, the story of the Fall of man, the historical and individual effects of the redemption, the rise of Christianity, and, drawing upon the most confusing of Biblical visions, the millenarian hopes of man. The story of "the Lord's dealings with" one soul which he had presented in *Grace Abounding,* in effect, was to be broadened so that he presented an account of God's dealing with the soul of man in the past, present, and future.

Inevitably, perhaps,[27] the central analogy proved inadequate to these themes. Using the image of the walled city to represent the state of man's soul historically, yet refusing to abandon the Biblical account of the cause of evil, for example, Bunyan gives a literal account of the fall of the angels and joins this to an allegorical account of the effects of man's fall upon his soul through the use of the fable of the tree of knowledge (pp. 9-15). Later, he passes over the Redemption lightly—Emmanuel refers to his sacrifice briefly in a speech (p. 75)—as an historical phenomenon and treats it allegorically primarily as a stage in the progress of the individual soul and only obliquely, and even obscurely, as an historical phenomenon in relation to the establishment of the primitive church (p. 106). When so much has been said, however, the fact remains that, regardless of the thematic complexity, the central metaphor dominates the narrative with remarkable consistency.

In contrast to the central analogy of *The Pilgrim's Progress,* that of *The Holy War* does not itself determine the narrative structure, but it does control the ways in which the narrative is developed. The plot is simple enough. As C. H. Firth points out:

> It is the siege and capture of the city of Man's Soul by the powers of evil, and the rule of those powers therein, followed by the siege of the same city by the powers of good and its recovery. Then the city that had once been weak grows strong and defends itself successfully.[28]

Though there are, thus, at least three major turning points in the action, the change in direction does not allow a bracing change in scene, a fresh beginning, or a rapid alteration of mimetic and allegorical scenes like that in *The Pilgrim's Progress*. Rather, to apply Professor Fletcher's generalization, "surprise diminishes as the analogy is extended,"[29] for the central analogy demands that the narrative develop primarily as a psychomachia through changes in the central image, or through central figures who, for the most part, are defined by the central image as sub-characters. New developments in the narrative, in brief, demand not simply that pilgrims be moved further along the Way, but that a whole series of existing images and relationships be altered in systematic, partially predictable, ways. The movement of the narrative does not at all suggest the subtle pulsations and changes of the spiritual life because the whole awkward cumbersome machinery of analysis must move with a change in the direction of the narrative.

The central metaphor also dominates the major figures. The central character, usually a representative member of the Elect, does not appear at all, of course, for he is simply present by implication in the central image. The central participants are largely restricted or controlled by their relationship to that metaphor. Some of them acquire stateliness, or even a certain ritualistic dignity—as Emmanuel does, for example—without acquiring the independent allegorical complexity or force of a Lady Meed or a Mutabilitie because their development is rigorously controlled with great consistency by their changing relationships as both moral types and metaphoric agents. The introductory schemata usually emphasize two sides of their natures, as moral types and metaphoric agents, and they participate in countless scenes and episodes without speaking or acting "out of character" in relation to either of those sides. There is no descent to the concrete so that, in Professor Fletcher's terms, their actions often appear "magically based."[30] Mr. Conscience has less freedom than a Lady Meed, for example, to act in typical ways because his functions restrict his mimetic development. The central figures who were examined earlier, in brief, do not exhibit extensive allegorical or mimetic development apart from the central metaphor.

The dominance of the central metaphor is especially evident in the settings of *The Holy War*. The secondary images extend the central one logically, economically, and precisely. Subordinate analogies such as "the understanding is darkened," for example, are transformed into narrative event through personifications, topographical images, and action thus:

> *Diabolus* thought not fit to let him [the Lord Mayor, previously identified with the understanding] abide in his former lustre.... Wherefore he darkened it, not only by taking from him his office and power, but by building a high and strong Tower, just between the Sun's reflections and the Windows of my Lord's Place.(p. 18)

The tower by the window is simply high and strong; there is no nonfunctional or adventitious mimetic detail. The state of consciousness is not "rendered" through an evocative symbol; rather, the initial figurative assertion is elaborated through imagery compatible with the central image and unequivocal in its revelations. It is not sensuous realization but precise oblique statement that is characteristic in the settings of *The Holy War*.

Logical compatibility, rather than appositeness for expressing a given situation or state of consciousness, is notable in *The Holy War*. Since the settings are elaborated as meticulously as, for example, Spenser's House of Pride or his House of Alma, a purely arbitrary relationship often exists between the concept and the image used to express it. For example, assuming the soul of man is a walled city and the senses are the five gates, Bunyan presents the Bible in this fashion:

> *Emmanuel* also, when he had thus set forward to go to recover the Town of *Mansoul,* took with him, at the commandment of his Father, fifty-four Battering Rams, and twelve Slings to hurl stones withal. Everyone of these was made of pure Gold, and these they carried with them, in the heart and body of their Army, all along as they went to *Mansoul.*

And, in the same scene, he elaborates through topographical names:

> Besides, there were Mounts cast up against it. The Mount *Gracious* was on the one side, and Mount *Justice* was on the other. Further, there were several small banks and advance-grounds, as *Plain-Truth-Hill* and *No-Sin-Banks,* where many of the Slings were placed against the Town. Upon Mount *Gracious* were planted four, and upon Mount Justice were placed as many, and the rest were conveniently placed in several parts round about the Town. Five of the best *Battering-Rams,* that is, the biggest of them, were placed upon *Mount Hearken,* a Mount cast up hard by *Ear-gate,* with intent to break that open. (pp. 69-70)

The fanciful, largely verbal, elaborations do not depend upon either a causal relationship between meaning and image, or even upon established Biblical or other arbitrary relationships between image and idea, so that they do, in fact, become intricate, complex, and ingenious without attaining the remarkable appositeness of settings in *The Pilgrim's Progress.* They are logically compatible with the central image, and they are unequivocal thematically.

Lacking the concrete realization and evocative power of the psychic settings in *The Pilgrim's Progress,* those of *The Holy War,* nevertheless, express complex psychic processes precisely. For example:

> For now could not *Mansoul* sleep securely as before, nor could they now go to their debaucheries with that quietness as in times past; for they had from the camp of *Shaddai* such frequent, warm, and terrifying alarms, yea, alarms upon alarms, first at one Gate and then at another, and again at all the Gates at once, that they were broken as to former peace. Yea, they had their alarms so frequently, and that when the nights were at longest, the weather coldest, and so consequently the *season* most *unseasonable,* that that Winter was to the Town of *Mansoul* a Winter by itself. Sometimes the Trumpets would sound, and sometimes the slings would whirl the stones into Town.

Sometimes ten thousand of the King's Soldiers would be running round the walls of *Mansoul* at midnight, shouting and lifting up the voice for the battel. Sometimes, again, some of them in the Town would be wounded, and their cry and lamentable voice would be heard, to the great molestation of the now languishing Town of *Mansoul.* (pp. 53-54)

The passage clearly lacks the visionary intensity of descriptions of comparable processes in *Grace Abounding* and *The Pilgrim's Progress*. Rather than visual allegories of states of consciousness, or intense dramatizations of harrowing conflicts like those of *The Pilgrim's Progress,* in brief, *The Holy War* typically exhibits, within the confines of the settings, narrative movement involving temporary obfuscation and expressing analysis of inner processes through the extension of the central metaphor.

It is, thus, evident that the development of settings, characters, and separate episodes exhibits a conspicuous shift in imaginative balance so that, though the impact of mimetic fullness and concreteness is sacrificed, greater dialectical precision and consistency are attained in *The Holy War.*

IV

There has been much objection to misplaced ingenuity among critics of *The Holy War.* John Tullock, for example, objects that there is "too much of the mere straggling play of fancy—catching at every point, and stretching its capricious tendrils around every clause, and even word."[31] Such objections are probably caused primarily by five methods of both introducing temporary obfuscation and stipulating the significance of narrative facts. These devices exhibit the author's ingenuity, or his fancy, rather than his imagination, and they encourage a reader to maintain an analytical attitude toward the narrative. They make stipulations less intrusive or more oblique, or, upon occasion, more interesting and emphatic, and they produce pleasurable moments of recognition when the reader penetrates the rhetorical facade. These devices are allusive symbols, related Biblical allusions, emblematic figures, embryonic personifications, and topographical names.

Both the devices that are primarily visual and allusive—allusive symbols, related Biblical allusions, and emblematic elements—and the devices that are primarily verbal—embryonic personification and topographical names—developed in a similar way from *The Pilgrim's Progress* to *The Holy War.* At the sacrifice of some of the impact they exhibited in the earlier masterpiece, both the "visual-allusive" devices and the "verbal" ones identify and stipulate in more oblique or less intrusive ways in *The Holy War* than they had in *The Pilgrim's Progress.*

First, the devices that are primarily verbal rather than allusive and visual. Embryonic personifications and topographical names appear in the introductory sketches of moral types and in various other parts of the allegorical narratives.

Those appearing in the introductory sketches constitute a kind of verbal filigree much like that described by C. S. Lewis as "mere characteristics of style, a form of poetic diction after the manner of the eighteenth century."[32] This filigree introduces obliqueness in the initial definition of such characters in *The Pilgrim's Progress* as Mr. Hold-the-World (p. 101), Mr. Anything (p. 99), and Formalist (p. 39). It introduces obliqueness, too, in the further analysis of the figures. Such obliquely-stated analysis appears, for example, in the statement that Temporary "dwelt in *Graceless*, a Town about two miles off of *Honesty*" (p. 151) or that Mr. Legality lived in the "village of Morality" (p. 19). Many of these definitions are figurative counterparts of the "insulting pedigree" which Professor Benjamin Boyce says was a familiar part of the polemic character.[33] Mr. By-ends, for example, was the grandson of a "Waterman, looking one way, and Rowing another," and his wife was "Lady *Faining's* Daughter." He also numbered among his kinsmen in the town of Fair Speech such figures as Lord Turn-about, Lord Time-server, and Lord Fair-Speech (p. 99). Although they scarcely give the "grandeur of generality" to the places or ideas, these embryonic personifications and topographical names function effectively as disguised statements and undoubtedly make some plain truths more interesting and emphatic.

Those in *The Holy War* typically express more extensive pedigrees and much more intricate, precise, and elaborate analyses:

> The *Doubters* are such as have their name from their nature, as well as from the Lord and Kingdom where they are born: their nature is to put a question upon every one of the truths of *Emmanuel*; and their country is called the Land of *Doubting*, and that Land lieth off, and furthest remote to the north, between the Land of *Darkness* and that called the *Valley of the Shadow of Death*. For though the Land of *Darkness*, and that called *the Land of the Shadow of Death*, be sometimes called as if they were one and the self-same place, yet indeed they are two, lying but a little way asunder, and the Land of *Doubting* points in and lieth between them. This is the Land of *Doubting*: and these ... are the Natives of that country. (p. 228)

Such oblique stipulations and analyses, involving astonishing numbers of embryonic, unvisualized personifications and topographical names, consistently encourage an analytical frame of mind and impede narrative movement in *The Holy War*.

The verbal devices appearing outside the sketches exhibit a similar loss of impact and growth in obliqueness and precision. Those in *The Pilgrim's Progress* produce a wide range of effects. On one hand, there are a great many that do little to humanize ideas or to give them authority or vitality. In the second edition, for example, Mr. Worldly-Wiseman warns Christian, "*Thou are like to meet with in the way which thou goest, Wearisomness, Painfulness, Hunger, Perils, Nakedness, Sword, Lions, Dragons, Darkness, and in a word, Death, and what not?*" (p. 18). These figures are so far from being developed as "characters" that they do not, in fact, appear at all, though, of course, Christian meets some of these dangers. Similarly, Great-heart reports to Christiana and Mercy that Simple, Sloth, and Presumption "prevailed with one *Short-wind*, with one *No-heart*, and with *Linger-after-lust*, and with one *Sleepy-head*, and with a young Woman her name was *Dull*, to turn out of the way" (p. 213). The figures are not developed. Moreover, such figures are treated with so little respect that they sometimes appear even in contradiction to narrative fact. Christian, for example, reports "*Blessed* Michael *helped me*" in the fight with Apollyan (p. 60), even though the warrior-angel had not been mentioned during the episode itself (pp. 57-60). Such figures, too, are treated with little respect in that doctrinal, rather than appropriately fictional, explanations of their significance or actions are given. Evangelist, for example, explains why Mr. Legality could not relieve Christian of his burden simply on the doctrinal basis, "Ye cannot be justified by the Words of the Law" (p. 23). Some of the names, in brief, merely identify and stipulate the significances of places and agents in the manner of the verbal filigree or poetic diction of the introductory sketches.

A few embryonic personifications and topographical names in *The Pilgrim's Progress*, on the other hand, become allegorical in a more strict sense,[34] even though they are scarcely developed beyond the possession of a name and the performance of an act or two. Among these are such figures as Help, who pulls Christian out of the Slough of Despond (p. 15), Good-will, who pulls Christian into the "Straight Gate" (p. 27), Watchful, who encourages Christian as he approaches the Palace Beautiful (p. 45) and Reliever, who rescues Christiana and Mercy (p. 195). These figures are developed indirectly, and they introduce sufficient temporary obfuscation to create a memorable moment of recognition. For example, Help, who pulls Christian out of the Slough of Despond (p. 15), is suitably enigmatic, forcing a reader to pause, even momentarily, to consider whether some inner resource, other men, or God himself—as Bunyan suggests in a marginal reference to Psalms 40:2—aids one in escaping despondency.

In some cases, such figures not only introduce temporary obfuscation but also create in the work itself a sense of vital external actuality. In the

Second Part, for example, the Good-will who pulled Christian into the Wicket-gate is replaced by a figure referred to as "the Keeper of the Gate" (p. 188). This figure says, "I grant Pardon ... by word, and deed" (p. 190), and he uses the Biblical sentence *"Suffer the little Children to come unto me"* (p. 189). The other characters consistently treat him with the reverence due a divine being. Mercy, for example, "fell to the Ground on her Face before him and worshipped," and said *"Righteous art thou O Lord..."* (p. 192). The "Keeper of the Gate," like the "Interpreter," in brief, is a functional name forcing a reader to pause, at least momentarily, and then to enjoy a memorable moment of recognition when they recognize that which had been concealed. The embryonic figures, thus, sometimes become significant sources of allegorical effects though, overtly, they are undeveloped. The verbal devices, thus, create a wide range of effects in both parts of *The Pilgrim's Progress.*

The verbal devices in *The Holy War*, in contrast, do not produce a wide range of effects, for they seldom heighten the immediate impact of the narrative since they involve little purposeful obscurity. For example, the following personifications express the idea that what St. Paul calls the "works of the flesh" still lurk about the walls of Mansoul: "the Lord *Fornication*, the Lord *Adultery*, the Lord *Murder*, the Lord *Anger*, the Lord *Lasciviousness*, the Lord *Deceit*, the Lord *Evil-Eye*, Mr. *Drunkenness*, Mr. *Revelling*, Mr. *Idolatry*, Mr. *Witchcraft*, Mr. *Variance*, Mr. *Emulation*" and so forth (p. 145). Only the social criticism implicit in the titles appears, surely, to differentiate the list from St. Paul's (Gal. 5:20). Again, the following place names express the idea that there are three kinds of Bloodmen, those who "did ignorantly what they did," those who did "superstitiously what they did," and those who "did what they did out of spite and implacableness": Bunyan says that some come from "Blind-Man-shire," others from "Blind-Zeal-shire," and others from the "Town of *Malice*, that is in the county of *Envy*" (p. 234). Do the names add anything else? Typically, neither these personifications nor these place names involve so much temporary obfuscation that they create memorable moments of recognition when the rhetorical facade is penetrated.

A second reason that the verbal devices do not heighten the impact of *The Holy War* is that, as was mentioned, there is a tremendous increase in the *number* of such personifications and topographical names. Literally hundreds of these figures and places appear, help to express one or two ideas, and disappear, leaving scarcely a trace behind. They are so numerous, in fact, that, as is illustrated in the St. Paul's list, they frequently constitute an awkward, cumbersome kind of disguised discourse that actually impedes narrative movement and, to that extent, weakens its impact.

ALLEGORICAL DEVELOPMENT / 121

The verbal devices in *The Holy War* also contrast strikingly to those in *The Pilgrim's Progress* in that, being more numerous, they introduce a greater amount of oblique expression without appreciably increasing the amount of ambiguity. The stipulations are unequivocal, whether the verbal devices express the most simple of authorial comments or the most complex of moral observations or analyses. The following narrative facts, for example, visibly suggest nothing more than that Mansoul's recent experience can now be of value to it. The narrator says Emmanuel "called one to him whose name was *Waiting*, and bid him, *Go quickly up to the Castle Gate, and inquire there for one Mr.* Experience." Mr. Experience, appropriately enough, is found "waiting to see the Captain train and muster his men in the Castle-yard." After Waiting brings Experience, Emmanuel appoints the latter a Captain among those guarding Mansoul (p. 135). Waiting is not seen again. A comparable lack of ambiguity is common in more complex sequences. For example, Mr. Wiseman might have observed that impudence, profanity, resentment of authority, contempt for the truth, indifference to God, pursuit of revenge, and numerous other evils spring from the desires of the flesh and the desire for the things of this world. He might have added that the desire for carnal things is born in the mind and that affection for vile things springs from the corrupted will. In *The Holy War* the narrator reports that, after Diabolus entered Mansoul, Lord Willbewill's Deputy, who was called "Vile Affection" because "he was wholly given to the flesh," married one Carnal-Lust, the daughter of Mr. Mind, and that they had children called Impudence, Blackmouth, Hate-Reproof, Scorn-Truth, Slight-God, and Revenge. The narrator adds, "These were all married in the Town, and also begot and yielded many bad brats, too many to be here inserted" (pp. 23-24). The latter expression of the moral observation or analyses seems scarcely more equivocal, surely, than the former one.

The verbal devices in *The Holy War*, in brief, introduce precise, oblique stipulations but contribute relatively little to the impact of the narrative. The range of effects is less extensive than in *The Pilgrim's Progress* largely because embryonic personifications and topographical names encode the language more consistently and intricately in *The Holy War*. The devices that are primarily visual and allusive, rather than verbal, exhibit a similar development. Allusive symbols, related Biblical allusions, and emblematic elements neither multiply as profusely nor becomes as prominent in *The Holy War* as the embryonic personifications and topographical names. Nevertheless, these devices are also exploited more fully and systematically in *The Holy War*, and they, too, contribute less than their predecessors to the impact of the narrative. Essentially, allusive symbols, related Biblical allusions, and emblematic elements are dispersed into many parts of

The Pilgrim's Progress so that they create a wide range of effects; these three devices are brought together in a relatively few passages in *The Holy War* so that, though their impact is less, they identify and stipulate in more oblique or less intrusive ways than those in *The Pilgrim's Progress*.

It is difficult to define the relationship of *The Pilgrim's Progress* to the emblem tradition, which has been studied separately by Professors Freeman and Sharrock,[35] and, perhaps, more difficult to define the relationship of the emblematic elements to others within the work itself. Professor Freeman says that one "cannot, in fact, in *The Pilgrim's Progress*, work out the point at which emblem writing stops and parable, illustration, and other adjuncts to the sermon begin."[36] She further points out that emblems "are part of Bunyan's habitual method of allegory. Consequently [she adds] there is much that is generally emblematic scattered all through the book."[37] Yet, manifestly, some passages adhere more closely to the traditional pattern of the emblem; these create quite different effects from those that are scattered throughout the book. These visual-allusive elements produce a wide range of effects in *The Pilgrim's Progress*.

Some emblematic passages, such as those in the significant rooms of the Interpreter (pp. 28-35, 201-03), augment the allegorical effects of both parts of *The Pilgrim's Progress*. They do so in the simple and relatively direct manner of the emblem book: they set forth one thing by another through visual detail and then explain that detail point by point as the verses of an emblem do. For example, the Interpreter shows Christian a "Picture of a very grave Person" who *"had eyes lift up to Heaven, the best of Books in its hand, the Law of Truth was written upon its lips, the World was behind its back; it stood as if it pleaded with Men, and a Crown of God did hang over its head."* This picture, for which Professor Sharrock found a probable source in the works of Whitney,[38] is explained by the Interpreter, who defines the significance of each visual detail:

> And whereas thou seest him with his eyes lift up to Heaven, the best of Books in his hand, and the Law of Truth writ on his lips: it is to shew thee, that his work is to know, and unfold dark things to sinners. ... And whereas thou seest the World as cast behind him, and that a Crown hangs over his head; that is, to shew thee, that slighting and despising the things that are present, for the love that he hath to his Masters service, he is sure in the world that comes next to have Glory for his Reward.... (p. 29)

Such "speaking pictures," involving little temporary obfuscation, serve didactic purposes in a relatively straightforward manner and, more important, keep a reader alert to the possibility that other narrative facts may "also mean" something else.

Other emblematic passages, in contrast, follow the emblem pattern less closely and, perhaps, create more significant allegorical effects. These scattered elements appear most obviously in such passages as the descriptions of Pope and Pagan (p. 65) or of the cave of Demas (pp. 106-08) in the first pilgrimage and the description of Prudence's examination of the children (pp. 231-35) and of events on Mounts Marvel, Innocent, and Charity (pp. 284-86) in the *Second Part*. Less obviously, they appear, perhaps, in the descriptions of Apollyon (p. 56) in *The Pilgrim's Progress* and of Heedless (p. 297) in the *Second Part*. In these passages, the departures from the norm represented by the "very grave Person" are in the direction of a fuller development of either the figures or the scenes. Emblematic figures typically have only one gesture or speech in *The Pilgrim's Progress*. Pope, for example, cries after Christian as he passes, *"You will never mend, till more of you be burned"* (p. 66). But the "Man in an Iron Cage" illustrates a further step in the assimilation of emblematic elements into the allegory, for he explains his own situation to Christian before the Interpreter points the moral, saying "Let this man's misery . . . be an everlasting caution to thee" (p. 35). The setting in which Pope and Pagan appear illustrates a fuller development of an emblematic setting. Unlike the setting in which the "very grave Person" appeared, the place of Pope and Pagan is not explicated point by point, yet it develops largely by visual means, supplemented only by brief explanatory phases, and expresses fairly unequivocal judgments about paganism and Roman Catholicism:

> At the end of this Valley lay blood, bones, ashes, and mangled bodies of men, even of Pilgrims that had gone this way formerly: And while I was musing what should be the reason, I espied a little before me a Cave, where two Giants, *Pope* and *Pagan*, dwelt in old time, by whose Power and Tyranny the Men whose bones, blood, ashes, etc. lay there, were cruelly put to death. . . . *Pagan* has been dead many a day; and as for the other, though he be yet alive, he is by reason of age, and also of the many shrewd brushes that he met with in his younger dayes, grown so crazy and stiff in his joynts, that he can now do little more then sit in his Caves mouth, grinning at Pilgrims as they go by, and biting his nails, because he cannot come at them. (p. 65)

The visual emphasis and the overt departures from the mimetic norm make this, and other, passages distinctively emblematic. These scattered emblematic elements, like the "very grave Person," keep the reader alert to "other" meanings, or simply say clearly what would be less interesting if announced directly. Moreover, they do not simply conceal a truth and reveal it more memorably later; they enhance additional allegorical effects as well.

The emblematic figures and settings scattered through both parts of *The Pilgrim's Progress* amplify the sense of wonder and mystery peculiar to allegorical narrative and fable. Coherent thematic patterns emerge from the mimetic incongruity of settings such as the place of Pope and Pagan, and the "lesson" or "meaning" of visual detail gains emphasis through implicit contrast with that mimetic norm. Such pictures do not create their effects through a symbolic coherence such as that in Spenser's den of Errour. Nor do they simply concentrate meaning as, for example, the picture of Marlow standing in the blood of his murdered native pilot epitomizes the exploitation theme in *The Heart of Darkness*. They violate the norm of probability and, at the same time, give numerous separate visual details a high thematic content despite their mimetic content. Flatterer, for example, appeared in the midst of a prosaic mimetic scene. He was "a man black of flesh, but covered with a very light Robe," (p. 133) a "false Apostle, that hath transformed himself into an Angel of Light" (p. 134). Flatterer led the pilgrims within the "compass of a Net . . . and with that, *the white robe fell off the black mans back*" (p. 133). Flatterer violates the norm of probability as Marlow does not and, so, sustains the shadowy atmosphere of significant fantasy. He also exhibits the curious "isolation" of much imagery in other allegories.[39] The thematic coherence emerging from apparent incongruity, the departures of characters and settings from the mimetic norm, the special emphasis gained thereby, and the descriptions that appear strangely meaningful in ways differing from those of common experience—these are the distinctive qualities of emblematic elements in *The Pilgrim's Progress*. The "speaking" visual detail adds a note of strangeness, not to beauty, but to a convincing mimetic surface, yet makes relatively unequivocal didactic disclosures. They introduce a pictoral, rather than dramatic, stress more characteristic of Spenser than of Bunyan.

Allusive symbols are images expressing ideas to which they are related by conventions outside the work of art. A cursory examination of Professor Walter Edward McNair's recent study of the "use and meaning" of about two hundred symbols in *The Pilgrim's Progress* "in terms of traditionally accepted Christian interpretation"[40] would suggest that the association of image and idea in allusive symbols were primarily dependent upon the Bible. However, as the late Professor Samuel C. Chew's *The Pilgrimage of Life* illustrates again and again, Biblical imagery had a tremendous influence upon both verbal and visual imagery in literature and graphic arts.[41] Many associations of image and idea could, therefore, have reached Bunyan through paintings, sculptures, tapestries, emblems, homilies, other religious treatises, romances, or other literary works, rather than directly from the Bible. This widespread use of Biblical imagery does not make it inappropriate to speak of these symbols as "allusive" ones, however, for—with rare exceptions[42]—they were probably derived directly from the Bible.[43]

Allusive symbols create allegorical effects similar to those produced by other minor devices and, perhaps, some major ones. They create temporary obfuscation and produce pleasurable moments of recognition. For example, Christian enters a setting containing a Cross and a Sepulcher. He is visited by the "shining ones," who may represent either inner or outer experience, and is given a "change of Raiment," a "mark in his fore-head," and a "Roll with a Seal upon it" (p. 38). Marginal Biblical allusions identify the sources of the symbols and indicate that Christian had experienced effectual calling, which came because of election rather than, as St. Augustine would have it, from baptism. Recognition of the Biblical text is necessary to an understanding of the event as it had not when a comparable stage of progress was earlier reported in *Grace Abounding:* "Now had I an evidence ... of my salvation from Heaven, with many golden Seals thereon, all hanging in my sight" (p. 40).

Allusive symbols also, of course, identify and stipulate the significance of experience in terms of an established system of belief, and they, too, gain emphasis by contrast to the mimetic norm. In the *Second Part,* for example, Christiana sits in an arbor to eat and says, "For I have here a piece of Pomgranate which Mr. *Interpreter* put in my Hand, just as I came out of his Doors; he gave me also a piece of a Honey-comb, and a little Bottle of Spirits" (p. 216), refreshments more closely associated with the promised land (Deut. 8:8) than with seventeenth-century England. These symbols are typical, too, in that they introduce a note of the strange or esoteric into dominantly mimetic scenes or settings.

Finally, in contrast to other devices, allusive symbols gain at least some of their emotive power from the fact that they *are* allusions. Even the simplest passage translating a Biblical image may be evocative of heroic or inspiring Biblical contexts. For example, Bunyan places a wall on each side of the straight and narrow path, which itself has a Biblical origin, and says the "Wall is called Salvation" (p. 37). A marginal reference (Isa. 26:1) leads a reader to "In that day shall this song be sung in the land of Judah: We have a strong city; salvation will *God* appoint *for* walls and bulwarks." The quotation could well arouse memories of the paean of praise from which it came. The cumulative effect of such allusive symbols is to create a constant awareness of the spiritual associations and authority behind the depicted journey.

In contrast to these in *The Pilgrim's Progress*, the emblematic passages and allusive symbols in *The Holy War* become less potent in emotive terms and more cryptic and precise as disguised discourse. This is true of both the emblematic appearances that identify the figure's significance, and the allusive symbols that are elaborated into cryptic and elliptical assertions. These devices appear elaborately and formally together in the emblematic descriptions of the forces Shaddai sends against Mansoul (pp. 37ff), those Emmanuel himself leads (pp. 68ff), and those Diabolus marshalls for the second (pp. 186ff) and third (pp. 229ff) assaults. Less varied than the epic catalogues of either Homer, Virgil, or Milton, these stiffly stylized passages are, nevertheless, unified so that their parts are mutually illuminating. First, the names of the Captain and his Ensign are given. These latter figures, as Froude remarks, are "counterparts of themselves."[44] Promise, for example, is the Ensign of Captain Credence, Expectation of Captain Good-hope, Piteful of Captain Charity, and so forth. Then there is a more-or-less elaborate description of the Captain's escutcheon together with a marginal Biblical reference. In describing many of these escutcheons Bunyan systematically uses Biblical imagery and stipulates the nature of the Captain through visual detail.

Allusive symbols and related allusions challenge the reader to discover further analogies that are, themselves, unexplained. The symbols stipulate obliquely. The intricacy of the process of reasoning involved is evident in the descriptions of some of Diabolus's followers. Captain Fury, for example, "had for his Scutcheon the Fiery flying Serpent" (p. 186). The symbol is appropriated from Num. 21:6 in which Moses's followers in the wilderness were complaining, despite the recent aid God had given them against their enemies, and "the LORD sent fiery serpents among the people, and they bit the people; and much people of Israel died." The further analogy, not explained by Bunyan, between those who doubt the beginnings of regeneration in themselves and those doubting followers of Moses makes clear why Captain Fury leads the Vocation-Doubters. Again, an allusion explains why Captain Damnation should lead the attack upon the soul of a man who doubts the grace of God. The allusion is to Matt. 22:13, the parable about the marriage of the king who said of the guest who wore no wedding garment, "Bind him hand and foot, and take him away, and cast him into outer darkness: there shall be weeping and gnashing of teeth." No explanation is given of the allegorical interpretation of the parable which would equate the man without a wedding garment with those suffering from the divine malediction. Again, the vision in Rev. 12:3, 4, 13, 15-17 supplied "the great Red Dragon" (p. 186) for the escutcheon of Captain Rage, leader of the Election-Doubters. In the Biblical passage "a great red dragon having

ALLEGORICAL DEVELOPMENT / 127

seven heads and ten horns, and seven crowns upon his head," opposed the birth of Christ, was defeated, and "went to make war with the remnant of his seed which keep the commandments of God, and have the testimony of Jesus Christ." The reader is given no aid in finding the analogy between the opposition of the dragon to the birth of Christ and the opposition to the birth of grace in the individual soul so that he may see why the red dragon is an appropriate symbol for the escutcheon of the leader of the Election-Doubters. The tenuity, the elliptical quality, the intricacy of allusion, in effect, is clearly far greater in *The Holy War* than in the other allegories.

The emblematic passages scattered through *The Pilgrim's Progress* have no counterparts in *The Holy War*. However, there are "emblematic" elements in these same formal descriptions. In them, the leaders, like the figures in the emblematic passages, are identified by the outward appearances of their escutcheons. In contrast to the point by point explanations of visual detail in *The Pilgrim's Progress,* these escutcheons are explained only by marginal Biblical references so that the visual images are, in effect, often more cryptic than those in the earlier masterpiece.

Varying degrees of difficulty are involved in understanding these escutcheons. In many cases the escutcheon is simply a visual representation of the verbal imagery of the Bible. For example, Captain Conviction's "Scutcheon was the Book of the Law wide open, from whence issued a flame of fire" (p. 37). This image was suggested by Moses's statement in Deut. 33:2, "The Lord came from Sinae ... and he came with ten thousand of saints: from his right hand *went* a fiery law for them." Only the phrase "fiery law" became visual. Captain Good-Hope's escutcheon, a symbol popular in the emblem books, is a bit more complicated. "Captain Good-Hope for a Scutcheon ... had *Three Golden Anchors*" (p. 68) and the allusion gives the source of the anchor as a symbol of hope: Heb. 6:19: "Which hope [God's Promise] we have as a anchor of the soul, both sure and steadfast, and which entereth into that within the veil." The context makes clear why there were three anchors, for in Heb. 6:17-18 God confirmed his promise by an oath by "two immutable things in which it was impossible for God to lie." A somewhat greater exercise of the fancy is needed, too, to understand why Captain Torment, leader of the Resurrection-Doubters "had the *Black Worm* for his Scutcheon" (p. 187), for the symbol is drawn from a refrain in Mark 9:44, 46, 48 which refers to hell "Where their worm dieth not, and the fire is not quenched." In this case the Biblical refrain, of course, supplies but part of the visual image. No reference is given to Job 24:20 in which man appears as food for worms. The systematic adaptations of verbal Biblical imagery into visual form gives the passages the appeal of the emblem, the precise stipulation of the allusive symbols, and, perhaps, the pleasure of the difficulty overcome.

The cumulative effect of these passages is seemingly that of a separate *tour de force,* interesting in its own right, but contributing little to the emotive power of the narrative or to sustaining a spectral atmosphere like that in the earlier pilgrimage. The visual-allusive devices, like the verbal one, in brief, exhibit a loss in impact as well as a gain in precision and intricacy in *The Holy War.*

CONCLUSIONS

John Bunyan described himself as a conscientious religious spokesman attempting to use fictional narratives for religious ends. His critics have described him in strikingly different terms. They have attempted to explain incongruities, inconsistencies, and irregularities in his narratives by describing him as a "simple and gifted" laborer or an "unconscious" artist. Professor Tindall's study of the conventions Bunyan shared with other "mechanick preachers" has apparently disposed of the legend of the "simple and gifted" laborer without eliminating the "unconscious" artist, who still lurks in the background of two recent major studies. It is not possible to demonstrate the accuracy of either of these sharply contrasting pictures in biographical terms, but their conflicting formal implications raise the question as to whether there is a meaningful, coherent pattern in the development of his narrative methods. Bunyan's picture suggests further that a fuller exploration of his professed goals and comments about his methods could isolate any such pattern that does exist.

Unresolved conflict is implicit in his description of his goals. He professed to teach, to please, to move, and, at the same time, to hold a mirror up to nature as an aid to introspection. These goals demanded that he both imitate external actuality and indicate the significance of these imitations. These goals necessarily involve conflict. The conflict involved in literal, or nonallegorical narrative methods is one between the didactic and mimetic principles; it threatens the basic illusion necessary to effective narrative art. A related unresolved conflict is implicit in his description of the allegorical method. The conflict is between the dialectical and mimetic principles; it places competing demands upon separate images and actions within the work of art and establishes two opposing kinds of relationships to external actuality. If these unresolved conflicts are considered in relation to the *development* of Bunyan's narrative methods, an unexpected pattern emerges: both the literal and the allegorical methods evolve in such a way that the conflict is gradually reduced.

In five major narratives, *Grace Abounding*, published in 1666; *The Pilgrim's Progress*, 1678; *Mr. Badman*, 1680; *The Holy War*, 1682; and *The Second Part of the Pilgrim's Progress*, 1684, Bunyan gradually reduced the conflict created by the mimetic and didactic principles. He did so by developing more effective methods for imitating external actualities and by suggesting or stipulating the significance of narrative material in more oblique or less intrusive ways.

The dominant movements in the development of nonallegorical, or literal, techniques between *Grace Abounding* and the *Second Part* are toward more effective imitation and more subtle or indirect stipulation of the significance of narrative facts. These dominant movements are intimately related, yet it would be inaccurate to say that the mimetic evolution gradually embodies a vision of actuality in artistic form and leaves behind an inert residue of direct preachments and contrived illustrative material. The manifestations of the didactic principle also change: they become more subtle or indirect in form; they become less inimical, or **more conducive, to the basic illusion necessary to effective narrative art.**

Granted some initial imaginative acceptance of a system of values that lacks universal appeal, the narratives, nevertheless, frequently create a more acute problem of belief and, in other ways, distract attention from, or dampen interest in, the complex of images and actions constituting their achieved artistic form. They do so most frequently through the direct characterization and through certain passages that may be called "applications." The applications exploit the illustrative capacities of characters and events, suggest an "official" interpretation, thus restricting a reader's own range of judgment, and, at times, include additional moral instruction and exhortation. These applications threaten the illusion at times in each of the narratives.

In *Grace Abounding*, which has prominent didactic characteristics aside from the applications, the narrator exercises the authority established by the narrative and impairs the illusion by voicing applications. The applications in the fictional narratives are voiced by the narrators and by certain characters who acquire authority from the narrative itself. Both the narrators and the authoritative speakers gradually change so that they become less inimical to an illusion.

The fictional speakers, who assume and exercise authority in each of the narratives, continue to restrict the reader's range of interest and to raise the spectre of didactic contrivance by using other characters as illustrations, by pointing the moral of separate episodes, and by moralizing about events at greater length than the dramatic occasion appears to demand. They gradually become less inimical to the illusion, or even to foster it, by voicing fewer, and shorter, discourses without a fairly direct thematic or dramatic sanction and by showing greater respect for the confines of the fictional world in which they live. The later commentary largely clarifies relationships within the work of art and alludes only very obliquely to external actualities.

The process by which the narrators gradually become less inimical to an illusion is more complicated because, aside from the effects of their stipulatory comments, they influence an illusion in more diverse ways. They continue to destroy the illusion in two principal ways. They distract attention from the story to the way it is told by changing their relationship to the story and the reader. They display little artistic detachment about their moral or religious themes; their narrative and linguistic choices consistently imply that they are deeply religious moralists. They gradually become less inimical to an illusion partially because they become less prominent as the scenic method of narration develops. They gradually destroy the illusion less often, too, by changing the two separate roles they play as figures in the foreground and as omniscient authors: they become less prominent as figures in the foreground, more bold and unobtrusive as omniscient authors, and less distracting in changing their relationship to the story and the reader.

Direct characterization much like certain homiletic and Theophrastan characters used as illustration in early treatises appears in each of the fictional narratives. They introduce a spirited group of minor wayward professors in *The Pilgrim's Progress,* a series of separate aspects of the nature of the central figure in *Mr. Badman,* and a number of minor figures in *The Holy War* and the *Second Part.* Delightful in themselves, these sketches are inimical to an illusion as direct characterization since they retain some of their didactic force and distract attention from the matter to the manner of its presentation because of their artificiality and abstractness. Some of the sketches, however, become analagous to the schemata of a visual artist; those sketches are elaborated so that they contribute to the dominant movement toward unobtrusive didacticism and more effective imitation. Some of the schemata in each narrative become more elaborate and more effective as direct characterization.

In *The Pilgrim's Progress* at least three minor figures benefit remarkably from elaborated schemata. The didactic overtones, the abstractness, and the artificiality of the schemata are reduced by a descent to the concrete, which suggests some of the complexity of "real" human experience; by a partial dispersal of the elements, which reduces the rigidity of the form, and, most notably, by stylized dialogue that extends the schemata. Some of the overtly self-revealing speeches enable a character to retain his identity in the midst of a dramatic scene. Others are more subtle; they have distinctive cadences and sentence patterns which obliquely and amusingly reinforce the schemata and enable three minor figures to become more convincingly complex.

The schemata in *Mr. Badman* become more effective as direct characterization through a further descent to the concrete that renders pictures of everyday life and manners with remarkable visual clarity. In contrast to the static figures of the earlier work, Mr. Badman is shown in successive schemata growing through time so that a new aspect of external probabilities is suggested. The third significant development in *Mr. Badman* is that a new kind of schema, a "portrait," shows the relationship between separate aspects of his nature and richly suggests the complexity of the "real" world.

The schemata of *The Holy War* constitute a new synthesis rather than a further realization of their mimetic capacities. The schema of central characters have a dual conceptual basis, and they are extended so that action is consistently extending metaphor as well as character. Although they do not show a further descent to the concrete, the schemata do not exhibit simple didactic impoverishment, for the abstractness of the schemata and of their extensions has become highly functional.

The elements of the schemata make, perhaps, their most effective mimetic contribution as direct characterization in the *Second Part*. The schemata introducing several major figures are subsumed in rapidly moving dramatic scenes so that the schemata create an effect of spontaneous disorder rather than of formal artificiality, and they are greatly elaborated and widely dispersed so that they contribute to convincing complexity of several central figures. The self-revealing speeches, too, characterize these figures more effectively in certain thematically-focused scenes, isolated by mere hints of artificiality, so that the revelation of character is more subtle and is itself enhanced through effective dramatic contrasts.

The effects of the elaborated schemata gradually merge with those of another method of revealing character which was developed, in a sense, from moral dialogues. In these discourses, the revelation of character was initially incidental to the presentation of ideas. It is, at any rate, clear that the mimetic principle is manifest in a characteristically dramatic way in Bunyan's first publication and that he developed the mimetic potentialities of narrative material most memorably through dialogue in fully developed dramatic scenes. These scenes reveal major and minor characters effectively, express the inner life forcefully, and explore the outer life of social life and manners vividly. Although emphasis varies from narrative to narrative, the dominant movement in the development of nonallegorical methods is toward a fuller realization of the potentialities of a scenic method of narration for sustaining an illusion.

In formal terms, there is a reduction in the proportions of narrative and expository material, an enlargement and refinement of separate scenes, a closer integration of successive scenes, and a fuller realization of the power of the dialogue to suggest immediacy and spontaneity, to externalize inner conflicts precisely, and to reveal a credible character through the substance of his speech. These separate developments do not at all proceed at a uniform rate, yet each of the narratives, except, perhaps, *The Holy War*, exhibits a fuller realization of the power of a scenic method of narrative to create and sustain an illusion.

Bunyan's spiritual autobiography represents a major step forward in dramatic development in that the style exhibits the qualities characteristic of Bunyan's best dialogue, the character of one central figure is revealed in an essentially dramatic way, certain interior monologues and dialogues attain the force of action in the dramatic present, the mimetic potentialities of some dialogue are realized, and six highly effective dramatic scenes re-create portions of the life of the young Bunyan.

The Pilgrim's Progress explores both inner and outer aspects of spiritual adventure, and it does so more extensively than the earlier narrative. In doing so, it reveals seven major dramatic developments: the narrative develops largely through dramatic scenes, many intense, sharply-focused effective scenes achieve a form that heightens their immediate dramatic impact, and three major characters are revealed primarily by dramatic means in both allegorical and mimetic scenes. The allegorical scenes, which allude indirectly to external actualities, both reveal self-consistent minor figures and explore the complex psychological conflicts of major ones primarily through dialogue; the mimetic ones, which allude directly to external actualities, exploit sharp dramatic contrasts extensively, and relatively subtle ones effectively. Both kinds of scenes exhibit potent dramatic immediacy, objectivity, and concentration.

Although *Mr. Badman* lacks the spiritual range and dramatic impact of *The Pilgrim's Progress*, it exhibits two significant dramatic developments. The first of these is that two major speakers reveal themselves through an extensive, continuing drama in the foreground and participate in a series of lively, subtle interactions, yet remain clearly differentiated. The second is that Bunyan's first important, fully-realized feminine character, Mrs. Badman, is revealed primarily through dialogue in this exploration of Puritan morality.

Though the dramatic elements are but a small part of the labyrinthian intricacy of *The Holy War*, this second allegory exhibits four major dramatic developments: many long, elaborate, formal scenes, unprecedented in earlier narratives, appear; speeches consistently convey a fuller impression of the narrative situation; effective, precise, dramatic contrasts are consistently sustained; and at least a dozen complex central figures consistently speak "in character" through countless scenes and episodes. Since the speakers in *The Holy War* create little human interest, these developments are, perhaps, more important as anticipations than as achievements.

The dramatic methods developed in the earlier narratives are evident at every turn during the depiction of the inexhaustible diversity of social life and manners in the *Second Part*. The *Second Part* is undoubtedly the most fully dramatic product of Bunyan's genius and, in a sense, the most fully human of the narratives. The narrative movement occurs so consistently in dramatic scenes that much of the work could easily be adapted to the stage. Among many highly effective scenes are a number of elaborate ones which create the effect, unprecedented in Bunyan's works, of a series of interactions among a group of characters. At least six fully-realized characters reveal themselves through a series of sharply-focused, rapidly moving, progressive scenes; they exhibit sustained contrasts so that they seem both self-consistent and complex. The inner life is externalized primarily by dialogue rather than by allegorical means, and, finally, scenes treating both the inner and outer lives of the central figures give unprecedented prominence to human emotions, sentiments, and relationships. The capacity of a scenic method of narration to create and sustain an illusion, in brief, is triumphantly realized in the final narrative, the *Second Part*.

The dominant movements toward more effective imitation and more subtle didacticism are, thus, evident in the development of literal narrative methods. The growth of the scenic method of narration, the elaboration of schemata to characterize major figures, the development of less distracting narrators, and the increased subtlety of suggestions about the significance of characters and events contribute to the reduction of conflicts between the didactic and the mimetic principles.

A similar reduction of conflict is evident in the development of allegorical methods. The nature of the central conflict differs in that the tension is created by two separate allegorical principles that Bunyan himself applied when he interpreted biblical passages allegorically. On one hand, there is the "dialectical" principle, which demands a series of precise, unequivocal, point by point correlations in an extended metaphor; on the other, there is the "mimetic" one, which demands that images and actions

CONCLUSIONS / 135

in an extended metaphor be "very natural," or level with the norm of common experience. The mimetic principle exerts a centripetal force; the dialectical one, a centrifugal force. Passages create strikingly different effects when one or the other of these principles is dominant, and isolated passages in which each is dominant appear in both parts of *The Pilgrim's Progress* and in *The Holy War*. Yet the dominant movement is clear from the contrasts between both parts of *The Pilgrim's Progress* and *The Holy War*. In the latter work, five oblique ways of stipulating and exploiting temporary obfuscation are used more extensively and systematically. The most significant reduction of conflicts, however, is produced by a shift in the imaginative balance, so that the dialectical principle, rather than the mimetic one, is almost invariably dominant in *The Holy War*. In the process, a method of giving unique, imaginative expression to the inner and outer effects of spiritual adventure and, at the same time, of partially controlling a reader's interpretation of that experience is transformed into an elaborate systematic method of expressing analyses and interpretations of such experience, indirectly yet precisely.

The allegorical potentialities of "very natural" images and actions are realized in *The Pilgrim's Progress*. The central characters, rather than the central metaphor, dominate the narrative. The rhythm of their inner lives determines the basic narrative movement, and the fundamental continuity springs from their spiritual vicissitudes, despite formal diversity. The allegory gives an incomparable picture of the inner and outward aspects of the life of spiritual adventure through dramatic scenes, which were discussed earlier, and settings, which were not discussed earlier. The "representative" settings in *The Pilgrim's Progress* sustain the illusion and extend the social range of the narrative; the "psychic" settings express states of consciousness so fully as to become evocative symbols of them. The five separate parts of these settings, anticipated in earlier works, are first fused in this masterpiece. The dramatic scenes and settings "open up" central and subordinate metaphors so fully that significant additional allegorical effects are attained. The mimetic fullness reinforces the effect of the conceptions embodied by the central figures, and the effect of that fullness is itself heightened by the conceptions these characters express. The mimetic fullness, further, lends emotive force to the central characters' effects as agents.

Although it was published after *The Holy War*, the *Second Part* also exhibits a rich mimetic fullness, as befits a continuation. The allegorical potentialities of "very natural" images and actions, however, are realized less extensively in the *Second Part* than in the earlier work. The central figures, to be sure, are developed fully as "very natural" fictional characters, but their functions as agents are few. The settings realize relatively few allegorical potentialities. Extensive changes in the weather and modifications in landscapes, as well as in the routes of individual pilgrims, enable some settings to function allegorically. A few settings, too, function as fixed points of known—but obliquely expressed—significance in the dramatic revelation of character. But very few settings in the *Second Part* produce powerful effects like those of the earlier "psychic" settings. On the whole, few allegorical potentialities of "very natural" images and actions are realized in the *Second Part*.

The imaginative balance has shifted in *The Holy War* so that mimetic fullness is less evident than dialectical precision and consistency. The development of separate episodes differs strikingly. Passages exhibiting an economic fusion of mimetic and dialectical elements are relatively rare in both parts of *The Pilgrim's Progress*; such passages are typical in *The Holy War*: mimetic development is limited, allusions to external actualities are few, and point by point correlations are precise and unequivocal. The shift is evident, too, because the central metaphor dominates the narrative. This dominance is evident because the narrative evolves primarily as a psychomachia and much awkward "machinery" moves with each change in the direction of narrative movement. The central metaphor also dominates the major characters so that there is no descent to the concrete, even when such characters remain long on the scene. They speak "in character" as both agents and types; they lack mimetic development, though they acquire a certain ritualistic dignity and, perhaps, a certain emotive power from ideas outside the work of art. The dominance of the central metaphor is evident, finally, in the fact that the inner life is explored only within the confines of the settings established by that metaphor. The balance has shifted, in brief, so that the dialectical, rather than the mimetic, principle is dominant in *The Holy War*.

In addition to the shift in imaginative balance, *The Holy War* exhibits a striking change in the following five devices: embryonic personifications, topographical names, emblematic elements, allusive symbols, and related biblical allusions. At the sacrifice of some of the impact they exhibited in the earlier masterpiece, both the "visual-allusive" devices and the "verbal" ones identify and stipulate in more indirect and subtle ways in *The Holy War*.

The verbal devices produce a wide range of effects in *The Pilgrim's Progress*, at times merely identifying or stipulating but often, too, heightening the immediate impact of the narrative. Those in *The Holy War*, in contrast, usually introduce little purposeful obscurity, create little impact, and often become so numerous that they impede narrative movement. Typically, they express unequivocal stipulations and identifications in treating both simple and complex themes.

The visual-allusive devices also lose impact as they gain precision and intricacy. The emblematic passages in *The Pilgrim's Progress* produce a wide range of effects. Some passages, conforming closely to the traditional didactic pattern, contribute little to the emotive force of the narrative; others, involving a fuller visual development of the settings or the figures, sustain a sense of wonder through contrast to the mimetic norm and give an aura of mystery to didactic disclosures. The allusive symbols in *The Pilgrim's Progress*, derived either directly or indirectly from the Bible, also create diverse effects. These visual-allusive devices, which appear together in four elaborate *tours de force* in *The Holy War*, do not greatly heighten the impact of the narrative. The allusive symbols, however, stipulate quite indirectly, and visual images, derived largely from the Bible, are more precise and cryptic than those in *The Pilgrim's Progress*.

It seems clear, then, that the loss of impact and the increase in stipulatory intricacy and precision evident in the use of these five devices enhance the effects of the shift of imaginative balance so that *The Holy War* became the least equivocal and most precise of Bunyan's analyses of the varieties of religious experience. This two-dimensional resolution of conflicts is parallel to the dominant movement noted in the examination of the literal or non-allegorical methods. Bunyan, thus, clearly developed his narrative art in such a way that he reduced the conflict created by the didactic and mimetic principles. He gradually developed more effective methods of imitating external actualities, and he gradually stipulated the significance of narrative materials in more oblique or less intrusive ways.

NOTES

CHAPTER ONE: INTRODUCTION

1. John Bunyan: *L'Homme et L'Oeuvre*, in *Etudes de Literature D'Art et L'Histoire* (Paris, n. d. [1948]), p. 260.
2. Future references to this, and other, minor treatises, which are in the text, are to *The Entire Works of John Bunyan*, ed. Henry Stebbing, 4 vols. (London, 1859-1860). Future references to the narratives, which appear in the text, are to the following editions: *Grace Abounding to the Chief of Sinners*, ed. Roger Sharrock (Oxford, 1962); *The Pilgrim's Progress from this world to that which is to Come*, ed. James Blanton Wharey, rev. Roger Sharrock (Oxford, 1960). The text refers to the Wharey-Sharrock edition of both parts of *The Pilgrim's Progress*. References to *Mr. Badman* are to the text in *Life and Death of Mr. Badman and The Holy War*, ed. John Brown (Cambridge, 1905), pp. 3-179. References to *The Holy War* are in the text in *The Holy War and The Heavenly Footman*, ed. Mabel Peacock (Oxford, 1892), pp. 1-254.
3. R. A. Knox, *Enthusiasm: A Chapter in the History of Religion with Special Reference to the XVII and XVIII Centuries* (New York, 1950), p. 154 suggests convincingly, if unconventionally, that the actual influence of Anabaptist ideas was extensive. Bunyan's use of the word suggests, at least, that it had no ill-savour for him early in his career. Later, he rejected "those factious titles of Anabaptists, Independents, Presbyterians" because "they naturally tend to divisions"—as Robert Southey points out in *The Pilgrim's Progress with a Life of John Bunyan* (Boston, n. d.), p. lxxi.
4. Knox, p. 134.
5. Frederick W. Farrer, *History of Interpretation* (New York, 1886), p. 147 points out that Philo, one of the most influential of the Alexandrians, introduced the Platonic theory into the Christian tradition of scriptural interpretation in maintaining that "the sacred books were written in a condition of ecstasy, which wholly obliterated the human powers. The

vocal organs of the prophets, without any co-operation on their part, were but used by a divine ventriloquism." Farrar further points out that it was Origen, "Father" of allegoric exegesis, who held this "theory of verbal inspiration" in its "strongest form," and who established the assumption that the Bible was "throughout homogeneous and in every particular supernaturally perfect" (pp. 189-90).

6. J. W. Blench, *Preaching in England in the late Fifteenth and Sixteenth Centuries: A Study of English Sermons 1450–c. 1600* (New York, 1964), p. 2.
7. James A. Froude, *Bunyan*, English Men of Letters (New York, 1880), p. 54.
8. Knox, p. 450.
9. The similarity to Plato's description is evident. In *Laws*, trans. R. G. Bury, Loeb Classical Library, 2 vols. (Cambridge, Mass., 1952), I, 305, Plato says the writer is "possessed by the Muse" so that he is "not in his senses, but resembles a fountain that gives free course to the upward rush of waters." In "Apology," *The Dialogues of Plato*, trans. B. Jowett, 2 vols. (New York, 1937), I, 405, Plato says that, like "diviners or soothsayers who also say many fine things, but do not understand the meaning of them," poets are instruments of higher powers. In "Phaedrus," *Dialogues*, I, 249, he speaks of the "madness of those who are possessed by the Muses." The Muses, he asserts, "taking hold of a delicate and virgin soul, and there inspiring frenzy, awakens lyrical and all other numbers; with these adorning the myriad actions of ancient heroes for the instruction of posterity."
10. Lawrence A. Sasek, *The Literary Temper of English Puritans*, Louisiana State Univ. Stud., Humanities Series, No. 9 (Baton Rouge, 1961), p. 110.
11. Ibid., p. 112.
12. Edward Wagenknecht, *Cavalcade of the English Novel* (New York, 1954), p. 23.
13. Earnest A. Baker, "John Bunyan," *The History of the English Novel: The Later Romances and the Establishment of Realism*, III (London, 1929), 50.
14. Froude, p. 109.
15. (New York, 1934).
16. Paul Elmer More, "Bunyan," *Shelburne Essays: Sixth Series: Studies in Religious Dualism* (New York, 1909), p. 198.
17. G. B. Harrison, *John Bunyan: A Study in Personality* (New York, 1928), p. 24.
18. Charles Firth, "John Bunyan," *Essays Historical and Literary* (Oxford, 1938), pp. 133-34.
19. Tindall, pp. 173; vii.
20. (New York, 1928).
21. Trans. Mrs. Bernard Wall (Cambridge, Mass., 1951), pp. 28, 131.
22. Hutchinson's University Library (London, 1954), pp. 120, 152.
23. Talon, p. 134.
24. Sharrock, pp. 141-42, 144.
25. Tindall, p. 182.
26. Ibid., p. 182.

27. Sasek, p. 35.
28. There are clearly meditative implications in Bunyan's use of "move" as well as in his description of this fourth basic goal. In *The Pilgrim's Progress and Traditions in Puritan Meditation* (New Haven, 1966), Professor V. Milo Kaufman establishes probabilities that these traditions influenced one narrative in a number of ways (pp. 156, 174, 197, 225, 245), yet he argues largely from Bunyan's practice rather than from his professions. His study suggests exciting possibilities with regard to the other narratives as well. Until such investigations have been made, however, it seems desirable to emphasize the oratorical, rather than the meditative, aspects of "move" because of this prominence and their unequivocal nature in context.
29. *The Poetry of Meditation: A Study in English Religious Literature of the Seventeenth Century* (New Haven, 1954) pp. 118-24.
30. "The Road of Excess," *Myth and Symbol: Critical Approaches and Applications*, ed. Bernice Slote (Lincoln, 1963), p. 14.
31. *Art and Illusion: A Study in the Psychology of Pictorial Representation* (New York, 1960), p. 261.
32. *Tropologia: A Key to Open Scripture Metaphors: Book II: Practical Improvement* (London, 1682), pp. 46-47.
33. "The Allegory as Employed by Spenser, Bunyan, and Swift" *PMLA*, IV (1889), 154.
34. *Tropologia*, II, 47.
35. Bunyan's inexact use of terms finds contemporaneous sanction in Keach's observation, "Rhetoricians make a difference between *Metaphors, Similies, Parables,* and *Allegories,* yet in Divinity there is none, but that Allegories are more large and continued" in "Epistle," *Tropologia:* II, sig. B1.
36. *Tropologia: A Key to Open Scripture Metaphors: Book I: Sacred Philology* (London, 1682), p. 200.
37. *Sacred Eloquence: Or, the Art of Rhetorick, As it is layd down in Scripture* (London, 1659), p. 20.
38. *Tropologia*, II, sig. B3.
39. *The Mysterie of Rhetorique Unvail'd* (London, 1657), p. 60.
40. *A Commentarie of M. Doctor Martin Luther Upon the Epistle of St. Paul to the Galatians* (London, 1603), pp. 217-18. Bunyan commended this work in *Grace Abounding*, p. 41.
41. *De Doctrina Christiana*, trans. J. F. Shaw, in *A Select Library of the Nicene and Post-Nicene Fathers of the Christian Church*, ed. Philip Schoff, Vol. II (Buffalo, 1887), p. 581.
42. Ibid., p. 537.
43. Ibid., p. 581.
44. Ibid., p. 537.
45. *Poetry Direct and Oblique* (London, 1948), p. 22.
46. *De Doctrina Christiana*, pp. 537, 581.
47. Bernard F. Huppé, *Doctrine and Poetry: Augustine's Influence on Old English Poetry* (New York, 1959), pp. 16-24 presents a precise description of St. Augustine's approach to Holy Scripture; the similarity referred to is evident even though Bunyan's generic term "similitude" is not used in the discussion of St. Augustine's position.

48. Blench, pp. 64-70.
49. *Dark Conceit: The Making of Allegory* (Evanston, 1959), p. 180. It could be objected that there would be no way to differentiate allegory from other fiction if the "fullest fictional manifestations of life" were actually achieved in the completion of the design. But Professor Honig, who appears to take *Moby Dick* as the norm for most things allegorical, argues that the "progression of an allegory is spiral—virtually simultaneously in all directions: backward to the thing represented . . . and forward and upward to the consummation of its meaning in the whole work" (pp. 179-80). The works of Jane Austen, for example, could not be considered allegory disguised by perfection because they lack the underlying design that would enable them to move in this three-dimensional way. In the terms used in this study, Jane Austen's works lack a central metaphor that would enable separate narrative facts to assume either direct, or indirect, or both kinds of relationships to external actualities. Allegory does not exist in a narrative simply because there is didactic impoverishment of mimetic fact; its presence depends primarily upon the presence of an analogy that suggests a series of comparisons.
50. Ibid., p. 129.
51. *Tropologia,* I, 38.

CHAPTER TWO: REPRESENTATION: DIDACTIC ELEMENTS

1. "John Bunyan," *Essays Historical and Literary* (Oxford, 1938), p. 166.
2. "*The Pilgrim's Progress:* A Study in Literary Immortality," *Essays in Appreciation* (New York, 1936), p. 62.
3. *John Bunyan: A Study in Personality* (New York, 1928), p. 182.
4. *John Bunyan: The Man and his Works,* trans. Mrs. Bernard Wall, (Cambridge, Mass., 1951), p. 164.
5. Firth, pp. 159, 152, 166.
6. Lowes, p. 68. A similar emphasis is evident in Ernest A. Baker, *The History of the English Novel: The Later Romances and the Establishment of Realism, III* (London, 1929), p. 77, and Paul Elmer More, "Bunyan," *Shelburne Essays, Sixth Series: Studies in Religious Dualism* (New York, 1909), p. 208.
7. *John Bunyan: Mechanick Preacher* (New York, 1934), pp. ix, 7.
8. Talon, p. 186.
9. Such identifications are the primary concern of Charles G. Harper, *The Bunyan Country: Landmarks of The Pilgrim's Progress* (Oxford, 1928); interesting speculations of this kind appear also in Vera Brittain, *Valiant Pilgrim: The Story of John Bunyan and Puritan England* (New York, 1950) and John Brown, *John Bunyan: His Life, Times and Work,* ed. James Blanton Wharey, rev. Frank Matt Harrison (London, 1928).
10. Firth, pp. 171-72.
11. Talon, *John Bunyan,* British Council Lectures (New York, 1956), p. 32.
12. Review of Robert Southey, "Life of John Bunyan" in *The Pilgrim's Progress with a Life of John Bunyan* (London, 1830) reprinted in *The*

Reader's Macauley, eds. Walter H. French and Gerald D. Sanders (New York, 1936), p. 234.
13. *The English Epic and its Background* (London, 1954), p. 392.
14. Lionel Stevenson, *The English Novel: A Panarama* (Boston, 1960), p. 43; Edward Wagenknecht, *The Cavalcade of the English Novel* (New York, 1954), p. 25.
15. Future references in the text refer to editions cited in note 2, p. 138.
16. *Gesta Romanorum: or, Entertaining Moral Stories*, eds. Charles Swan, Wynnard Hooper (London, 1876), p. 253. The "Applications" also often contain allegorical elucidations (pp. 19, 135) as well as additional moral instruction and exhortation (pp. 31, 347).
17. Tindall, p. 23.
18. *The Rise of Puritanism* (New York, 1938), pp. 114-20.
19. Tindall, p. 37.
20. *The Rhetoric of Fiction* (Chicago, 1961), p. 158. Professor Booth discusses this problem more fully on pp. 71-75.
21. *Rise of Puritanism*, p. 115.
22. Bunyan himself had used the secular rhetorical device, the dialogue, in his first published work, *Some Gospel Truths Opened*. He presented a few conflicting ideas in this form during the course of the treatise (I, 68, 71, 81), and he wrote a full recapitulation "by way of question and answer" (I, 84) at the end of it.
23. *John Bunyan*, Hutchinson's University Library (London, 1954), p. 83.
24. It is customary to assume that Mr. Sagacity was an experiment that failed. Professor Talon speculates that Bunyan "simply wants to make a variation," and he says Bunyan "gets rid of the old man" with "charming ingenuousness" (p. 155). Professor Sharrock speculates that "Bunyan's story-teller's instinct prompts him to drop Sagacity with a disarming naiveté when he has related Christiana's journey as far as the Wicket-gate" (p. 144). "Sagacity is abandoned," he suggests, "not because Bunyan's intelligence informs him that immediacy is the essence of a dream narration, but because he can now see without him" (p. 142). But there is no conclusive evidence that Mr. Sagacity was *intended* to tell the whole story. He is introduced as one who is to go "some part of the way" (p. 174) with the Dreamer. His offer to "give you an account of the whole of the matter" clearly refers to his earlier claim that he was "upon the spot at the instant" that Christiana prepared to go on a pilgrimage (p. 177). He is dismissed when his initial advantage over the Dreamer is about to become meaningless. He leaves when the pilgrims are at the wicket gate; they are soon to be under the direction of the Interpreter and, not long thereafter, of a heroic successor of Mr. Recorder, Great-heart himself. Great-heart also knows what has happened in that country since the Dreamer's last visit (p. 213), and, more important, he renders the authority of merely human sagacity relatively unimportant since he is an experienced servant of the Interpreter. Mr. Sagacity's departure is analogous to the point in *The Holy War* at which, after the appearance of the Lord High Secretary, Mr. Conscience becomes the Subordinate-Preacher. Perhaps Mr. Sagacity is not at all evidence of Bunyan's "charming ingenuousness"

or his "disarming naiveté"; it seems at least equally possible to see him as evidence of Bunyan's concern for the religious authority of the speaker.
25. *A Serious Call to a Devout and Holy Life* (London, 1906), p. 138.
26. The few sketches in the first edition of *Grace Abounding* were less fully developed than those in the early treatises. Typical examples are those of his wife's father and the "Antient Christian" (pp. 8, 55). The few fuller sketches, such as that of the "poor man" who became a "devilish *Ranter*" (pp. 16-17, were added in the third edition, which was published between 1672 and 1674 (p. xxxvii). These later sketches lack the concentration, the polish, and the manifest satiric intent of those in *The Strait Gate*.
27. James F. Forrest, "Bunyan's Ignorance and Flatterer: A Study in the Literary Art of Damnation," *SP*, LX, No. 1 (1963), p. 13; Harrison, pp. 155-60; Edwin Honig, *Dark Conceit: The Making of Allegory* (Evanston, 1959), p. 100; Lowes, p. 50; Talon, pp. 167-68. The possible sources and influences are unclear because of the wealth, rather than the paucity, of possibilities. G. R. Owst traces in *Literature and Pulpit in Medieval England* (Cambridge, 1933) a tradition, which he dates from the thirteenth century, among writers of pulpit manuals and treatises. They were "accustomed to illustrate each separate 'branch' of Vice or Virtue" with brief sketches of "contemporary men and women and their ways" (p. 87). Owst suggests that Bunyan's sketches, and other echoes of medieval sermons which he found in Bunyan's allegories, could have been a product of oral tradition among provincial ministers; Professor J. W. Blench's subsequent study, *Preaching in England in the late Fifteenth and Sixteenth Centuries* (New York, 1964) makes clear that sketches not unlike Bunyan's own were not unusual in the early seventeenth century (pp. 301-12). Professor Benjamin Boyce emphasizes the close relationship between "moralistic and didactic" sketches and Theophrastan ones in *The Theophrastan Character in England to 1642* (Cambridge, Mass., 1947), pp. 296-300. And he emphasizes the diffusion of the Theophrastan influence by 1661 in *The Polemic Character: 1640-1661* (Lincoln, 1955), p. 12. The wealth of possibilities appears to make certitude impossible.
28. *Polemic Characters*, pp. 12-15.
29. Sharrock, *John Bunyan*, p. 131.
30. *Bunyan*, English Men of Letters (New York, 1880), p. 109.
31. Bollingen Series XXXV, No. 5 (New York, 1960).
32. Gombrich, p. 88.
33. Ibid., p. 116.
34. Ibid., p. 74.
35. Ibid., p. 173.
36. Ibid., p. 90.
37. Ibid., p. 370.
38. Bunyan suggests that a similar process was involved. In *Grace Abounding* he suggests that early sketches were modified to "match" specific persons during oral delivery (p. 124). In *Mr. Badman* he emphasized that he was using authentic material (p. 141) and sometimes specific incidents (p. 146) as a basis for his depictions.
39. In *Aspects of the Novel* (New York, 1927), E. M. Forster distinguishes "flat" and "round" characters in the novel. He says flat characters

"in their purist form . . . are constructed around a single idea or quality: when there is more than one factor in them, we get the beginning of the curve towards the round. The really flat character can be expressed in one sentence such as 'I will never desert Mr. Micawber.'" The "round" characters, in contrast, have more than "one factor" in them and are capable of surprising a reader in a convincing way (pp. 103-04; 118).
40. *Theophrastan Character,* pp. 27-36.
41. *Sacred Eloquence: Or, the Art of Rhetorick, as it is layd down in Scripture* (London, 1659), p. 68.
42. *The Mysterie of Rhetorique Unvail'd* (London, 1657), pp. 153-54.
43. *Sacred Eloquence,* p. 68.
44. Lowes, p. 54.
45. *The Road of Life: A Study of Pilgrim's Journey,* 2 vols. (New York, n. d.), II, 14.
46. The term "portrait" is borrowed from Professor Boyce, who uses it in discussing three permutations of the polemic character which are not unlike Bunyan's portrait of Mr. Badman—*Polemic Character,* pp. 44, 55-56, 60.

CHAPTER THREE: MIMETIC DEVELOPMENT

1. References in this chapter are to those cited in note 2, p. 138.
2. *John Bunyan,* British Council Lectures (New York, 1956), pp. 17-21.
3. Such colloquial vigor as that which conveys a sense of the immediacy and spontaneity of rapid dramatic interactions in Bunyan's fictional narratives is, of course, nearly attained at times in works which Professor Charles C. Mish classifies as "merry tales" and "jest-biographies" in "Introduction," *Short Fiction of the Seventeenth Century* (New York, 1963), p. xiii. The following passage, for example, is from "Long Meg of Westminster," which Professor Mish reprinted:

> "What's the matter?" "Oh, Meg," quoth he, and fetched a great sigh, "I am arrested and, alas, utterly undone, for if I go to prison I shall have so many actions clapped on my back as I shall never be able to come out." "Arrested?" quoth Meg, "what, in our house? Why, Master Baily, is this a neighborly part, to come into our house and arrest our guests? Well, 'tis done and past, and therefore play the good fellow. Take an angel," quoth she, "and see him not. Here be none that be blabs; hold thy hand, here's the money, man, I'll pay it for the gentleman myself." "No," quoth the Baily, "I cannot do it, for the creditor stands at the door." "Bid him come in," quoth Meg, "and we will see if we can take up the matter." (p. 95)

Such vigorous colloquial dialogue as this is not uncommon in the "merry tales" reprinted by Professor Mish in "The Tinker of Turvey," pp. 129, 133, 148-49. The more aristocratic contemporaneous romances, of course, do not imitate the cadences of animated conversation in this way.
4. Bunyan's biographer treats *Grace Abounding* as an unquestionable authority, though he disagrees with Bunyan about a few matters of emphasis in John Brown, *John Bunyan: His Life, Times, and Work,* rev. Frank Mott Harrison (London, 1928), pp. 17-20, 56-58.

5. The experience behind *Grace Abounding* probably contrasts conspicuously with the formed experience embodied in the work itself because Bunyan is clearly one of those "religious geniuses" for whom, William James asserts, it is "normal" to be subject to "abnormal psychical visitations," to be "creatures of exalted emotional sensibility," to have "led a discordant inner life," to have suffered "melancholy during a part of their career," to have been "liable to obsessions and fixed ideas," and to have "fallen into trances, heard voices, and seen visions"—*The Varieties of Religious Experience* (London, 1929), pp. 6-7. The precise nature of the relationship between the perception and the expression of the experience, of course, is indeterminable, but the thoroughness with which the record of the complex process is molded into the conventional form of an "enthusiastic autobiography" is demonstrated in William York Tindall, *John Bunyan: Mechanick Preacher* (New York, 1934), pp. 23-32.
6. A number of their earlier appearances are described in Ronald A. Knox, *Enthusiasm: A Chapter in the History of Religion with Special Reference to the XVII and XVIII Centuries* (New York, 1950), pp. 139-42.
7. *John Bunyan: A Study of Personality* (New York, 1928), p. 109.
8. John J. O'Meara, *The Young Augustine: The Growth of St. Augustine's Mind up to his Conversion* (London, 1954), p. 10.
9. *John Bunyan*, British Council Lecture, p. 16.
10. "*The Pilgrim's Progress*: A Study in Literary Immortality," in *Essays in Appreciation* (Boston, 1936), p. 45.
11. O'Meara, p. 11.
12. "Introduction," *Grace Abounding*, p. xxiii.
13. *Essays in Appreciation*, p. 60.
14. "Spiritual Autobiography in *The Pilgrim's Progress*," RES, XXIV (1948), p. 103.
15. Ed. F. J. H. Harvey (London, 1913), pp. 57, 212, 334, 379.
16. *Seven Champions*, p. 59; *The Faerie Queene*, reprinted in *The Poetical Works of Edmund Spenser*, ed. J. R. Smith and E. D. Selincourt (London, 1959), p. 60, cant. (I, xi, 29).
17. John Prideaux, *Sacred Eloquence: Or, The Art of Rhetorick, As it is layd down in Scripture* (London, 1659), p. 68; John Smith, *The Mysterie of Rhetorique Unvail'd* (London, 1657), pp. 153-54.
18. *Faerie Queene*, p. 19 (I, iv, 4-5).
19. "Of Spenser's Allegorical Characters" in *Spenser's Critics*, ed. William R. Mueller (Syracuse, N. Y., 1959), p. 60.
20. *Faerie Queene*, pp. 19-22 (I, iv, 12-36).
21. Ibid., p. 19 (I, iv, 8-10).
22. Ibid., p. 22 (I, iv, 37).
23. *Seven Champions*, p. 57.
24. At one point, for example, Wiseman says he will tell about two "judgments" for "cursing and swearing." After the first story is told, however, Bunyan attributes the second one to Attentive (pp. 38-40). Or, again, the author so far ignores the narrative framework that he has Attentive explain that he asked a question, "*Not for mine own sake, but for others*" (p. 166), though ostensibly, no others are present.
25. The possible influence of Dent's work, which Bunyan mentioned in *Grace Abounding* as a part of his first wife's dowry (p. 8), is evaluated

in J. B. Wharey, "Bunyan's *Mr. Badman, MLN, XXXVI* (1921), pp. 65-79. Professor Wharey concludes that "the Pathway had left a lasting impression on Bunyan's mind" (p. 79), but both Professor Talon—*John Bunyan: The Man and his Works*, trans Mrs. Bernard Wall (Cambridge, Mass., 1951), p. 226—and Professor Tindall (p. 197) point out that neither the form nor the substance of Dent's popular work was so unusual that one must assume a direct debt on Bunyan's part.

26. Brown, pp. 160-62.
27. *Mechanick Preacher*, p. 200.
28. Bonamy Dobrée, "Bunyan: Mr. Badman," *Variety of Ways: Discussions on Six Authors* (Oxford, 1932), surely does less than justice to Bunyan in saying he "evidently took into account the frailty of the average reader, who then, as now, liked to feel his flesh creep. The love of horror is never absent from man's make-up.... Bunyan, at any rate, persuades his reader to follow the tale by promising him a sugar-plum at the end" (p. 41).
29. At times, a bit of verbosity obstructs even *The Plaine-Man's Pathway to Heaven*, 21st ed. (London, 1931), pp. 31-37; 71-74.
30. In S. H. Butcher, ed. *Aristotle's Theory of Poetry and Fine Art*, 4th ed. (London, 1907), p. 45, Aristotle says "the misfortunes of men like ourselves" arouse fear in tragedy, and Butcher points out that the "effect of tragedy, as described in the *Poetics*, mainly hinges" upon this "inner likeness." He argues persuasively, "So much human nature must there be in him [the hero] that we are able in some sense to identify ourselves with him, to make his misfortune our own" (p. 260). The ideal tragic hero, he argues further, must have "so large a share of our common humanity as to enlist our eager interest and sympathy" (p. 317).
31. "Bunyan," *Shelburne Essays: Sixth Series: Studies in Religious Dualism* (New York, 1909), p. 210.
32. "John Bunyan," *Essays Historical and Literary* (Oxford, 1938), pp. 142-43.
33. Brown, p. 310; Mabel Peacock, ed. "Introduction," *The Holy War*, p. xxviii.
34. Sharrock, *John Bunyan* (London, 1954), p. 131; Froude, *John Bunyan*, English Man of Letters (New York, 1880), p. 134.
35. In Emanuel Ford, "The Most Pleasant History of Ornatus and Artesia," reprinted in *Shorter Novels: Seventeenth Century*, ed. Philip Henderson (London, 1962), pp. 7-143, the narrative elements seem significant primarily insofar as they provide occasion for relatively formal speeches. The similarity of Ford's work to Bunyan's is most evident in the studied rhetorical pattern, not merely of the formal addresses (p. 113), or the soliloquies (p. 27), but even in the incidental speeches (p. 19) of Ford's characters. An even more elaborate pattern appears in the popular romantic tale by Aneas Sylvius, "Eurialus and Lucretia," reprinted in *Short Fiction of the Seventeenth Century*, ed. Charles C. Mish (New York, 1963), pp. 291-337. When he solicits Pandalus's aid in his illicit affair with Lucretia, Eurialus makes an uninterrupted speech of about eight hundred words expressing his esteem and friendship for Pandalus, describing the irrestible power of their love, summarizing their inadequate attempts to resist this passion, setting forth the social consequences of discovery,

explaining specifically how Pandalus may help, promising suitable rewards, and concluding with a passionate peroration: "I commend to your care and fidelity, Lucretia, myself, our love, our reputation, the honor of your family; they are all in your power. It lies in your hands to ruin all, or to preserve all" (pp. 327-29). Professor Harold Golder passes over the possible *stylistic* influence of romances lightly in "John Bunyan's Hypocricy," *North American Review*, CCXXIII (1926), pp. 323-32, though the "new" emphasis upon rhetorical form is quite striking in *The Holy War*.
36. Cf. E. M. W. Tillyard, *The English Epic and its Background* (New York, 1954), pp. 402-03. The lack of such dignity is especially evident when Bunyan treads in Milton's footsteps. The mere memory of the "great consult" in Pandemonium, for example, spoils the effect of Bunyan's depiction of a similar debate (pp. 27-30), and similar disparities in conception and tone are evident when Bunyan treats the material of *Paradise Regained*, which is reprinted in *The Complete Poetical Works of John Milton*, ed. Harris Francis Fletcher (New York, 1941), pp. 391-436. Emmanuel said to Diabolus:

> Thou knowest that all that thou has now said in this matter is nothing but guile and deceit, and is, as it was the *first*, so is it the *last* Card that thou hast to play. Many there be that do soon discern thee when thou showest them thy cloven foot.... (p. 85)

Milton's Jesus, in contrast, said to Satan, "Deservedly thou grievest, composed of lies, / From the beginning, and in lies wilt end" (p. 400; Bk. I, 11. 407-08). Again, Emmanuel asks Diabolus, "But if Righteousness be such a Beauty-spot in thine eyes now, how is it that Wickedness was so closely stuck to thee before?" (p. 85). Jesus, in contrast, asked Satan:

> But what concerns it thee when I begin
> My everlasting kingdom, why art thou
> Solicitous, what moves thy inquisitious?
> Knowest thou not that my rising is thy fall,
> And my promotion will be thy destruction? (p. 416; Bk. III, 11. 198-202)

37. Professor Talon—*The Man and his Works*, p. 256—points out that Bunyan expressed his admiration for one Robert Audley in describing Mr. Conscience's resistence to the new king (pp. 18-20). In Professor Rhodes Dunlap's terms—"Allegorical Interpretation of Renaissance Literature," *PMLA*, LXXXII (1967), 42—the historical allusions must be classified as "specific or closed allegory" in these passages because the parallels, which are described in detail by Brown, pp. 317-18, are very precise, but the subsequent actions of the moral type are clearly of the "open" variety.
38. The central doctrines underlying Bunyan's treatment of the conscience as a complex faculty of the soul are set forth in Heinrich Heppé, *Reformed Dogmatics Set Out and Illustrated from the Sources* rev. and ed. Ernst Bizer, trans. G. T. Thomson (London, 1959). The conscience makes man aware that "he is a transgressor against God's commandment and thereby guilty in God's sight; and yet by his natural knowledge of God he knows God only as a righteous judge of good and evil." This knowledge

is innate and indestructible, but it "cannot ensure any man peace with God or be in any sense a *religio* satisfying to Himself or to man" (p. 4). It was the function of the conscience to teach men "to distinguish right from wrong" and to recognize "not only the law of God, but also his own appointment to a covenant of works" (p. 285). The conscience does not contribute to effectual calling since the "adoption of the individual into the covenant of grace . . . is effected and realized (since natural man is utterly incapable of raising himself to God), solely by the grace of the H. Spirit" (p. 388). The "inward efficacy of the H. Spirit" is indispensible both to the "calling of the elect" (p. 517) and to later sanctification (p. 116).

39. The discussions between Messrs. By-ends, Money-Love, Love-All, and Hold-the-World, which suggest group interactions briefly (pp. 101-04), were not added until the third edition, which was not published in 1670— "Introduction," *Grace Abounding,* p. xiv.

CHAPTER FOUR: ALLEGORICAL DEVELOPMENT

1. *English Puritanism and its Leaders* (London, 1861), p. 472.
2. References in the text are cited in note 2, p. 138.
3. *John Bunyan: The Man and His Work,* trans. Mrs. Bernard Wall (Cambridge, Mass., 1951), p. 256.
4. George A. Watrous, ed. *Literary Essays of Thomas Babington Macaulay* (New York, 1900), p. 246. (This essay was contributed to the *Encyclopedia Britannica* in May, 1854).
5. *John Bunyan: A Study in Personality,* pp. 198-99.
6. Chapter I of the present study discusses these terms more fully. The following discussion is much indebted to Edwin Honig, *Dark Conceit: The Making of Allegory* (Evanston, 1959), and Angus Fletcher, *Allegory: The Theory of a Symbolic Mode* (New York, 1964).
7. *Allegory,* pp. 177-78.
8. C. S. Lewis, *Allegory of Love: A Study in Medieval Tradition* (Oxford, 1936), p. 69.
9. *Allegory,* pp. 81-82.
10. *The Pilgrim's Progress with a Life of John Bunyan* (Boston, 1830), pp. lxxxii-lxxxiii.
11. "John Bunyan," *Essays Historical and Literary* (Oxford, 1938), pp. 152, 159, 166. A similar emphasis upon the "realism" of the settings is evident in Earnest A. Baker, *The History of the English Novel: The Later Romances and the Establishment of Realism,* III (London, 1929), p. 77; Paul Elmer More, *Shelburne Essays, Sixth Series: Studies in Religious Dualism* (New York, 1909), p. 208.
12. The most systematic of these is Charles G. Harper, *The Bunyan Country: Landmarks of The Pilgrim's Progress* (Oxford, 1928). A well-illustrated supplement is Vera Brittain, *Valiant Pilgrim: The Story of John Bunyan and Puritan England* (New York, 1950). Valuable discussion appears in John Kelman, *The Road of Life: A Study of Pilgrim's Journey,* 2 vols. (New York, n. d.), I, 93 and Talon, p. 186.
13. *Literary Essays,* p. 245.

14. "John Bunyan's Hypocrisy," *North American Review*, CCXXIII (1926), 330; "Bunyan's Valley of the Shadow," *MP*, XXVII (1929), 64, 66, 68.
15. This emphasis is the inverse side of Professor Honig's emphasis (p. 70) upon the freedom from "realistic" criterion the dream artifice gives the allegorist and of Tullock's emphasis (p. 480) upon the influence of the Bible upon Bunyan's perceptions. The reasons that emblematic elements, which are discussed later in this chapter, could well have seemed more "real" or "natural" to Bunyan's contemporaries than to subsequent readers are suggested in Samuel C. Chew, *The Pilgrimage of Life* (New Haven), p. 277.
16. "Space and the Hero in *The Pilgrim's Progress*: A Study in the Meaning of an Allegorical Universe," *Etudes Anglaises*, XIV (1961), 125-27.
17. Golder, "John Bunyan's Hypocrisy," p. 326.
18. Kelman, II, 204-05.
19. *The Rise of Puritanism* (New York, 1938), p. 212.
20. *Allegory*, p. 198.
21. The paragraphs treating these effects undoubtedly owe much to Professor Honig's illuminating discussion of "dialectical transfer" in *Dark Conceit*, pp. 137-45, though the underlying assumptions, conclusions, and critical terms differ from those of Professor Honig. Here as elsewhere, Professor Honig's wonderfully expressive critical terms are avoided because they imply too much; they consistently imply a whole, closely-integrated, theoretical system.
22. Chew, p. 131.
23. *John Bunyan* (New York, 1904), p. 146.
24. Examples are: Firth, pp. 144-45; Roger Sharrock, *John Bunyan* (London, 1954), pp. 134-35. A detailed exploration of historical significance is C. H. Firth, "Bunyan's *Holy War*," JEGP, I (1913), pp. 141-50.
25. *John Bunyan: A Study in Personality*, p. 202.
26. G. R. Owst, *Literature and Pulpit in Medieval England* (Cambridge, 1933), pp. 77-80, traces the "use of the figure of the 'Castle of Mansoul' in English preaching" from the "end of the twelfth century" to the fifteenth and suggests that Bunyan may have heard it used among village preachers. Professor Sharrock, *John Bunyan*, pp. 118-19, refers to similar besieged castles in literature of the fifteenth and sixteenth century and points out that Bunyan himself had "developed in an extended simile the conception of the heart as the chief fortress of the soul, which, if well manned, could keep the rest of the town in subjection to its rightful prince" in *A Treatise of the Fear of God*. In William Haller, *The Rise of Puritanism* (New York, 1938), Professor Haller describes the "soldier who, having been pressed to serve under the banners of the spirit, must exact faithfully his part in the unceasing war of the spiritual against the carnal man" (p. 142) as one of the two "eternal images" which, "for at least a century," were a "chief mode of stimulating popular imagination" among reforming Puritan spiritual preachers (p. 25). James Blanton Wharey, *A Study of the Sources of Bunyan's Allegories* (Baltimore, 1904), says Richard Bernard's *Isle of Man or the Legal Proceedings in Manshire against Sin*, a "remarkably popular" book which had reached

the fourteenth edition by 1668 (p. 78), contains "the germ of Bunyan's second great allegory" in that "both allegories have as their root-idea the contest for supremacy in the human soul between the forces of good and the forces of evil" and concludes that Bunyan's indebtedness to Bernard is "almost a certainty" (p. 89). Fletcher, p. 151, finds the "battle" one of "two basic forms" that allegories resolve themselves into.

27. Macaulay discusses the inevitable limitations of "human ingenuity" in a review of Robert Southey, "Life of John Bunyan," in *The Pilgrim's Progress with a Life of John Bunyan* (London, 1930), which is reprinted in *The Reader's Macaulay*, eds. Walter H. French and Gerald D. Sanders (New York, 1930), p. 234.
28. "Bunyan's *Holy War*," p. 141.
29. *Allegory*, p. 81.
30. Ibid., p. 198.
31. *English Puritanism and its Leaders*, p. 461.
32. *Allegory of Love*, p. 167.
33. *The Polemic Character: 1640-1661* (Lincoln, 1955), p. 29.
34. Herbert Eveleth Greene, in "The Allegory as Employed by Spenser, Bunyan, and Swift," *PMLA*, IV (1889), refuses to "admit that a prolonged personification is genuine allegory" because nothing is hidden by "representing in action an abstract quality named for itself" (p. 152), but he later adds that "personifications may become allegorical, not by virtue of being personifications, but by taking part in allegorical action" (p. 181).
35. Roger Sharrock, "Bunyan and the English Emblem Writers," *RES*, XXI (1945), pp. 105-16; Rosemary Freeman, *English Emblem Books* (London, 1948), pp. 1-2; 212-22.
36. *English Emblem Books*, pp. 219-20.
37. Ibid., p. 222.
38. "Bunyan and the English Emblem Writers," p. 107.
39. This curious "isolation" is examined in Fletcher, *Allegory*, pp. 100-08.
40. "John Bunyan's Use of Symbols in *The Pilgrim's Progress*" Unpubl. diss. (Emory, 1956), p. 1.
41. (New Haven, 1962), pp. 106, 124, 127.
42. Captain Charity, who "for his Scutcheon had three naked Orphans imbraced on the bosom" in *The Holy War* (p. 68), is one such exception, for Bunyan's reference (1 Cor. 13) leads to an inspired description of clarity that does not even suggest the image of the babies. Such children were a part of a tradition in treating charity, for they appeared with Spenser's Charissa—I, x, 30-32—in "innumerable examples" in the five arts—Chew, p. 131—and in emblems—Freeman, p. 227. The visual convention, rather than the Bible, appears to be the source.
43. The probability is suggested by the close relationship between certain passages in *The Holy War* and a minor treatise, *The Barren Fig-tree*, which was published in the same year. As he explicates and moralizes about the parable of the barren fig tree (Luke 13:6-9), Bunyan draws from various parts of the Bible additional tropes and reasons them into conformity with both the idea and the image of the barren fig tree. He amasses a whole series of "matching" allusive symbols within three pages: the fruitless branch, the withered plant, and the plant not planted by God

(II, 246-49). In *The Holy War* he wrote of Captain Execution, his "Scutcheon was a Fruitless Tree, with an Axe laying at the root thereof" (p. 37), and he allowed the Captain to use at least four of the symbols he had amassed in the treatise in a speech (pp. 46-47). The known veneration for Biblical association of image and idea, which he frequently revealed (IV, 124; I, 72), lends further support to the suggestion that he usually drew his allusive symbols directly from the Bible.

44. James Anthony Froude, *Bunyan*, English Men of Letters (New York, 1880), p. 129.

REFERENCES

Aristotle. *Aristotle's Theory of Poetry and Fine Art,* ed. and trans. S. H. Butcher, 4th ed. London, 1907.

Augustine, St. *De Doctrine Christiana,* trans. J. F. Shaw, in *A Select Library of the Nicene and Post-Nicene Fathers of the Christian Church: II,* Philip Schoff. Buffalo, 1887.

Baker, Ernest A. *The History of the English Novel: The Later Romances and the Establishment of Realism, III.* London, 1929.

Bernard, Richard. *Isle of Man, or the Legal Proceedings in Manshire against Sin.* London, 1668.

Blench, J. W. *Preaching in England in the Late Fifteenth and Sixteenth Centuries: A Study of English Sermons: 1400–c. 1600.* New York, 1964.

Booth, Wayne C. *Rhetoric of Fiction.* Chicago, 1961.

Boyce, Benjamin. *The Polemic Character: 1640-1661.* Lincoln, Nebraska, 1955.

———. *The Theophrastan Character in England to 1642.* Cambridge, Mass., 1947.

Brittain, Vera. *Valiant Pilgrim: The Story of John Bunyan and Puritan England.* New York, 1950.

Brown, John. *John Bunyan: His Life, Times, and Work,* rev. Frank Mott Harrison. London, 1928.

Bunyan, John. *The Entire Works of John Bunyan,* ed. Henry Stebbing. 4 vols. London, 1859–1860.

———. *Grace Abounding to the Chief of Sinners,* ed. Roger Sharrock. Oxford, 1962.

———. *The Holy War and the Heavenly Footman,* ed. Mabel Peacock. Oxford, 1892.

———. *The Life and Death of Mr. Badman and The Holy War,* ed. John Brown. Cambridge, 1905.

———. *The Pilgrim's Progress from this World to That which is to Come,* ed. James Blanton Wharey, rev. Roger Sharrock. Oxford, 1960.

Chew, Samuel C. *The Pilgrimage of Life.* New Haven, 1962.

Dent, Arthur. *The Plaine-Man's Pathway to Heaven.* 21st ed. London, 1931.

Dobrée, Bonamy. "Bunyan: Mr. Badman," *Variety of Ways: Discussions on Six Authors.* Oxford, 1932.

Dunlap, Rhodes, "The Allegorical Interpretation of Renaissance Literature," *PMLA,* LXXXII, No. 1 (1967), 39-43.

Farrer, Frederick W. *History of Interpretation.* London, 1886.

Firth, Charles H. "Bunyan's *Holy War,*" *Journal of English Studies,* I (January, 1913), 141-50.

———. "John Bunyan," *Essays Historical and Literary.* Oxford, 1938.

Fletcher, Angus. *Allegory: The Theory of A Symbolic Mode.* New York, 1964.

Ford, Emanuel. "The Most Pleasant History of Ornatus and Artesia," *Shorter Novels: Seventeenth Century,* ed. Philip Henderson, London, 1962.

Forrest, James F. "Bunyan's Ignorance and Flatterer: A Study in the Literary Art of Damnation," *Studies in Philology,* LX, No. 1 (1963), 12-22.

Forster, E. M. *Aspects of the Novel.* New York, 1927.

Freeman, Rosemary. *English Emblem Books.* London, 1948.

Froude, James A. *John Bunyan,* English Men of Letters, New York, 1880.

Frye, Northrup. "The Road of Excess," *Myth and Symbol: Critical Approaches and Applications,* ed. Bernice Slote. Lincoln, Nebraska, 1963.

Gesta Romanorum: or, Entertaining Moral Stories, ed. Charles Swan, Wynnard Hooper. Anon. London, 1876.

Golder, Harold. "John Bunyan's Hypocrisy," *North American Review,* CCXXIII (1926), 323-32.

Gombrich, E. H. *Art and Illusion: A Study in the Psychology of Pictorial Representation,* Bollingen Series, XXXV, No. 5. New York, 1960.

Green, Herbert Eveleth. "The Allegory as Employed by Spenser, Bunyan, and Swift," *PMLA,* IV (1889), 145-93.

Haller, William. *The Rise of Puritanism. . . .* New York, 1938.

Harper, Charles G. *The Bunyan Country: Landmarks of The Pilgrim's Progress.* Oxford, 1928.

Harrison, G. B. *John Bunyan: A Study in Personality.* New York, 1928.

Heppé, Heinrich. *Reformed Dogmatics Set Out and Illustrated from the Sources,* rev. and ed. Ernst Bizer, trans. G. T. Thomson. London, 1950.

Honig, Edwin. *Dark Conceit: The Making of Allegory.* Evanston, 1959.

Huppe, Bernard F. *Doctrine and Poetry: Augustine's Influence on Old English Poetry.* New York, 1959.

James, William. *The Varieties of Religious Experience.* London, 1929.

Johnson, Richard. *The Seven Champions of Christendom*, ed. F. J. H. Harvey. London, 1913.

Kaufman, U. Milo. *The Pilgrim's Progress and Traditions in Puritan Meditation*. New Haven, 1966.

Keach, Benjamin. *Tropologia: A Key to Open Scripture Metaphors: Book I: Sacred Philology*. London, 1682.

———. *Tropologia: A Key to Open Scripture Metaphors: Book II: Practical Improvement*. London, 1682.

Kelman, John. *The Road of Life, A Study of Pilgrim's Journey*. 2 vols. New York, [n. d.]

Knox, Ronald A. *Enthusiasm: A Chapter in the History of Religion with Special Reference to the XVII and XVIII Centuries*. New York, 1950.

Law, William. *A Serious Call to a Devout and Holy Life*. London, 1906.

Lewis, C. S. *Allegory of Love: A Study in Medieval Tradition*. Oxford, 1936.

Lowes, John Livingston. "*The Pilgrim's Progress*: A Study in Literary Immortality," *Essays in Appreciation*. New York, 1936.

Luther, Martin. *A Commentarie of M. Doctor Martin Luther Upon the Epistle of St. Paul to the Galations*. London, 1603.

Macaulay, Thomas B. *Literary Essays of Thomas Babington Macaulay*, ed. George A. Watrous. New York, 1900.

———. *The Reader's Macaulay*, eds. Walter H. French and Gerald D. Sanders. New York, 1936. Reprints review of Robert Southey. "Life of John Bunyan," *The Pilgrim's Progress with a Life of John Bunyan*. London, 1830.

Martz, Louis L. *The Poetry of Meditation: A Study in English Religious Literature of the Seventeenth Century*, New Haven, 1954.

McNair, Walter Edward. "John Bunyan's Use of Symbols in *The Pilgrim's Progress*," Unpubl. diss. Emory University, 1956.

Milton, John. *Paradise Regained*, reprinted in *The Complete Poetical Works of John Milton*, ed. Harris Francis Fletcher. New York, 1941.

Mish, Charles C. *Short Fiction of the Seventeenth Century*. New York, 1963.

More, Paul Elmer. "Bunyan," *Shelburne Essays: Sixth Series: Studies in Religious Dualism*. New York, 1909.

O'Meara, John J. *The Young Augustine: The Growth of St. Augustine's Mind up to his Conversion*. London, 1954.

Owst, G. R. *Literature and Pulpit in Medieval England*. Cambridge, 1933.

Plato. "Apology," *The Dialogues of Plato*, trans B. Jowett. 2 vols. New York, 1937.

Prideaux, John. *Sacred Eloquence: Or, the Art of Rhetorick, As it is layd down in Scripture*. London, 1659.

Sasek, Lawrence A. *The Literary Temper of the English Puritans*, Louisiana State University Studies, Humanities Series, No. 9. Baton Rouge, 1961.

Sharrock, Roger. "Bunyan and the English Emblem Writers," *Review of English Studies*, XXI (1945), 105-16.

———. *John Bunyan*, Hutchison's University Library. London, 1954.

———. "Spiritual Autobiography in *The Pilgrim's Progress*," *Review of English Studies*, XXIV (1948), 102-20.

Smith, John. *The Mysterie of Rhetorique Unvail'd*. London, 1657.

Southey, Robert. *The Pilgrim's Progress with a Life of John Bunyan*. Boston, 1930.

Spenser, Edmund. *The Faerie Queene*, reprinted in *The Poetical Works of Edmund Spenser*, eds. J. C. Smith and E. De Selincourt. London, 1959.

Stevenson, Lionel. *The English Novel: A Panarama*. Boston, 1960.

Sylvius, Aneas. "Eurialus and Lucretia," in *Short Fiction of the Seventeenth Century*, ed. Charles C. Mish (New York, 1963), pp. 291-337.

Talon, Henri A. *John Bunyan*, British Council Lectures. New York, 1956.

———. *John Bunyan: The Man and His Works*, trans. Mrs. Bernard Wall. Cambridge, Mass., 1951.

———. *John Bunyan: L'Homme et L'Oeuvre*, in *Etudes en Literature D'Art et D'Histoire*. Paris, 1948.

———. "Space and the Hero in *The Pilgrim's Progress*: A Study in the Meaning of an Allegorical Universe," *Etudes Anglaises*, XIV (1961), 124-30.

Tillyard, E. M. W. *The English Epic and its Background*. New York, 1954.

———. *Poetry Direct and Oblique*. London, 1948.

Tindall, William York. *John Bunyan: Mechanick Preacher*. New York, 1934.

Tullock, John. *English Puritanism and its Leaders*. London, 1861.

Wagenknecht, Edward. *Cavalcade of the English Novel*. New York, 1954.

Wharton, Thomas, "Of Spenser's Allegorical Characters," *Spenser's Critics*, ed. William R. Mueller. Syracuse, N. Y., 1959.

Wharey, James Blanton. *A Study of the Sources of Bunyan's Allegories*. Baltimore, 1904.

———. "Bunyan's *Mr. Badman*," *Modern Language Notes*, XXXVI, No. 2 (1921), 65-79.

White, William Hale. *John Bunyan*. New York, 1904.

INDEX

allegorical method, Bunyan's use of, 8, 13, 14, 19, 94, 95, 110, 111, 122, 129, 130, 134
allegorical principles, Bunyan's use of, 14, 95, 110
allegorical scenes as dramatic method, 67, 69-71, 75, 88, 106, 107, 110, 114, 133
allegorical techniques in development of conflict, 12-14, 23, 95
allegorical vehicles, development of, 14, 111
allegory: Bunyan's description of, 15, 16: Honig, Edwin, description of, 20, 141n
allusive symbols as narrative device, 117, 121, 124, 125, 136
Anabaptist, 4
Anglican Church, 60
Antigone, resemblance to Mrs. Badman, 80
Apollyon, 68, 69, 71-73, 85, 98, 119
artifice, 8
Atheism, narrator's struggle with, 29
Atheist, 29, 30, 67, 76, 112
Attentive, 31, 37, 76-79, 85
autobiography in Bunyan's works, 25, 27, 28, 64, 133, 145n

Badman, Mr., 24, 30, 49, 50, 76, 77: death of, 77, 80, 81
Badman, Mrs., 37, 80, 83, 133: death of, 81
Balzac, Honoré de, narrative detail likened to, 22

Barren Fig-Tree, The, 20, 83, 150n
Beulah, 36
Bevis of Southampton, 6
Bible, interpretation of, 4, 29, 60, 116, 127, 134
biblical allusions as narrative device, 17, 117, 120, 121, 136
Boanerges, Captain, 84, 85
Bolder, 37
Booth, Wayne C., 28, 142n
Boyce, Benjamin, 40, 118
Brisk, Mr., 25
Bubble, Mme, 41
Bunyan, John: conscious artist, 7, 129; mirror images, 9-11; preacher, 3, 27, 28, 129; religious spokesman, 3-8, 28, 39, 129; unconscious artist, 6, 7, 129
By-ends, 29, 30, 41, 43, 46, 48, 49, 67, 70, 89, 109, 112, 118
By-Path Meadow, 109

Carnal-Security, Mr., 84
Celestial City, 33, 34, 106, 107
characters, minor; see figures, minor
characters, major; see figures, major
Christian, 13, 25, 26, 29, 30-33, 35, 36, 42, 44, 45, 50, 54, 58, 66, 68, 72, 76, 84, 88-90, 98, 105, 106, 109, 112, 119, 122
Christiana, 26, 33, 38, 41, 43, 49, 54-56, 58, 80, 89, 91, 109, 113, 125
Ciceronian goals, Bunyan's use of, 8
climactic order, 60, 65, 68
Conceit, Country of, 112

[156]

INDEX / 157

Coleridge, Samuel Taylor, creation of illusion, 14
colloquial style as narrative technique, 57, 59, 69, 82, 88, 144n
Confession of My Faith, A, 4
consciousness, state of, 103, 105, 115
Conscience, Mr., 30, 53, 85-87, 115
Conviction, Captain, 84, 85, 127
Cordelia, resemblance to Mrs. Badman, 80
Cymbal, 4, 5

Defoe, Daniel, narrative detail likened to that of, 22
Dent, Arthur, 79, 146n
Despair, Giant, 58, 71, 109
Destruction, City of, 53, 106-09
Diabolus, Tyrant, 37, 52, 83, 85, 86, 113, 115, 126
dialectic principle as allegorical device, 14, 18, 20, 21, 23, 95, 96, 134-36
dialectic process to extend metaphors, 21, 52, 103, 104, 110
dialectical patterns, 21, 22, 96, 108
dialogue, interior, as dramatic device, 62, 63
didactic contrivance to reduce illusion, 30, 36
didactic intrusion by narrators and authoritative characters, 29, 37, 38, 43
didactic principle, Bunyan's use of, 12, 22, 24, 26, 129, 130, 137
Diffidence, 71, 109
Divine Emblems, 9
Donne, John, 52, 61
Doubting Castle, 101, 109
dramatic contrast, between characters, 75, 82, 84, 87, 88
dramatic development, through dialogue, 80, 82, 85
dramatic integration, in *The Holy War*, 31
dramatic scenes, in *Pilgrim's Progress*, 67, 68, 97, 105, 112, 132-35
Dreamer, 33-36, 38, 88, 101, 109, 110

Ebal and Gerizim, 9, 16
Elect, 9, 51, 60, 108, 113
emblematic elements, as narrative device, 117, 121-24, 127, 136
embryonic personifications, as narrative device, 117-20, 136
Emmanuel, 30-32, 34, 36, 37, 83, 85-87, 113-15, 121, 126
Enchanted Grounds, 108, 110, 112
Envy, 74, 75

Evangelist, 31
Evil-Questioning, Mr., 41
Execution, Captain, 83, 84
exempla, as figurative device, 14
Exposition on the First Ten Chapters of Genesis, An, 18, 19

Fable, 16
Faithful, 29, 43, 46, 58, 67, 68, 70, 74, 75, 84, 89, 90, 92, 96, 98, 109
False-Peace, 30
Fancies, 16
Fearing, Mr., 55, 109
Feeble-mind, Mr., 33, 42, 54, 91, 109
fictional narrative, in *Grace Abounding*, 6, 10, 30, 31
fictional type, 52, 74, 86, 87
Fielding, Henry, didactic approach to the ideas of, 27
figurative language in narrative context, 33, 61
figures, major, (central), 48, 51, 54, 59-61, 66, 69, 70, 73, 76, 83, 85, 92, 98, 106-08, 114, 115, 131-35
figures, minor, 35-38, 43, 46, 63, 64, 70, 71, 85, 91, 131
Firth, Charles, realism in *Pilgrim's Progress*, 24, 25, 82, 99, 114
Flatterer, 109, 112, 124
Fletcher, Angus, use of allegory by, 97, 106, 114, 115
Formalist, 73
Formality, 109
Fox, George, 4
Froude, James Anthony, 5, 41, 82, 126
Fruitless Professor, Downfall of the, 20
Frye, Northrup, central dilemma of literature, 13
Fury, Captain, 126

Gaius, 30, 58
George on Horseback, 5, 6
Gesta Romanorum, 27
Godly-fear, Mr., 84
Golder, Harold, 99; biblical settings romanticized, 149n
Gombrich, E. H., illusion in narrative literature, 14, 42
Good-Hope, Captain, 127
Grace Abounding: analogies and symbols, 102, 103; autobiography, 30; informative, 8, 27, 29; religious authority, 28, 130; religious purpose, 3, 5, 6, 9, 10, 11, 26
Great Difficulty of Going to Heaven, The, 40

Great-Heart, Mr., 17, 30-33, 42, 49, 53, 55, 58, 89, 90, 92, 113, 119
Groans of a Damned Soul, 4
Greene, Hubert Eveleth, parable and metaphor, 15

Haller, William, Puritan influences, 27, 28, 102
Harrison, G. B., view of Bunyan as conscious artist, 7, 24, 60, 94, 113
Heart of Darkness, The (Conrad), 124
Help, 104, 105
Herbert, George, spiritual style of, 61
Hill Difficulty, The, 13
Hold-the-World, Mr., 40, 69, 70, 118
Holy City, The, 3, 16, 17, 19, 26
Holy War, The: allegorical significance, 94, 110; dialectical principles, 23, 96, 120; religious purpose, 5; scenic methods, 82, 133-35, 137; verbal devices, 120, 121, 128
Honest, 24, 30, 53-55, 58, 89, 91
Honig, Edwin, allegorical method, 20, 141n
Hopeful, 29-32, 43, 67, 68, 74, 76, 77, 84, 89, 92, 96, 98, 109, 112
hortatory, literal technique, 12
Humiliation, Valley of, 68, 70, 72, 109
Hypocrisy, 73, 109

Ignorance, 30, 34, 43-45, 49, 53, 67, 69, 73, 85, 112
Incredulity, Mr., 83, 85
illusion, 12-14, 23, 27, 29-34, 36, 37, 42, 131
interior dialogue; see dialogue, interior
interior monologue; see monologue, interior
Interpreter, 30, 32, 92, 122, 125
Instruction for the Ignorant, 8
introspection, 9

Jacobean quibble, 40
James, 56, 58, 59, 90, 91
Jerusalem Sinner Saved, 8
John Bunyan: Mechanick Preacher (Tindall), 6
Johnson, Richard, 68

Keach, Benjamin, parable and allegory as narrative devices, 14, 15, 20
Kelman, John, imitative accuracy, 49

Law, William, character development, 39

Legality, Mr., 118, 119
Lewis, C. S., verbal style in *Pilgrim's Progress,* 118
literal techniques, 12, 13, 22, 61, 102, 129, 130, 133, 137
Light for them that Sit in Darkness, 3, 4
Little-faith, 53, 110, 111
Lord High Secretary; see Secretary
Lowes, John Livingston, realism in *Pilgrim's Progress,* 24, 25, 49, 62
Lucifera, 71-73
Luther's definition of allegory, 16, 140n

Macaulay, didactic principle in allegory, 25, 94, 99
McNair, Walter E., symbols in *Pilgrim's Progress,* 124
major character: see figures, major
Malice, Town of, 120
Mansoul, Town of, 34, 36, 37, 52, 83-87, 113, 116, 120, 121, 126; derivation of name, 149n
Martz, Louis L., introspection, 9
Matthew, 56, 58, 89, 90
Maul, Giant, 33, 92, 109
metaphor, 12-15, 18-21, 33, 40, 95, 96, 134; central, 12, 15, 20, 22, 26, 29, 34, 51, 53, 91, 97, 98, 101, 110, 112-15, 117, 135, 136
Mercy, 25, 34, 38-39, 53, 54, 56, 58, 59, 80, 91, 92, 108, 113, 119, 120
Milton, John, use of metaphor by, 28, 51, 64, 126; vs. Bunyan, 147n
minor character; see figures, minor
mimesis, literal technique, 12, 19
mimetic elements, in narrative art, 14, 82
mimetic material, as illustrative functions, 11, 12, 22, 27, 28
mimetic norm, 100-02, 123
mimetic potentialities, of allegory, 20; through dialogue and narrative scenes, 58, 63, 88, 132
mimetic principles, 12, 14, 18, 22, 24, 25, 57, 95-97, 129, 130, 134-37
mimetic scenes, 67, 69, 70, 73, 88, 92, 106, 107, 110, 114, 124, 125, 133
Mind, Mr., 53, 121
mirror images, Bunyan's use of, 9-11
Mistrust, 109, 112
Moby Dick (Melville), 13, 141n
monologue, interior, as dramatic device, 62, 63, 81
Morality, Village of, 109, 118
More, Hannah, 25

Nashe, narrative detail likened to, 22
nonallegorical technique; see literal
  techniques
novel of manners, as in *Second Part*, 58
objective drama, as in *Grace Abounding*,
  62
obscurity, Bunyan's view of, 17, 22;
  St. Augustine's view of, 17, 18
Obstinate, 73
Old Testament, 18, 19
omniscient authors, 35, 38, 131
omniscient narrator, 36-38

Pagan, 123, 124
Palace Beautiful, 119
parable, 14, 15, 21
Pharisee and the Publican, The, 10
Pilgrim's Progress, The: allegorical
  aspects, 97, 104, 114, 122, 123, 124;
  central metaphor, 13; mimetic art,
  11, 22, 25, 75, 112, 114; religious
  authority, 28; religious purpose, 5,
  6, 10, 17, 105; verbal devices, 136
Plain of Ease, 102
Plato, 4, 139n
Platonic theory, 5; transformation into
  scriptural interpretation, 138n
Pliable, 73
polemic character, 40, 46, 118
Pope, 123, 124
predestination, 9
Prejudice, Mr., 36
Presumption, 108, 119
Prideaux, John, 15, 46
Profitable Meditations, 8
progressive revelation in *Pilgrim's
  Progress*, 50
prosopopoeia, 46, 70
Prywell, Mr., 87
Puritan morality, 9, 133

Quakers, 4, 102

Recorder, 36, 53, 86, 113
Red Cross Knight, 13, 71, 72
Reliever, Mr., 91, 119
religious conversion in *Pilgrim's
  Progress:* process of, 11, 13, 26,
  60, 98; process of in *Grace Abound-
  ing*, 60, 66
Resurrection of the Dead, The, 18, 111
Roman Catholicism as emblematic
  setting, 123

Sagacity, Mr., 7, 38, 142n
St. Augustine, 17, 18, 60, 125, 140n
Saint's Knowledge of Christ's Love, 16
Sartre, approach to didactic ideas of,
  27
satiric art, character contrast, 73
satiric intent in *The Strait Gate*, 40
*Second Part of the Pilgrim's Progress,
  The:* interaction of characters, 89,
  134; mimetic method, 93, 135
schemata, 48-51, 53, 54, 85, 88, 131,
  132
Secret, Mr., 91
Secretary, Lord High, 85-87
Senecan seesaw, 40, 41, 46
settings, "psychic," 100, 102, 104,
  106, 108, 116
Shaddai, 30, 37, 85, 116, 126
Shame, 51, 70, 72, 73, 83, 85, 98
Sharrock, Roger, 7, 36, 41, 65, 66,
  82, 122
Shaw, G. B., approach to didactic
  ideas of, 27
Shepherds, 30, 32, 89
Sighs from Hell, A Few, 5, 8, 15, 39,
  47
similes, as literary device, 14, 16
similitude, as literary device, 14, 16,
  18, 19, 20, 140n
Simple, 108, 119
Sincere, Town of, 111
Slay-good, Giant, 33, 90, 109
Slough of Despond, 102, 104, 105,
  109, 119
Sloth, 108, 119
Socratic method, 32
Solomon's Temple Spiritualized, 3, 16,
  17, 19
Some Gospel Truths Opened, 4, 9, 10,
  31, 39, 47, 57
Southey, Robert, comments on
  Pilgrim's Progress, 98
Spenser, Edmund, 20, 51, 71
Stand-fast, Mr., 30, 53, 54, 91
Strait Gate, The, 40, 43, 44, 49, 119
Stupidity, Town of, 53
Superstition, 74

Talkative, Mr., 5, 29, 43, 46, 47, 53,
  69, 73, 76, 85, 89, 112
Talon, Henri, on Bunyan as conscious
  artist, 3, 7, 24, 25, 59, 61, 94, 99
Temporary, 31
Tempter, 64, 70, 73

Theophrastan character, 40, 42, 46, 131
Theophrastan form, 43
Tillyard, E. M. W.: on *Pilgrim's Progress*, 17; on *Mr. Badman*, 25
Timorous, 109, 112
Tindall, William York, Bunyan as conscious artist, 6, 25, 27, 77, 129
topographical names, 116-20
Torment, Captain, 127
Trinity and a Christian, Of the, 4
Tullock, John, on *The Holy War*, 94, 117

Una, 13
Understanding, Lord, 29, 85

Vain-hope, 45
Valiant-for-Truth, 30, 53, 91
Valley of the Shadow of Death, 102, 118
Vanity Fair, 67, 74, 101, 107
verbal dictation theory, 4
verisimilitude, as literary device, 37

Warton, Thomas, view on emblematic elements of Spenser and Bunyan, 71
Water of Life, The, 15, 19
White, William Hall, 110
Whitefield, George, 5
Willbewill, Lord, 36, 52, 53, 85
Worldly-Wiseman, Mr., 29-31, 37, 38, 50, 76-80, 109, 119